Business Companion:
CHINESE

TIM DOBBINS
PAUL WESTBROOK

Translation and culture notes by
WENQING ZHOU

Edited by
ZVJEZDANA VRZIĆ

LIVING LANGUAGE®
A Random House Company

To my sons, Matt and John Dobbins, for continuously teaching me the universal language of not taking one's self too seriously. To my parents, Christine and Peter, for letting me spend my most joyous years of childhood in the Spanish culture of Quito, Ecuador. To my brother, Dan, for his unconditional support of my vision to help others communicate beyond their differences. And finally, for his editorial input, to Christopher Warnasch, who has never, until now, had a book dedicated to him. *Pax Domini.*

—*Tim Dobbins*

To businessmen and -women around the globe who are practicing the noblest of professions: business.

—*Paul Westbrook*

Copyright © 2001 by Living Language, A Random House Company
Maps © 1998, Fodor's Travel Publications

Published by Living Language, A Random House Company, New York, New York.
Random House, Inc., Toronto, London, Sydney, Auckland
www.livinglanguage.com
Living Language and colophon are registered trademarks of Random House, Inc.
Manufactured in the United States.
Design by Wendy Halitzer
Library of Congress Cataloging-in-Publication Data available
ISBN 0-609-80629-7
10 9 8 7 6 5 4 3 2 1
First Paperback Edition

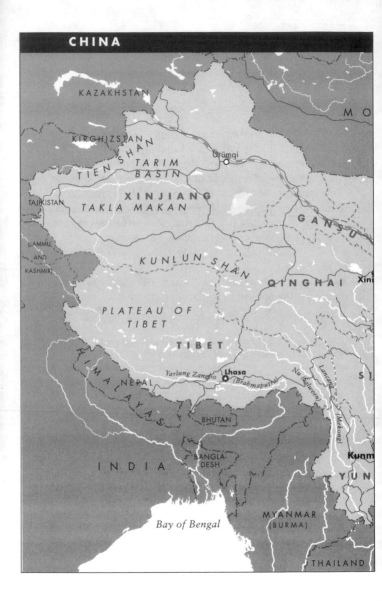

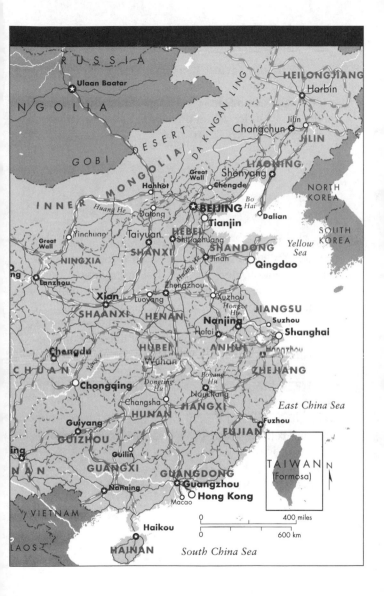

ACKNOWLEDGMENTS

Thanks to the Living Language staff: Lisa Alpert, Elizabeth Bennett, Christopher Warnasch, Suzanne McGrew, Marina Padakis, Helen Tang, Elyse Tomasello, Fernando Galeano, and Pat Ehresmann. Thanks also to An Chen.

AUTHOR INFORMATION

Timothy Dobbins, M. Div., is a communications and strategic alignment specialist. As president of Leadership Technologies, Inc./Cultural Architects™. com, he provides advice, direction, and conflict management skills. An Episcopal priest, he was educated in the United States and Jerusalem, and has studied at the C. G. Jung Institute in Zurich. He lives in Philadelphia and New York City.

Paul Westbrook has a broad business background and has worked for major corporations and business consulting firms. He is now running his own financial and retirement firm, WestBrook Financial Advisers, in Ridgewood, New Jersey. He is the author of *Word Smart for Business* and *Math Smart for Business*, both published by Random House.

CONTENTS

Preface

It can be said that business is the basis of human relationships. The opportunity to interact with people beyond our own "hometown experience" is both a growing necessity and a challenging adventure. Business never stops. Journeying from one country to another becomes easier every day. *Business Companion: Chinese* is written for people in the global marketplace of today's world.

But, you don't need to cross borders to experience the people and cultures of other lands. In today's global marketplace, business is conducted without borders. The telecommunications revolution allows the businessperson to travel to distant lands measured not in miles but in megahertz.

Do business in Hong Kong, Mexico City and Berlin, without ever leaving your desk. Of course, a great deal of global business is conducted in English. Yet, these interactions are enhanced and strengthened by the strategic use of key words and phrases in the others' native tongue, and placed in letters, conversations and over the Internet.

The primary aim of this book, then, is to provide you with the tools to put language to work for you, even if you don't have the time for a traditional language course. Whether you travel to work in foreign lands by plane, train, ship, telephone or computer, this book will increase your business self-confidence and help you develop the power of using a foreign language. After all, communicating on a global level will only continue to be essential in the workplace of the 21st century.

The second, and subtler purpose of this book is to offer you proven and effective ways to communicate the keywords and phrases themselves. This aim has to do with enhancing your global communication skills. Whenever business leaders ask me to help them and their companies create, shape and sustain a new organizational culture, I try to help them use the talents, insights and creative energy of their employees. In guiding this collective leadership effort, I am amazed at how broad and deep is the desire for learning one of the core competencies of global business today: key words and phrases in a foreign language. Developing your foreign language skills and practicing them in the context of the scenarios in this book, will improve your chances for business success.

To assume that English is the only language necessary for successful business interactions is to limit yourself to fewer growth possibilities and maybe even to offend potential clients or associates. In fact, speaking the words and phrases of another language is only part of the equation to more effective communication.

Just as important is your understanding of them when they are used in dialogue. When you begin to read, mark, learn and "inwardly digest" the material in this book, you will be seen as a person willing to expand your communication horizons beyond what's comfortable. You will reveal an intellectual curiosity that will gain the respect of your business partners and your colleagues. Now, let's go to work!

—*Tim Dobbins*

ORGANIZATION OF THE PHRASEBOOK

Even if you don't have the time to immerse yourself in yet another general Chinese course, this phrasebook will help you do business in China or Taiwan in spite of it. While it provides you with basic phrases and expressions you need to make an appointment or introduce yourself in a meeting, it also contains a wealth of business-related terminology and phrases that you would have a hard time finding.

This book can be used either as a reference or as a continuous read, where you will find interesting commentary and helpful cultural information in addition to abundant language material.

Pīnyīn Romanization System and Tone Marks

The most commonly used Chinese transcription system—*pīnyīn*—is described in this section. It is a phonetic spelling system most helpful if your goal is to acquire speaking and listening skills in Chinese. The chart of tone marks is added to help you master Chinese pronunciation.

Chapters 1–6

Chapters 1–6 provide over 1,000 phrases and sentences to be used when on the telephone, in a negotiating meeting, at a dinner table with your business associate or when settling down in your office abroad.

Dialogues

Each chapter has several dialogues recreating a variety of business situations to help you experience the language as it is really used.

Key Words

Here, we provide lists of the key terms you will need to remember from each section or subsection. In order to make them easy to locate, we put them in shaded boxes, with a key icon in the top right corner.

Culture Notes

Culture notes are interspersed throughout the chapters, and provide you with fascinating and useful information about business-related behavior abroad. Their location in the text is marked by a globe icon.

Appendices

Appendices provide such useful information as measurements used in China and Taiwan, holidays celebrated, or interesting Web sites. Appendix D has a grammar summary; a list of "emergency" Chinese words written in Chinese characters is given in Appendix E.

Glossary of Industry Specific Terms

This section contains a very thorough glossary of the terminology used in a wide range of industries.

General Glossary

English-Chinese and Chinese-English, the glossary lists the basic vocabulary words and specific business terminology used in the six chapters of the book.

CD

If you acquired our package including the CD, you will be able to listen to more than 600 phrases from the book. You can just listen, or listen and repeat during a pause provided between the recordings. All the words, phrases and sentences that are recorded come from Chapters 1–6 and appear in **boldface type.**

PĪNYĪN ROMANIZATION AND TONE MARKS

The Chinese language does not have an alphabet. Each word or a syllable is represented by a character, which may be composed of just one stroke (line) or as many as several dozen. To represent Chinese sounds for those who do not read characters, various systems of romanization have been devised. You will learn *pīnyīn*, the standard system used in China and the one most commonly used in the United States.

Each syllable in Chinese has an initial consonant sound and a final vowel sound. There are twenty-three initial sounds and thirty-six final sounds. Here is how each sound is written in *pīnyīn*, with its approximate English equivalent.

INITIAL SOUNDS

Chinese Sound	Approximate English Sound
b	<u>b</u>ear
p	<u>p</u>oor
m	<u>m</u>ore
f	<u>f</u>ake
d	<u>d</u>are
t	<u>t</u>yke
n	<u>n</u>ow
l	<u>l</u>earn
z	yar<u>ds</u>
c	i<u>ts</u>
s	<u>s</u>ing
zh	ju<u>dge</u>
ch	chur<u>ch</u>
sh	<u>sh</u>hhh!
r	<u>r</u>ubber

j	just
q	cheetah
x	shoe
g	get
k	cow
h	help
y	yes
w	want

FINAL SOUNDS

Chinese Sound	Approximate English Sound
a	ma
ai	my, but shorter
ao	pout
an	élan
ang	throng
o	or
ou	float
ong	long
e	bet
ei	day
en	under
eng	lung
i (after z, c, s, zh, ch, sh)	bird
i	it
ia	yah
iao	meow
ian	yan
iang	yang
ie	yes
iu	yo-yo
iong	young
in	sin

ing	si<u>ng</u>
u	fl<u>u</u>
ua	s<u>ua</u>ve
uai	<u>wi</u>de
uan	<u>wan</u>
uang	<u>wong</u>
uo	<u>wo</u>n't
ui	<u>weigh</u>
un	<u>won</u>
ü	rh<u>eu</u>matic
üan	like *ü* above with <u>an</u>
üe	like *ü* above with n<u>et</u>
ün	like *ü* above with <u>an</u>
er	met<u>er</u>

TONE MARKS

Getting the tones right is the most difficult part of Chinese pronunciation. Here's a table that can help.

Tone	Pīnyīn Mark*	Example	How you pronounce it	Similar English intonation
First tone	—	mā "mother"	Pronounce the word in an even manner, but with a high-pitched voice.	Say "yes" as if you were answering a telephone, with a high-pitched but even voice.
Second tone	´	má "hemp"	Pronounce the word with a rising intonation.	As in English questions. Say "yes" as in a question: "Yes? Or, no?"
Third tone	ˇ	mǎ "horse"	Pronounce the word by starting close to the bottom of your voice range, and let your voice first dip to the bottom, then rise to about the middle of your range.	This is the trickiest tone. Say "yes" as if you're querying a statement somebody just made: "Yeees?! And then what?"
Fourth tone	`	mà "to scold"	Pronounce the word by starting high, dropping your voice quickly to the bottom of your range.	Say "yes" as if you are answering a question in a somewhat abrupt and angry manner: "Yes! Now, stop it!"
Neutral	(No mark)	ma - question particle	Pronounce it lightly, as if it had no tone.	Pronounce "yes" without thinking and without any distinct melody, as when you're reading a word out of the dictionary.

*Note that the shape of the pīnyīn tone marks suggests the "movement" of your voice, that is, the fall and rise of the pitch of your voice.

1 GETTING STARTED

Business is global, business is fast-paced, and business is high-tech. There is an energy and urgency underlying our activities and communications. The new century is alive and in motion.

High-tech tools give instant access to clients and associates. Finding the right way to communicate is the key to success in business as much as it is in our private lives. Learning the following greetings, introductions or openers will go a long way. When you say "Hello!" to someone in his or her native language you show your willingness to make an effort in their tongue and you also make a great first impression.

We cover a bunch of subjects, all of which will get you started doing business successfully overseas. Here is a summary of sections in this chapter:

Saying Hello
Introducing Oneself and
  Getting Names Right
Introducing Others
Thank You and Please
Small Talk
Presenting Your Business and
  Department
Telephone: Making a Call
Telephone: Getting Through
Telephone: Why You Are Calling
Setting the Time for the
  Appointment or Meeting
Talking to Machines: Voice Mail
  and Answering Machines
Telling Time and Giving Dates

Business Letters
E-mail and Internet

So let's start with the basics—the opener, the ice-breaker, the hand offered in greeting.

SAYING HELLO

"Wènhǎo"

SHǏMÌSĪ XIĀNSHENG: *Nín* hǎo. Wǒ shì Shǐmìsī Xiānsheng.*

LǏ XIĀNSHENG: *Wǒ shì Lǐ Xiānsheng. Wǒ cóng shí diǎn jiù kāishǐ děng nǐ.*

SHǏMÌSĪ XIĀNSHENG: *Shì de. Dùibuqǐ, wǒ chí dào le. Jìchéngchē sījī mí le lù.*

LǏ XIĀNSHENG: *Hǎo la. Qǐng jìn lái zùo ba.*

"Saying Hello"

MR. SMITH: *Hello, I am Mr. Smith.*

MR. LI: *I am Mr. Li. I have been waiting since 10.*

MR. SMITH: *Yes. I'm sorry to be late. The taxi driver got lost.*

MR. LI: *Well, come in and have a seat.*

Your knowledge of Chinese customs and culture will give you an advantage in doing business abroad. Be observant and follow your host so you can avoid drinking from the finger bowl. At the first meeting with your Chinese partners, stick to handshakes. The Chinese often accompany the handshake with a nod or slight bow.

---

*Nín is the polite form of the pronoun *nǐ.*

Key Words

Good-bye	Zàijiàn
Hello	Nǐ hǎo
Introduce oneself/ someone (to)	Ràng wǒ lái jièshào wǒ zìjǐ/mǒurén . . .
Name	Míngzi/Xìngmíng
It's nice to meet you.	Hěn gāoxìng rènshi nǐ.
Repeat (to)	Chóngfù/Zài shūo yī biàn
Thank you.	Xièxie.
You're welcome.	Bù yòng xiè./Bié kèqi.

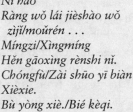

Good morning/afternoon/ evening/night.

Zǎoshàng hǎo./Xiàwǔ hǎo./Wǎnshàng hǎo or **Wǎn'ān***.

Good-bye.
Zàijiàn.

Hello.
Nǐ hǎo.

See you soon/later.
Zàihùi./Děng hǔi'r zàijiàn.

See you tomorrow/next week/next year.
Míngtiān jiàn./Xià zhōu jiàn./Míngnián jiàn.

It's a pleasure to see you again.
Hěn gāoxìng yòu jiàn dào nǐ.

It's great to see you again.
Yòu jiàn dào nǐ tài hǎo le.

How are you?
Nǐ hǎo ma?

It's a pleasure to finally meet you.
Zǒngsuàn jiàn dào nǐ le, shízài ràng rén gāoxìng.

I'm glad to meet you in person. (We've spoken on the phone so many times.)
Hǎo gāoxìng jiàn dào nǐ běnrén. (Wǒmen zài diànhùa shàng yǐ tán gùo dūocì.)

Hi! How are you doing?
Nǐ hái hǎo ma?

I'm honored to be here.
Lái zhèlǐ, wǒ gǎndào fēicháng róngxìng.

I'm so glad to be here.
Hěn gāoxìng lái zhèlǐ.

---

*Chinese use an apostrophe to separate syllables whose pronunciation is unclear. For example, *wanan* could be *wa'nan* or *wan'an*.

INTRODUCING ONESELF AND GETTING NAMES RIGHT

Names are important for a business relationship. Get them right! Since a person's name is critically important to that person, if you get it wrong it can mean an unsuccessful business connection.

If a person's name seems long or difficult, ask what he or she prefers to be called. Use that name. You should know that in many cultures the use of nicknames is less common then in United States, especially in the office. If they want to use their full names—then, it's up to you to learn them. It's part of doing business abroad. No one said it was going to be easy. At the same time, English names can be just as difficult for your foreign contacts, so be as patient and flexible as you would expect others to be.

Chinese always put the family name (last name or surname) first, followed by their given name (first name). Most names in China consist of three characters, that is, one character for the last name, and two characters for the first name, for example, *Mǎ* (last name) *Xiǎo-hóng* (first name). However, more people are using single-character first names nowadays, for example, *Gāo* (last name) *Yuán* (first name). Also, a limited number of last names in China are formed of two characters, for example, *Ōuyáng*, *Sīmǎ*. If a person has a title, such as Director (*Chǎngzhǎng*), or Chairman (*Zhǔxí*), it is considered respectful and good manners to address him or her by using the family name followed by the title, for example, Director Liu (*Liú Chǎngzhǎng*), or Chairman Mao (*Máo Zhǔxí*).

My name is . . .	Wǒ (de míngzi) jiào . . .
I am . . .	Wǒ shì . . .

What is your name?	Nǐ jiào shénme míngzi?
You are . . . ?	Nǐ shì . . . ?
Can you please repeat your name?	Qǐng chóngfù yīxià nǐ de míngzi.
Can you please write your name down for me?	Qǐng nǐ wèi wǒ xiě yīxià nǐ de míngzi.
How do you spell that?	Zěnme xiě?
My name is . . . but everyone calls me . . .	Wǒ jiào . . . dàn dàjiā dōu jiào wǒ . . .
My name is . . . but I like to be called . . .	Wǒ jiào . . . dàn wǒ xǐhuān bié rén jiào wǒ . . .
My name is spelled . . .	Wǒ de míngzi shi zhèyàng xiě de. . .
My title/position is . . .	Wǒ de zhíchēng/zhíwèi shì . . .
How do you do?	Nǐ hǎo.
It's a pleasure to meet you. I am . . .	Hěn gāoxìng rènshì nǐ. Wǒ shì . . .
It's nice to meet you. I'm . . .	Néng jiàn dào nǐ tài hǎo le. Wǒ shì . . .
So, we finally meet.	Wǒmen zhōngyú jiànmiàn le.
Please call me.	Qǐng dǎ diànhùa gěi wǒ.
Please/Let's keep in touch.	Qǐng/ràng wǒmen bǎochí liánlùo.

INTRODUCING OTHERS

Wang, may I introduce you to . . .	Wáng, ràng wǒ lái jièshào yīxià . . .
I'd like to introduce you to . . .	Wǒ xiǎng gěi nǐ jièshào yīxià . . .
Ms. Zhāng, this is . . .	Zhāng Xiǎojie, zhè shì . . .
Have you met Mr. Zhong?	Nǐ jiàn guo Zhōng Xiānsheng ma?
It's important for you to meet . . .	Ràng nǐ gēn . . . rènshì shì hěn zhòngyào de.
You should meet . . .	Nǐ děi gēn . . . rènshì.

5

THANK YOU AND PLEASE

Thank you (very much).	(Fēicháng) **xièxie.**
You're welcome.	**Bù yòng xiè.**
Please.	**Qǐng.**
Excuse me.	**Dùibuqǐ.**
Sorry.	Hěn **bàoqiàn.**
I'm so sorry.	**Fēicháng bàoqiàn.**
It doesn't matter.	**Méiguānxì.**
That's fine/OK.	**Kěyǐ/Xíng.**

SMALL TALK

When you make even a stumbling attempt at small talk, you show that you're willing to put yourself out there and make an effort. You don't need to be perfect, you just need to show you'll take the lead and try your best to make a great first impression.

Americans are a "chatty" bunch of people. People in other cultures do not feel as pressed to make "small talk" and keep the conversation going when there is not much to be said. So don't be impatient or offended if there are moments when people don't have anything to say to you, and don't try to impose conversation upon others. Learning to communicate in other languages and cultures is like learning to dance—relax and let the music lead you.

Chinese are not interested in "small talk" as we know it. Instead, they tend to get into more personal topics, such as your age, marital status and salary! So don't be surprised if someone asks you those questions as you try to make small talk. Chinese believe that asking personal questions is a way to show a genuine interest in the other person, and a way to start a friendly relationship, which they find indispensible for doing business. A safe way to start a conversation and avoid overly personal questions is to say a few words in Chinese, or ask questions such as "Which school did you go to?", "Where did you learn your English?", "Have you been to the United States?", "Which part of China are you from?", or "Have you always lived in Beijing [or whatever place you happen to be in]?".

"Liáotiān"

GAŌ XIĀNSHENG: *Fēixíng yúkùai ma?*

JIÉKÈSÙN XIĂOJIE: *Yŏu diăn dòngdàng, dàn fànshí què hĕn hăo.*

GAŌ XIĀNSHENG: *Hùoxŭ méiyŏu zhè jiā cāngŭan de hăo chī ba.*

JIÉKÈSÙN XIĂOJIE: *Nĭ yĭqián lái zhèlĭ chī gùo ma?*

"Small Talk"

MR. GAO: *How was your flight?*

MS. JACKSON: *It was somewhat turbulent. But surprisingly the food was good.*

MR. GAO: *Probably not as good as in this restaurant.*

MS. JACKSON: *Have you eaten here before?*

Key Words

English	Yīngwén/Yīngyŭ
How do you say . . . in Chinese?	. . . yòng zhōngwén zĕnme shūo?
Language	Yŭyán
Today	Jīntiān
Tomorrow	Míngtiān
Weather	Tiānqì/Qìhòu

How are you?	Nǐ hǎo ma?
So how have you been?	Nǐ jìnlái hái hǎo ma?
How are you feeling this morning?	Nǐ jīntiān gǎnjúe zěnmeyàng?
Very well./Fine. Thank you. And you?	Hěn hǎo./Hái hǎo. Xièxie. Nǐ ne?
It's very hot/cold today.	Jīntiān hěn rè/lěng.
What beautiful weather/lousy weather.	Tiānqì zhēn hǎo/hùai.
It's supposed to rain/to snow/to be nice tomorrow.	Tīngshuō míngtiān tiānqì hěnhǎo/yào xià yǔ/yào xià xǔe.
Is it always this hot here?	Zhèlǐ zǒng shì zhème rè ma?
I'm looking forward to working with you.	Wǒ qīdài zhe yǔ nǐ yīdào gōngzùo.
I am looking forward to our time together.	Wǒ pànwàng yǔ nǐ gòng dù shígūang.
Me too.	Wǒ yě shì.
I'd like to keep in touch with you.	Wǒ xiǎng yǔ nǐ bǎochí liánlùo.
I'll give you a call when I get back.	Děng wǒ húiqù hòu zài gěi nǐ dǎ diànhùa.
Please call me.	Qǐng dǎ diànhùa gěi wǒ.
I want to try to use your language.	Wǒ xiǎng shǐyòng nǐmen de yǔyán.
I'm afraid I'm not very good at it.	Kǒngpà wǒ hái bù shúliàn.
Please be patient with me.	Qǐng nàixīn yīdiǎn.
Unfortunately, I speak only English.	Yíhàn de shì, wǒ zhǐ néng shūo yīngyǔ.
I'd like to learn (some words in) your language.	Wǒ xiǎng xúe yīdiǎn nǐmen de yǔyán (wénzì).
Can you teach me some words in your language?	Nǐ néng jiāo wǒ yīdiǎn nǐmen de yǔyán ma?
Of course, it would be my pleasure.	Dāngrán kěyǐ la.

How do you say . . . ?   **Nǐ zěnme shūo . . . ?**
Can you say that again?   **Kěyǐ zài shūo yībiàn ma?**
Please, repeat.   Qǐng chóngfù yī xìa.
How do you write that?   Nà ge zěnme xiě?

On weather

If you're completely stuck for topics, yes, there's still the weather. When in doubt, talking about the weather is the safest subject.

"Tiānqì"
JIÉKÈSÙN XIǍOJIE: *Tiānqì xiǎnrán yǐjīng biàn le.*
GĀO XIĀNSHENG: *Shì ya. Zúotiān tiānqì qínglǎng, xiànzài què qīngpén dàyǔ.*
JIÉKÈSÙN XIǍOJIE: *Xiànzài shì yǔjì ma?*
GĀO XIĀNSHENG: *Bù shì. Jiù jīntīan xià yǔ.*

"The Weather"
MS. JACKSON: *The weather sure has changed.*
MR. GAO: *Yes. Yesterday it was clear, but now it's raining very hard.*
MS. JACKSON: *Is this the season for rain?*
MR. GAO: *Not really. It's just a rainy day.*

Key Words	
Clear	Qínglǎng
Cold	Lěng
Cool	Liángshǔang
Hot	Rè
Rain (to)/Rainy Day	Xià yǔ/Yǔ tiān
Snow (to)	Xià xǔe
Stormy	Fēngbào
Temperature	Wēndù

Warm Weather	Nǔanhuo Tiānqì
What's the temperature?*	Shénme wēndù?
It's 15 degrees Celsius.	Shì shíwǔ dù.
What's the average temperature this time of year?	Měinián zhè ge shíhòu de píngjūn wēndù shì dūoshǎo?
What's the weather report?	Tiānqì yùbào shūo shénme ne?
What's the forecast for tomorrow?	Míngtiān tiānqì yùbào rúhé?
It's going to stay nice.	Tiānqì hùi yīyàng hǎo.
It's going to be cloudy.	Jiāng shì yīntiān.
It should be sunny.	Hùi shì qíngtiān.
The forecast is for warm weather.	Tiānqì yùbào qìhòu nǔanhuo.
We're going to have . . .	**Tiāngqi hùi . . .**
fine weather.	**hěn hǎo.**
good weather.	hǎo.
hot weather.	hěn rè.
bad weather.	hěn hùai.
Will it . . .	**Hùi . . .**
rain?	**xià yǔ ma?**
snow?	**xià xǔe ma?**
How are the road conditions between . . . and . . . ?	**Zài . . . yú . . . zhījiān lù de qíngkùang zěnmeyàng?**
It's very foggy.	**Yǒu wù.**
It's very slippery.	**Lù tài húa.**
The roads have been plowed.	Lùmiàn yǐ qīngsǎo gùo le.

---

*Please refer to Appendix A for the Celsius and Fahrenheit conversion table.

PRESENTING YOUR BUSINESS AND DEPARTMENT

Following the initial greetings and introductions, you may wish to identify your company, organization, group and/or position in it. Never take for granted that others know your role.

The name of my company is . . .	Wǒmen gōngsī de míngzi shì . . .
I/We specialize in . . .	Wǒ/wǒmen zhuānmén zùo . . .
My department is . . .	Wǒmen bùmén shì . . .
I am with . . .	Wǒ zài . . .
I work with . . .	Wǒ wèi . . .
I'm . . .	Wǒ shì . . .
president of . . .	de zǒngcái.
vice president of . . .	de fù zǒngcái.
in charge of operations.	fùzé jīngyíng yèwù de.
the chief financial officer.	shǒuǒuxí kuàijì.
the treasurer.	chūnà/cái wù zhǔ guǎn.
the general counsel.	tōngfǎ lǜshī.
a director.	zhǔrèn.
a manager.	jīnglǐ.
the leader of our team.	zǔzhǎng.
in administration.	gǎo xíngzhèng de.
in customer service.	gǎo gùkè fúwù de.
in finance.	gǎo cáiwù de.
in human resources.	gǎo rénshì de.
in the legal department.	zài fǎzhìbù.
in marketing.	gǎo tūixiāo de.
in production.	gǎo jiāgōng de/zài shēng chǎn bùmén.
in sales.	gǎo xiāoshòu de.

A note about the word *director*. In the U.S., the word can either mean a member of the board of directors, the highest management level in a corporation, or, it can mean some lower level of management. Commonly, a director reports to a vice president and has managers report to him or her. However, in many countries, the word *director* or *managing director* refers to one of the highest levels of management, equivalent to the president in some U. S. organizations.

In Chinese, *dǒngshì* (director of the board), *zhǔrèn* (department director) and *chǎngzhǎng* (factory director) define different positions in a company, even though they can all be translated as a "director" in English. When in doubt, ask for clarification. Otherwise, you may end up talking to the wrong person in the hierarchy.

Business cards

If you are offering your business card, be careful to follow the appropriate cultural norms of the country in which you are doing business. In general, never force a card on a potential client. Ask if you may give him or her one. It is also good etiquette, as well as natural, to ask for one of his or her cards.

Don't stuff it into your pocket immediately! Don't write a restaurant's telephone number on the back of it (at least not in front of the person)! Be sure to actually take a look at it and note what's on it—to some people it actually matters. Then put it away carefully.

One last point. You are likely to hand out more business cards than at home, so bring plenty.

When doing business in China, it is considered polite to have your business cards in both English and Chinese. Make sure you present your business card with both hands and the lettering facing up. This is an old-fashioned courtesy many westernized Chinese no longer practice, but most people will appreciate that you are making an attempt to follow the etiquette of the land.

"Bàngōng Huìyì"

QIÓNGSĪ XIǍOJIE: *Xià Xiǎojie, zhè shì wǒ de míngpiàn. Wǒ de diànhuà haòmǎ shì yī sān sì èr sān èr sì. Kěyǐ bǎ nǐ de míngpiàn gěi wǒ ma?*

XIÀ XIǍOJIE: *Dāngrán kěyǐ. Zhè'r gěi nǐ.*

QIÓNGSĪ XIǍOJIE: *Kàn qǐlái nǐ shì zài Xīndà bàngōnglóu gōngzuò. Zhèlǐ hái yǒu nǐ de diànzǐ yóujiàn dìzhǐ.*

"A Meeting at the Office"

MS. JOHNSON: *Ms. Xia, this is my card. You will see that my phone number is 134–2324. My e-mail address is also included. May I have one of your cards?*

MS. XIA: *Sure. Here you go.*

MS. JOHNSON: *Oh, I see that you work out of the Xinda office. I see your e-mail address here.*

Here is my business card.	**Zhè shì wǒ de míngpiàn.**
You will see that our telephone number is . . .	**Wǒmen de diànhuà hàomǎ shì . . .**
Our address is . . .	**Wǒmen de dìzhǐ shì . . .**
Our e-mail is . . .	**Wǒmen de diànzǐ yóujiàn dìzhǐ shì . . .**
May I have one of your business cards?	**Kěyǐ yào yī zhāng nǐ de míngpiàn ma?**
Do you have a business card?	**Nǐ yǒu míngpiàn ma?**
Your company has very nice business cards.	**Nǐmen gōngsī de míngpiàn hěn piàoliang.**

Your card looks very professional.	Nǐ de míngpiàn hěn zhuānyèhuà.
Your logo is very nice.	Nǐ de biāoshì hěn hǎo kàn.
Could you pronounce your name for me?	**Kěyǐ wèi wǒ niàn yī xià nǐ de míngzi ma?**
Could you repeat your name?	Kěyǐ chóngfù yī xià nǐ de míngzi ma?
Could you repeat the name of your firm?	Kěyǐ chóngfù yī xià nǐmen gōngsī de míngzi ma?

TELEPHONE: MAKING A CALL

When you're trying to be understood in another language, using a telephone is not as simple as picking up the receiver. Here's the vocabulary and phrases you need to make this common business activity a success.

"Dǎ Diànhuà"
XĪNKÈLÁI XIĀNSHENG: *Qǐng chóngfù yī xià diànhuà hàomǎ.*
JIĒXIÀNSHĒNG: *Hàomǎ shì yī sān sì, èr sān èr sì. Wǒ xiànzài jiù gěi nǐ jiē hào.*
XĪNKÈLÁI XIĀNSHENG: *Xièxie.*

"On the Phone"
MR. SINCLAIR: *Would you repeat that number, please?*
OPERATOR: *The number is 134–2324. Let me transfer you now.*
MR. SINCLAIR: *Thank you.*

Key Words	
Answer (to)	*Húi/dáfù*
Answering machine	*Liúyánjī*

Be on hold (to)	*Děnghòu*
Busy	*Zhànxiàn*
Call (to)	*Gěi . . . dǎ diànhùa*
Calling card	*Diànhùakǎ*
Cellular phone	*Yídòng diànhùa/Shǒujī*
Dial (to)	*Bōhào*
Extension	*Fēnjī*
Hang up (to)	*Gùa diào diànhùa*
Line	*Diànhùaxiàn*
Local call	*Duǎntú diànhùa/Běn shì diànhùa*
Long-distance call	*Chángtú diànhùa*
Message	*Liúyán*
Number	*Hàomǎ*
Operator	*Jiēxiànyúan*
Put on hold (to)	*Ràng . . . bié gùa diào*
Telephone	*Diànhùajī*
Transfer (to)	*Jiē . . . /Zhǔan . . .*
Voice mail	*Yǒu shēng yoújiàn*

I'd like to place a call.	Wǒ yào dǎ diànhùa.
How can I make a phone call?	Zěnyàng dǎ diànhùa?
Where can I make a phone call?	Zài nǎlǐ kěyǐ dǎ diànhùa?
Is there a telephone booth here?	Zhè'r yǒu diànhùatíng ma?
How much does a local call cost?	Shìnèi diànhùa shōufeì dūoshǎo?
How can I use my calling card on this phone?	Zěnyàng shǐyòng wǒ de diànhùakǎ dǎ diànhùa?
How can I make a local call?	Zěnyàng dǎ shìnèi diànhùa?
How can I make a long-distance call?	Zěnyàng dǎ chángtú diànhùa?

How can I make a conference call?	Diànhùa hùiyì zěnyàng dǎ?
How do I get an outside line?	Zěnyàng jiē wàixiàn?
How can I call the United States?	Zěnyàng gěi Měigúo dǎ diànhùa?
Please . . .	Qǐng . . .
call this number.	dǎ zhè ge hàomǎ.
dial this number.	bō zhè ge hàomǎ.
forward this call.	zhuǎn yī xià diànhuà.
get an operator.	zhǎo jiēxiànshēng.
redial this number.	zài bō zhè ge hàomǎ.
transfer this call.	zhuǎn yī xià diànhùa.
I need to call . . .	Wǒ yào gěi . . . dǎ diànhùa.
I would like to leave a message.	Wǒ xiǎng liúyán.
No one is answering.	Méi rén jiē diànhùa.
Please hang up.	Qǐng guà diào diànhùa.
My party hung up.	Dùifāng bǎ diànhùa guà dùan le.
I was put on hold.	Tā ràng wǒ děnghòu.
Please put me on speaker.	Wǒ yào shǐyòng diànhùa yángshēngqì.
I have you on speaker.	Wǒ xiànzài yòng yángshēng qì gēn nǐ shuōhùa.
How do I redial?	Zěnyàng chóng bō hàomǎ?
How do I transfer this call?	Zěnme zhuǎnjiē diànhùa?
I'd like to check my voice-mail.	Wǒ xiǎng tīngtīng wǒ de yǒushēng yóujiàn.
How do I make a recording?	Zěnyàng lùyīn?
Do you have a/an . . .	Nǐ yǒu . . .
answering machine?	liúyánjī ma?
calling card?	diànhùakǎ ma?

direct line?	zhíxiàn ma?
switchboard?	jiēhàotái ma?
telephone directory?	diànhùa zhǐnán ma?
contact list?	liánlùo míngdān ma?

I would like to buy a . . .	Wǒ xiǎng mǎi . . . *
car phone.	qìchē diànhùa.
cellular phone.	yídòng diànhùa/shǒujī.
portable phone.	shǒujī.
video phone.	yǐngxiàng diànhùa.

Does your office have . . .	Nǐmen bàngōngshì yǒu . . .
e-mail capability?	diànzǐ yoújiàn ma?
Internet access?	diànnǎo wǎnglùo ma?
Web access?	wǎngyè wǎnglùo ma?

The line is busy.	Zhànxiàn.
We have a bad connection.	Xiànlù bù hǎo.
We got cut off.	Wǒmen bèi gùa duàn le.

TELEPHONE: GETTING THROUGH

The first word you are likely to hear on the phone in China is *wèi*. It's equivalent to the telephone "hello" we use in America. *Wèi* is also repeatedly used during phone calls as a way of ensuring that the other person is still there, or to fill in the gaps in a conversation.

After hearing *wèi*, you can ask for a person you wish to talk to. Normally, Chinese callers do not introduce themselves first. If you are asked to identify yourself, state the name of your company (Say something like: "I am from Beijing Jeep Company.") rather

---

*The words "buy" and "sell" in Chinese have the same sounds—*mai* in each case—but "buy" uses the 3rd tone while "sell" uses the 4th tone.

than your own name because your company often gets more respect.

"Dǎ Tōng Le"
SHĬMÌSĪ XIĀNSHENG: *Wèi.*
TÁN XIĀNSHENG: *Wèi. Zhè shì Tán Xiānsheng.*
SHĬMÌSĪ XIĀNSHENG: *Nǐ hǎo. Wǒ yào zhǎo Hùa Xiānsheng.*
TÁN XIĀNSHENG: *Qǐng děng yī xià. Duìbuqǐ, Hùa Xiānsheng bù zài. Nǐ yào liúyán ma?*
SHĬMÌSĪ XIĀNSHENG: *Wǒ yào. Qǐng gàosù tā gěi Xī'érdùn Fàndiàn dǎ diànhùa, zhǎo Shǐmisī Xiānsheng. Hàomǎ shì yī èr sān sì wǔ sì liù. Wǒ de fángjiān hàomǎ shì wǔ èr sān.*
TÁN XIĀNSHENG: *Wǒ hùi zhǔang tā.*

"Getting Through"
MR. SMITH: *Hello?*
MR. TAN: *Hello. This is Mr. Tan speaking.*
MR. SMITH: *Hello. I would like to speak to Mr. Hua.*
MR. TAN: *Please hold . . . I'm sorry, but Mr. Hua is not here. May I take a message?*
MR. SMITH: *Yes. Please tell him to call Mr. Smith at the Hilton Hotel, number 123–4546. My room number is 523.*
MR. TAN: *I will give him this message.*

Hello?	**Wèi.**
This is . . . calling/ speaking.	**Zhè shì . . .**
I'd like to speak to . . .	**Wǒ yào zhǎo . . .**
May I speak to . . . ?	Kěyǐ zhǎo yī xìa . . . ma?
Do I have the office of . . . ?	Zhè shì . . . de bàngōngshì ma?

Could you connect me with . . . ?	Kěyǐ gěi wǒ jiē . . . ma?
Extension . . . please.	Qǐng jiē . . . fēnjī.
Please put me through to . . .	Qǐng jiē . . .
I don't mind holding.	Wǒ kěyǐ děnghòu.
Is . . . available?	. . . zài ma?
Is . . . in the office?	. . . zài bàngōngshì ma?
When do you expect . . . to return?	Nǐ zhīdào . . . shénme shíhòu huílái ma?
He/she is busy/not available right now.	Tā/tā xiànzài hěn máng/bù zài.
He/she is not at his/her desk.	Tā/tā bù zài zuòwèi shàng.
He/she is in a meeting.	Tā/tā zài kāihuì.
He/she is out to lunch.	Tā/tā qù chī zhōngwǔfàn le.
He/she is out of town/ away from the office.	Tā/tā bù zài chénglǐ/ bàngōngshì.
Yes, I understand.	Wǒ zhīdào le.
I'm sorry, I did not understand.	Duìbuqǐ, wǒ méi dǒng.
Could you repeat that?	Kěyǐ chóngfù yī xià ma?
Okay.	Hǎo.
Could you repeat your name?	Kěyǐ chóngfù yī xià nǐ de míngzi ma?
Could I ask you to spell that please?	Kěyǐ tì wǒ pīnxiě yī xià ma?

TELEPHONE: WHY YOU ARE CALLING

I'm calling to follow up with/on . . .	Wǒ dǎ diànhùa lái shì xiǎng kànkan . . .
I am calling/would like to arrange an appointment with . . .	Wǒ dǎ diànhùa/xiǎng yú . . . ānpái yūehùi.
The reason for my call is . . .	Wǒ dǎ diànhùa lái shì wèi . . .

19

I'm calling at the request of . . .	Wǒ gěi nǐ dǎ diànhùa shì yào . . .
I'm calling to tell you . . .	Wǒ gěi nǐ dǎ diànhùa shì yào gàosù nǐ . . .
This call is in reference to . . .	**Gěi nǐ dǎ diànhùa shì guānyú . . .**
. . . asked me to call him/ her this morning.	. . . yào wǒ jīntiān zǎoshàng gěi tā/tā dǎ diànhùa.
I'm returning . . . call.	Wǒ shì gěi . . . húi diànhùa.
You may remember . . .	Nǐ huòxǔ hái jìdé . . .
Who's calling?	**Zhè shì shúi ya?**
Hold the line.	**Děng yī xià.**
You have a call on line 1.	**Yī hào xiàn yǒu nǐ de diànhùa.**
You have the wrong number.	**Nǐ dǎ cùo hàomǎ le.**

SETTING THE TIME FOR THE APPOINTMENT OR MEETING

Appointments are generally made over the telephone. While it is true that more arrangements are now being made by e-mail, it's to your advantage to speak to the person directly or to his or her secretary, or leave a message. These days, busy people receive many e-mails per day. You don't want your request for an appointment to get lost in that e-mail sea.

"Yuēhùi"

JIÉKÈSÙN XIǍOJIĚ: *Wǒmen xiǎng zài shí diǎn kāishǐ kāihùi.*

ZHŪ XIĀNSHENG: *Wǒmen kěyǐ zǎo yìdiǎn'r ma? Jiǔ diǎn bàn hǎo ma?*

JIÉKÈSÙN XIǍOJIE: *Kěyǐ. Wǒmen jiǔ diǎn bàn yǐqián dào nǐmen bàngōngshì.*

ZHŪ XIĀNSHENG: *Húitóu jiàn.*

"Setting the Appointment"

MS. JACKSON: *We would like to start the meeting at 10.*

MR. ZHU: *Could we start earlier, say 9:30?*

MS. JACKSON: *Fine. We'll be in your office before 9:30.*

MR. ZHU: *See you then.*

Key Words

Appointment	Yuēhùi
Beginning/End	Kāishǐ/jiēshù
Calendar	Rìlì
Cancel an appointment (to)	Qǔxiāo yuēhùi
Day	Tiān/Báitiān
Earlier	Zǎo yīdiǎn'r
Later	Wǎn yīdiǎn'r
Make an appointment (to)	Yuēhùi
Meeting	Hùiyì
Okay	Hǎo/Xíng
Schedule	Shíjiān biǎo
Start	Kāishǐ
Time	Shíjiān
Week	Xīngqī/Zhōu

Time

I'd like to meet with you tomorrow.	Wǒ xiǎng gēn nǐ míngtiān jiànmiàn.
Would next week be okay?	Xià ge xīngqī kěyǐ ma?
How does Thursday/next week look?	Xīngqī sì zěnmeyàng/Xià ge xīngqī zěnmeyàng?

21

Does he/she have room on his/her calendar for . . .	Tā/Tā háiyǒu shíjiān . . . ma?
It's important to meet soon.	Jíshí jiànmiàn shì hěn zhòngyào de.
I can't meet (with you) next week.	Wǒ xià xīngqī bù néng (yú nǐ) jiànmiàn.
I'm not available/busy tomorrow.	Wǒ míngtiān méiyǒu shíjiān/ hěn máng.
At what time will the meeting begin?	Hùijiàn shénme shíhòu kāishǐ?
What time do we begin?	Wǒmen shénme shíjiān kāishǐ?
When will the meeting be over?	Hùiyì shénme shíhòu jiēshù?
When do we finish?	Wǒmen shénme shíhòu jiēshù?
Tomorrow is fine/ excellent.	Míngtiān kěyǐ/Míngtiān tài hǎo le.

Place and directions

Where shall we meet?	Wǒmen zài nǎ'er jiànmiàn?
Do you wish to meet in my office?	Nǐ yùanyì lái wǒ bàngōngshì jiànmiàn ma?
Shall I come to your office?	Shì wǒ lái nǐ de bàngōngshì ma?
Where is your office/ hotel?	Nǐ de bàngōngshì/lǚgǔan zài nǎr?
Could you fax me a map please?	Nǐ kěyǐ bǎ dìtú chúanzhēn gěi wǒ ma?
Please wait while I get a pencil and some paper.	Qǐng děng yī xià, ràng wǒ ná zhāng zhǐ hé bǐ.
Do you need directions to my office?	Nǐ xūyào lái wǒ bàngōngshì de lùxiàn ma?

| I will meet you in my office/the lobby of the hotel. | **Wǒmen zài nǐ bàngōngshì/ lǚguǎn méntīng jiànmiàn.** |
| Where is the hotel? | Lǚguǎn zài nǎr? |

Completing the Conversation

Thank you very much for your assistance.	**Fēicháng gǎnxiè nǐ de xiézhù.**
It's been a pleasure/great to talk to you.	**Yú nǐ jiāotán hěn gāoxìng/tài hǎo le.**
I'm very glad we were able to talk.	Néng yú nǐ jiāotán wǒ hěn gāoxìng.
I can't believe we finally connected!	Wǒmen zhōngyú liánxì shàng le. Wǒ zhēn bù gǎn xiāngxìn!
I look forward to the meeting.	**Wǒ pàn zhe yú nǐ jiànmiàn.**
I look forward to hearing from/talking to you again.	Wǒ pàn nǐ de xiāoxí/zài yú nǐ jiāotán.
Take care, and I hope to see you soon.	Qǐng bǎozhòng, xīwàng hěn kuài zàijiàn.

Other Helpful Phrases While on the Telephone

Yes, I understand.	Shì de. Wǒ míngbái.
I'm sorry. I did not understand you.	Duìbuqǐ. Wǒ bù míngbái.
Could you please repeat that/your name?	Kěyǐ chóngfù yī xià nà ge/nǐ de míngzi ma?
Could you please spell your/the name for me?	Kěyǐ wèi wǒ pīnxiě yī xià nǐ de/nà ge míngzi ma?
All right/Okay.	**Hǎo./Xíng.**
Sure.	**Dāngrán kěyǐ.**

May I read the number back to you?	Ràng wǒ gěi nǐ niàn yī xià hàomǎ, hǎo ma?
Could you please speak louder?	**Qǐng dà shēng yī diǎn, hǎo ma?**
This is a bad line. Let me call you back.	**Zhè tíao xiàn bù hǎo. Ràng wǒ gěi nǐ dǎ húilái.**

TALKING TO MACHINES: VOICE MAIL AND ANSWERING MACHINES

When leaving a message on an answering machine, remember to speak slowly and repeat important information, such as telephone numbers, names, and specific times.

Answering machines are still not common in China, so the Chinese are not used to leaving messages. In business interactions, it is important to make appointments in advance and to be there on time. In personal interactions, people tend to be much more casual, and often just drop by or call to make instant arrangements.

"Liúyán"

QIÓNGSĪ XIĀNSHENG: *Sòng Xiānsheng, zhè shì Àilìxìn de Qióngsī Xiānsheng. Wǒ zài Xīěrdùn Fàndiàn. Zhèlǐ de diànhuà hàomǎ shì yī èr sān sì wǔ liù qī. Wǒmen shuō guo wǎnshàng bā diǎn zhōng gēn nǐ chīfàn. Nǐ kěyǐ dào fàndiàn lái jiē wǒ ma? Zài shuō yī biàn, wǒ zài Xīěrdùn Fàndiàn, diànhuà shì yī èr sān sì wǔ liù qī. Qǐng gàosu wǒ nǐ shìfǒu kěyǐ zài bā diǎn zhōng lái jiē wǒ.*

"Leaving a Message"

MR. JONES: *Mr. Song, this is Mr. Jones of Ericsson. I'm staying at the Hilton Hotel. The telephone here is 123–4567. I would like to meet you for dinner at 8:00 P.M. as we had talked about. Could you pick me up at the hotel? Again, I'm at the Hilton, telephone number 123–4567. Let me know if you can pick me up at 8.*

Key Words

Answering machine	Liúyánjī
Message	Xìnxí
Pound key	Jǐngzìjiàn
Pound sign	Jǐngzìhào
Voice mail	Yǒushēn yóujiàn

I would like to leave a message.	Wǒ xiǎng liú ge yán.
Could you take a message?	Nǐ kěyǐ chuán ge hùa ma?
Could you transfer me to his voice mail?	Qǐng gěi wǒ zhǔan tā de liúyánjī.
Please tell . . . I will call later/in two days.	Qǐng gàosu . . . wǒ dāihuì'r zài dǎ guòlái/gùo liǎng tiān zài dǎ.
Please tell . . . to give me a call as soon as possible.	Qǐng gāosu . . . jìnkuài gěi wǒ dǎ diànhùa.
I will call back again later.	Wǒ děng yìhùi'r zài dǎ laí.
May I ask who is calling?	Nǐ shì shúi?
Would you like to leave a message?	Nǐ yào liú yán ma?
Would you like to leave your name and number?	Nǐ xiǎng liú xià nǐ de míngzi hé diànhùa hàomǎ ma?
Please hold while I try that extension.	Qǐng bié gùa, wǒ gěi nǐ jiē fēnjī.

25

Is there anything you would like me to tell . . . ?	Nǐ hái yǒu bié de shì yào wǒ gàosu . . . ma?
This is . . . I'm away from my desk.	**Zhè shì . . . Wǒ xiànzài bù zài.**
You have reached . . .	**Zhè shì . . .**
I'm away from the office until . . .	**Wǒ xiànzài bù zài bàngōngshì, yào . . . cái húilái.**
I'm on vacation until . . .	. . . zhīqián, wǒ zài dùjià.
I'm on the other line.	**Wǒ zài lìng yī tiáo xiàn shàng.**
Please call back after 9:00 A.M. on Monday, June 1st.	Qǐng zài liù yuè yī hào xīngqī yī zǎo shàng jiǔ diǎn yǐhòu zài dǎ laí.
Please leave a message.	**Qǐng liúyán.**
Leave a message after the tone.	Tīng dào xìnhào hòu, qǐng liúyán.
Please leave your name, number, and a brief message, and I will call you back.	Qǐng liú xià nǐ de míngzi, diànhuà hàomǎ hé jiǎndǔan de liúyán. Wǒ huì gěi nǐ húi diànhuà.
If you wish to speak to my assistant, please dial extension . . .	**Nǐ rúgǔo xiǎng gēn wǒ de zhùshǒu tōnghùa, qǐng bō fēnjī . . .**
To return to an operator, please press 0 now.	Yào zhǎo jiēxiànshēng, qǐng àn líng.
To return to the main menu, please press 4.	Yào húi dào zhǔ mùlù, qǐng àn sì.
To leave a message, press # now.	Yào liúyán, qǐng àn jǐngzìhào.
To speak to an operator, press # now.	Yào yú jiēxiànshēng tōnghùa, àn jǐngzìhào.
To return to the main menu, press # now.	Yào húi dào zhǔ mùlù, qǐng àn jǐngzìhào.

| If you have a Touch-Tone phone press 1 now. | Nǐ rúguǒ shǐyòng ànjiàn shì diànhuàjī, qǐng àn yī. |
| If you have a rotary phone, please stay on the line. | Rúguǒ nǐshǐyòng de shì xuànzhuǎn bōhào jī, qǐng liú zài xiàn shàng. |

TELLING TIME AND GIVING DATES*

"Shíjiān"

GĀO XIĀNSHENG: *Xiànzài shì shénme shíjiān?*
SHǏMÌSĪ XIĀNSHENG: *Zhèlǐ shì shàngwǔ shíyī diǎn bàn (sānshí). Wǒ xiǎng nǐmen bǐ wǒmen zǎo sān gè xiǎoshí.*
GĀO XIĀNSHENG: *Shì de. Zhèlǐ xiànzài shì xiàwǔ liǎng* diǎn bàn sānshí*. Wǒ xiànzài hěn máng. Nǐ kěyǐ zài yī gè xiǎoshí yǐhòu zài dǎ lái ma?*
SHǏMÌSĪ XIĀNSHENG: *Hǎo. Wǒ yī gè xiǎoshí yǐhòu zài gěi nǐ dǎ lái. Yě jiùshì nǐmen de xiàwǔ sān diǎn bàn.**

"Telling Time"

MR. GAO: *What time do you have?*
MR. SMITH: *It is 11:30 A.M. here. I believe you are three hours ahead of us.*
MR. GAO: *Yes. It is 2:30 P.M. here. I'm busy right now. Could you call in one hour?*
MR. SMITH: *Yes, I'll call you back in one hour, at 3:30 P.M. your time.*

| What time is it? | Xiànzài shénme shíhòu? |
| It's 10:30 A.M. | Shàngwǔ shí diǎn bàn. |

----

*Please refer to the section *Telling Time* in Chapter 6 for additional ways of expressing time.
*The number 2 is pronounced *èr* generally in Chinese but when followed by a classifier, *liǎng* is used instead of *èr*.
Bàn means half in Chinese; here you can either say *bàn* or *sānshí* (thirty).

What day is it?	Jīntiān shì shénme rìzi?
It's Monday.	Xīngqī yī.
What month is it?	Xiànzài shì jǐ yuè?
It's November.	Shíyī yuè.
What year is it?	Jīnnián shì nǎ yī nián?
It's the year 2000.	Èr líng líng líng nián.
It's morning.	Xiàn zài shì zǎoshàng./ shàngwǔ.
It's noon.	Xiàn zài shì zhōngwǔ.
It's afternoon.	Xiàn zài shì xiàwǔ.
It's evening.	Xiàn zài shì wǎnshàng.
It's midnight.	Xiàn zài shì bànyè.
Five minutes/two hours ago.	Wǔ fēn zhōng/liǎng gè xiǎoshí zhīqián.
In twenty minutes/a half hour/an hour.	Èrshí fēn zhōng/bàn gè xiǎoshí/yī gè xiǎoshí yǐhòu
What time do we begin?	Wǒmen shénme shíhòu kāishǐ?
When is the meeting over?	Hùiyì shénme shíhòu jiéshù?

BUSINESS LETTERS

No, the business letter is not a relic of the pre-Internet era. A well-written letter on your company's letterhead is still an effective means of communications and in fact may never go out of style.

The business letter is also effective as a follow-up thank-you "note." People appreciate receiving even a short personalized business note. It says you care. It tends to build relationships, which is the bedrock of success in business or in any walk of life.

In business, nonprofit, or governmental agencies, you are often trying to win over people to do something, or at least convince them to think well of you, so when you write a business letter, let it represent you at your best.

The Greeting

Dear . . .	Zūnjìng de . . .
Mr., Mrs., or Ms.	Xiānsheng, Tàitai, Xiǎojie
Sir(s)/Madam(s)	Xiānsheng/Nǚshì
Director	Zhǔrèn/Chǎngzhǎng
Doctor/Dr.	Yīshēng/Bóshì
Professor	Jiàoshòu
Dear Mr. Schurz	Zūnjìng de Sūérzī Xiānsheng
Dear Ms. Zhu	Zūnjìng de Zhū Xiǎojie

Stating the Purpose

This should be done right up front. Don't beat around the bush.

I am writing . . .	Gěi nǐ xiěxìn shì wèile . . .
to accept . . .	jiēshòu . . .
to ask . . .	xùnwèn . . .
to answer . . .	dáfù . . .
to apologize . . .	dàoqiàn . . .
to confirm . . .	quèrèn . . .
to commend . . .	biǎoyáng . . .
to inform . . .	tōngzhī . . .
to provide . . .	tígòng . . .
to recommend . . .	tuījiàn . . .
to reject . . .	jùjúe . . .
to request . . .	yāoqiú . . .
to submit . . .	tíjiāo . . .
to thank you . . .	gǎnxiè . . .

Or you may wish to start more informally.

In connection with . . .	Yǒuguān . . .
In regard to . . .	Gūanyú . . .
In response to . . .	Dáfù . . .

Instead of calling . . .	Zhìyú . . .
On behalf of . . .	Dàibiǎo . . .
With reference to . . .	Yǒuguān . . .

You may wish to organize your letter with bullets:

• This is the first point

• This is the second point

Or perhaps numbers:

1. This is the first point

2. This is the second point

Other Important Phrases

The purpose of this letter is . . .	Cǐ xìn de mùdì shì . . .
The mission of our business (organization) is to . . .	Wǒmen gōngsī (zǔzhī) de shǐmìng shì . . .
Our strategic goals include . . .	Wǒmen de zhànlüè mùbiāo bāokùo . . .
The quality assurance team wishes to present its report on . . .	Zhíliàng bǎozhèng xiǎozǔ xīwàng zuò yǒuguān . . . de bàogào.
It has come to our attention that . . .	Wǒmen zhùyì dào . . .
We regret to inform you . . .	Wǒmen yíhàn de tōngzhī nǐ . . .
Could you please provide me/us with . . . ?	Kěyǐ qǐng nǐ wèi wǒ/wǒmen tígòng . . . ma?
Unfortunately we cannot accept/agree/complete . . .	Yíhàn de shì wǒmén bù néng jiēshòu/tóngyì/wánchéng . . .
In consultation with . . .	Tōngguò yú . . . xiéshāng . . .
In reviewing your proposal . . .	Kàn le nǐmen de tí'àn . . .

In going over the contract, I/we discovered . . .	Zài yuèdú hétóng de shíhòu, wǒ/wǒmen fāxiàn . . .
While reviewing the financial statements . . .	Zài shěnyuè cáiwù bàobiǎo de shíhòu . . .
It is my/our pleasure to accept your proposal.	Wǒ/wǒmen hěn gāoxìng jiēshòu nǐmen de tí'àn.
Would you contact us at your earliest convenience?	Qǐng nǐmen jìnkuài yú wǒmén qǔdé liánxì.
Enclosed is . . .	Fùshàng . . .
Enclosed please find . . .	Shùnbiàn fùshàng . . .

The Closing

Thank you for your attention to this matter.	Gǎnxiè nǐ duì cǐ shì de guānzhào.
I look forward to hearing from you.	Wǒ pàn nǐ de húiyīn.
Please let me know if I can provide further information.	Rú hái xūyào wǒ tígòng bié de xìnxí, qǐng tōngzhī wǒ.
Please contact me at the following telephone number or e-mail address.	Yú wǒ liánxì, qǐng shǐyòng yīxià diànhùa hàomǎ hùo diànzǐ yóujiàn dìzhǐ.
I look forward to receiving . . .	Wǒ qīdài zhe . . .
your response to this letter.	nǐ duì cǐ xìn de dáfù.
your proposal(s).	nǐ de tí'àn.
the contract.	hétóng.
your evaluation.	nǐ de pínggū.
your call.	nǐ de diànhùa.
your order.	nǐ de dìngdān.
the samples.	shōudào yàngpǐn.

the corrected statements.   xiūgǎi hòu de shēngmíng.
additional information.   gèng duō de xìnxī.

Salutations

Sincerely,   Chéngzhì de,
Signed,   Qiānzì,

Yours truly,   Nǐ zhēnchéng de,
Yours sincerely,   Chéngzhì de,

Best wishes,   Zhìyǐ zuì liánghǎo de
                                  zhùyuàn,

With affection,   Shēnqíng de,

Zhōngguó Běijīng*
Cháng'ān Jiē 123 hào
ABC Gōngsī
Qiáo Xiānghé Xiānsheng

Zūnjìng de Qiáo Xiānsheng:
Xièxie nǐ duì hétóng tíchū de zēngbǔ. Wǒmen zhè dùi
hétóng yǒu suǒ gǎijìn. Yī, liǎng tiān zhīnèi, wǒmen huì
bǎ rèn wéi hétóng de dìnggǎo jì gěi nǐ qiānzì.
Nǐ rúguǒ háiyǒu shénme wèntí, qǐng láixìn gào zhí.

Chéngzhì de,

Zhānnéfō Shǐmìsī
Èr líng líng yì nián sì yuè èrshí rì*

April 20, 2001

Mr. Xianghe Qiao
ABC Corporation
123 Chang'an Street
Beijing, China 100020

---

*A Chinese letter usually does not bear the address of the addressee inside the
letter.
*You can use Arabic numbers here with the Chinese character *nián* (year), *yuè*
(month) and *rì* (date).

Dear Mr. Qiao:

Thank you for the additions to the proposed contract. We agree that this will improve the contract. We will be sending the final version of the contract to you for your signature in a couple of days.

If you have any questions, please let me know.

Sincerely,
Jennifer Smith

In Chinese, *dear* can be translated as *zūnjìng de* or *qin'ai de*. The former is the term used to start a business letter, while the latter is a term of endearment that has no place there. Also, when you address the envelope in Chinese, you should put the addressee's address in the upper left corner; on the envelope, the addressee's name and address are in the middle and the sender's name and address lower right hand corner. The order of information in the address is in the reversed order from the one we use. That is, first write the country, the state or province, the city, the street, the company, and then the name of the person. The date is not at the beginning of the letter but at the end, just below your signature.

E-MAIL AND INTERNET

In a few short years e-mail and the Internet have gone from a curiosity to an essential part of our existence. Here's an important tip if you wish to impress others and get ahead in your organization: Use complete sentences and proper grammar. Don't use e-mail slang, such as: gtg, for "got to go." Using the correct language and grammar communicates that you're a professional. And check the spelling in your messages! Nothing turns off other professionals more than careless errors.

 The Internet etiquette is the same in China as it is in the United States The only thing you do have to remember is that, apart from big companies, most people in China do not have unlimited access to the Web and are charged by the minute for their connection time. As a result, you may not get your response as promptly as you expect. It may be wise to follow your e-mail with a phone call or a letter if it is something important.

Key Words

Desktop computer	Tái shì diànnǎo
Laptop computer	Shǒutí diànnǎo
Computer disk	Diànnǎo cípán
CD-ROM disk	Léishè guāngdié
E-mail or electronic mail	Diànzǐ yóujiàn
Server	Sìfúqì
Browser	Liúlánqì
Send/Receive e mail (to)	Fā/Jiēshōu diànzǐ yóujiàn
Check/Download e-mail (to)	Chákàn/Xiàzài diànzǐ yóujiàn

More computer talk

Cyberspace	Diànzǐ kōngjiān
Database	Shùjùkù
Download (to)	Xiàzài
File	Wénjiàn
Flat-panel display	Píngbǎn xiǎnshì
Help	Qiúzhù
Home page	Zhǔyè
Hypertext	Chāojí wénjiàn

Internet	Yīn tè wang/Diànnǎo wǎngluò
Link	Liánjiē
Mailing List	Tóusòng míngdān
Mainframe	Zhǔ jìsuanjī
Modem	Shùjùjī
Multimedia	Duō méi tǐ
Network	Wǎnglu hiò
Online Service	Xiànshàng fúwù
Portable	Shǒutí shì
Reboot	Chóngxīn kāijī
Search engine	Jiǎnsuǒ yǐnqíng
Surf	Wǎngshàng chōnglàng
Technical support	Jìshù fúwù
URL	Zhǔyè dìzhǐ
Videoconferencing	Yǐngxiàng huìyì
Virtual reality	Xūnǐ xiànshí
Web page/site	Yèmiàn/Yèzhǐ
World Wide Web	Quánqiú zīxún wǎng

What you need to do

Log on/off (to)	Qiān rù/chu
Forward e-mail (to)	Bǎ diànzi yóujiàn zhuǎnjì gěi . . .
Open a file (to)	Dǎkāi wénjiàn
Reply to an e-mail (to)	Huídá diánzi yóujiàn
Search the Internet/ Web (to)	Jiǎnsuǒ guójì wǎngluò
Send a file (to)	Jìsòng wénjiàn
How do I turn the computer on?	**Zěnyàng dǎkāi diànnǎo?**
How to I dial up?	**Zěnyàng bōhào líanjiē?**
Do I need a password?	**Wǒ xūyào mìmǎ ma?**
What is the password?	Mìmǎ shì shénme?
Do you have an IBM-compatible computer?	**Nǐ de diànnǎo gēn IBM jiānróng ma?**

Do you have a Mac computer?	Nǐ yǒu Mac diànnǎo ma?
What word processing software do you use?	**Nǐ shǐyòng shénme yàng de wénzì chùlǐ ruǎnjiàn?**
What spreadsheet software do you use?	**Nǐ shǐyòng nǎ gè diànzǐ biǎo gé ruǎnjiàn?**
What database software do you use?	Nǐ shǐyòng nǎ gè shùjùkù ruǎnjiàn?
What presentation software do you use?	Nǐ shǐyòng nǎ gè túxiàng zhǎnshì ruǎnjiàn?
How can I get Word/ WordPerfect on this computer?	Zěnyàng zài zhè tái diànnǎo shàng ānzhuāng Word/ WordPerfect?
How can I get Excel/ Lotus 1-2-3 on this computer?	Zěnyàng zài zhè tái diànnǎo shàng ānzhuāng Excel/ Lotus 1-2-3?
How can I get PowerPoint on this computer?	Zěnyàng zài zhè tái diànnǎo shàng ānzhuāng PowerPoint?
How can I get Dbase on this computer?	Zěnyàng zài zhè tái diànnǎo shàng ānzhuāng Dbase?
Do you have Internet capability?	**Nǐ kěyǐ shàng diànnǎo wǎngluò ma?**
Do you have e-mail capability?	Nǐ yǒu diànzǐ yóujiàn ma?
How can I get AOL on this computer?	**Zěnyàng bǎ zhè tái diànnǎo jiē shàng Měiguó Xiànshàng liánjiē?**
How do I . . .	**Zěnyàng . . .**
log on?	**qiān rù/dēng rù?**
check my e-mail?	jiǎnchá wǒ de diànzǐ yóujiàn?
access a Web site?	jìnjiē wǎngzhǐ?
search the Web?	jiǎnsuǒ wǎngyè?
bookmark a Web site?	gěi wǎngyè zuò jìhào?
print this page?	dǎyìn wǎngyè?
print this document?	dǎyìn wénjiàn?

send an e-mail?	jìfā diànzǐ yóujiàn?
send this document to someone?	bǎ zhè gè wénjiàn fā gěi . . . ?
forward this message to someone?	bǎ zhè ge xìnxí zhuǎnfā gěi . . . ?
attach a file to an e-mail?	bǎ wénjiàn fùjiā zài diànzǐ yóujiàn hòumiàn?
Do I leave the computer on?	**Wǒ ràng diànnǎo kāi zhe ma?**
How do I turn the computer off?	**Zěnyàng gūandiào diànnǎo?**

2 GETTING INVOLVED

Conducting business overseas adds an unusual dimension to your work. Not only do you need to transact sales, negotiate contracts, communicate plans, and receive feedback on products and services, but also you need to do it in a foreign place and even in a foreign tongue.

As a general principle, don't assume that your own ways of doing business apply in other countries and cultures. Be cautious until you know the culture you're dealing with, and take an active role in learning about it. For example, in some cultures, it is bad form to be overly assertive, a common U.S. business trait. In the course of this chapter, and indeed, this whole book, we give you tips on how to proceed.

Business Companion, however, is not content to just help you with the language and culture, we also want to remind you of how to handle your business successfully. For instance, in talking about business presentations we not only give you the words *easel*, *slide projector*, and *refreshments*, but we also want to provide you with a review of what makes a presentation successful. Thus, we mix language and culture with the ideas on how to make your business successful.

Here are the most common business situations you'll be confronting in your work and learning about in this chapter:

> **The General Business Meeting**
> **The Presentation or Speech**
> **The Sales Call or Meeting**
> **The Negotiating Meeting**

The Training Session
The Trade Show
Attending a Conference or
    Seminar
Conducting an Interview

Now let's get involved.

THE GENERAL BUSINESS MEETING

What's the purpose of the meeting? If you're in charge, make it clear. You owe it to the participants. If you're a participant, find out ahead of time, so you can successfully contribute.

If you are leading the meeting, you need to make sure things are organized on two levels: the purpose of the presentation and the details—announcements, agenda, room arrangements, presentation equipment, and any refreshments.

A last-minute question to ask is: Is there anything else that needs to be on the agenda to make the meeting more successful?

Finally, during the meeting, make sure you encourage the participation of everyone. By the end of the meeting, call on those who have not participated much or not at all for their comments.

So let's go have a meeting.

————————

"Kāihuì"

SHǏMÌSĪ XIĀNSHENG: *Huìyì yìchéng shàng zěnme méiyǒu tí jiézhǐ qīxiàn?*

QIÓNGSĪ XIǍOJIE: *Hǎo zhǔyì. Ràng wǒmen jīntiān xiàwǔ tǎolùn wán Tuánduì Lìliàng wěiyúanhùi de bàogào yǐhòu zài tíchū ba.*

CHÁNG XIĀNSHENG: *Gànmá bù zài míngtiān zǎoshàng lái tǎolùn ne? Wǒmen jīntiān xiàwǔ bù*

yīdìng néng wánchéng wěiyúanhùi de bàogào,
érqiě dào shíhòu yě bù yīdìng měi gè rén dōu hái
zài zhè'r.

QIÓNGSĪ XIĂOJIE: *Nàyàng gèng hǎo. Wǒmen jiù*
míngtiān zǎoshàng lái tǎolùn ba.

"At the Meeting"

MR. SMITH: *Why were deadlines left out of the*
agenda?

MS. JONES: *That's a good point. Let's put that*
in for later this afternoon, after we finish our
discussion on the Team Force committee
report.

MR. CHANG: *Why not discuss it first thing tomor-*
row morning? We may not finish the committee
report until late this afternoon and not everyone
will be here.

MS. JONES: *That's an even better idea. We'll dis-*
cuss it first thing tomorrow morning.

Chinese usually hold meetings in their offices or company's conference rooms. Occasionally, they'll suggest to meet you in your hotel. When that happens, Chinese will appreciate it if you are a good host, so prepare or offer drinks and refreshments. When you come to meet a group of people, remember to greet the person with the highest rank first, before turning to others. Also, ask for a list of participants beforehand, so you can learn to pronounce their names correctly. If you are in a group, the leader of the team should go in first and wait to be seated; the principal guest is usually escorted by the main host to the seat of honor, facing the entry door.

Key Words

Agenda	(Huìyì) yìchéng
Answer	Dáfù
Cancel a meeting (to)	Qǔxiāo huìyì
Committee	Wěiyuánhùi
Deadline(s)	Jiézhǐ qīxiàn
Decision(s)	Juédìng
Discussion	Tǎolùn
Facilitator	Xiétiáorén
Feedback	Fǎnkùi
Information	Xìnxí
Have a meeting (to)	Kāihùi
Lead a meeting (to)	Zhǔchí hùiyì
Materials	Zīliào
Meeting	Hùiyì
Participant	Cānjiāzhě
Problem solving	Jiějué wèntí
Purpose	Mùdì
Question	Wèntí
Schedule	Shíjiānbiǎo
Schedule a meeting (to)	Ānpái huìyì shíjiān
Set an agenda (to)	Zhìdìng hùiyì yìchéng
Team building	Tuánduì jiànshè

Hello.	Nǐ hǎo.
Good morning/afternoon/ evening.	Zǎoshàn hao./Xiàw hao./ Wǎnshàng hǎo.
Welcome to . . .	**Huānyíng nǐ dào . . .**
My name is . . .	Wǒ jiào . . .
I am . . .	Wǒ shì . . .
I want to introduce . . . myself. the participants. the secretary.	**Wǒ xiǎng jièshào yī xià . . .** wǒ zìjǐ. cānjiā zhě. mìshū.

| the administrative assistant. | xíngzhèng zhùlǐ. |
| the recorder. | jìlùyuán. |

Please introduce yourself. Qǐng jièshào yī xià nǐ zìjǐ.

Before we begin the meeting, let's introduce ourselves. Zài kāihùi yǐqián, ràng wǒmen zùo gè zìwǒ jièshào.

Beginning on my left/ right please state your name, company, and position (title). Ràng wǒmen cóng zuǒ/ yòubiān kāishǐ, qǐng shūochū nǐ de míngzi, gōngsī hé zhíwèi.

Yìchéng: **Tuándùi Lìliàng Wěiyuánhùi**

Shàngwǔ	9:00	Hùiyì kāishǐ
	9:10	Chóngwēn shàngcì hùiyì jìlù
	9:20	Tǎolùn liǎng ge xíngzhèng bùmén de hébìng
		Chéngxù wèntí
		Xīn de zǔzhī jiégòutú
		Duōyú rényúan de ānzhì wèntí
	10:30	Kāfēi xiǎoxí
	10:45	Fēnsàn tǎolùn—jiějúe wèntí
	11:45	Fēnsàn tǎolùn hùi bào
	12:00	Wǔcān
Xiawu	1:00	Tǎolùn xīn de chéngxù
	4:30	Hùiyì jiéshù

Agenda: **Team Force Committee**

9:00 A.M.	Opening
9:10 A.M.	Review of last meeting
9:20 A.M.	Discussion of merging the two administrative departments
	Handling of procedures
	New organization chart
	Outplacement
10:30 A.M.	Coffee break
10:45 A.M.	Breakout sessions— Handling problems

11:45 A.M.	*Reporting on the sessions*
12:00 P.M.	*Lunch*
1:00 P.M.	*Discussion of new procedures*
4:30 P.M.	*Close*

Purpose of the Meeting

The purpose of this meeting is . . .	Zhè cì hùiyì de mùdì shì . . .
Today's meeting concerns itself with . . .	Jīntiān hùiyì shì guānyú . . .
I've been asked to lead this discussion about . . .	Wǒ bèi zhǐdìng lái zhǔchí zhè cì yǒuguān . . . de tǎolùn.
This morning/afternoon/ evening we'll be discussing . . .	Jīntiān shàngwǔ/xiàwǔ/ wǎnshàng, wǒmen jiāng tǎolùn . . .
I'm sure you all know why we are here.	Wǒ xiāngxìn nǐmen dōu zhīdào wǒmen wèi shénme dōu zài zhèlǐ.
Let's begin by going over the agenda.	Ràng wǒmén xiān kàn yī xià hùiyì yìchéng.
Are there any questions about the agenda?	Dùi hùiyì yìchéng yǒu shénme wèntí ma?
Yes, I have a question.	Wǒ yǒu yī gè wèntí.
Yes, please, what is your question?	Nǐ yǒu shénme wèntí? Qǐng shuō ba.
Who determined/set the agenda?	Shuí júedìng/zhìdìng cǐ hùiyì yìchéng?
I set the agenda.	Wǒ júedìng de.
The agenda was determined by the committee.	Hùiyì yìchéng shì yóu wěiyùanhùi jùedìng de.
The agenda was determined in our last meeting.	Hùiyì yìchéng shì wǒmen shàng cì kāihùi jùedìng de.
Is the agenda complete?	Zhè shì wánzhěng de hùiyì yìchéng ma?

Does everyone have a copy of the agenda?	Měi gè rén dōu yǒu huìyì yìchéng le ma?
Does anyone need a copy of the agenda?	Hái yǒu shúi xūyào huìyì yìchéng?
Is there anything that needs to be added to the agenda?	Hái yǒu shénme shìqíng xūyào zēngtiān dào yìchéng zhōng qù ma?
Has everyone received the materials?	Dàjiā dōu ná daò zīliào le ma?

Schedule

We will have a coffee break at . . . *	Wǒmen zài . . . xīuxi hē kāfēi.
10:15 A.M.	shàngwǔ shí diǎn shíwǔ fēn
10:30 A.M.	shàngwǔ shí diǎn bàn (sānshí)
2:30 P.M.	xiàwǔ liǎng diǎn bàn (sānshí)
3:00 P.M.	xiàwǔ sān diǎn
Lunch will be served at . . .	Wǔcān zài . . .
12:00 P.M.	zhōngwǔ shí'èr diǎn.
12:30 P.M.	xiàwǔ shí'èr diǎn bàn (sānshí).
Lunch will last . . . an hour. an hour and a half.	Wǔcān shíjiān shì . . . yī gè xiǎoshí. yī gè bàn xiǎoshí.
The meeting will continue at 2:00 P.M.	Huìyì zài xiàwǔ liǎng diǎn jìxù jìnxíng.
The meeting should be over at . . .	Huìyì yào zài . . .

---

*For more on how to tell time in China, please refer to the section *Telling Time* in Chapter 6.

| 4:30 P.M. | xiàwǔ sì diǎn jiéshù. |
| 5:00 P.M. | xiàwǔ wǔ diǎn jiéshù. |

Let's begin.	**Zánmen kāishǐ ba.**
Does anyone have any questions before we begin?	**Zài kāishǐ yǐqián, shuì hái yǒu wèntí ma?**
Does anyone have a question on the first subject?	Shuí duì dì yī gè zhǔtí háiyǒu wèntí?
Not everyone has spoken.	**Bù shì měi gè rén dōu fā le yán.**
Mr. Wang, do you have something to add?	**Wáng Xiānsheng, nǐ háiyǒu shénme xūyào bǔchōng ma?**
We have not heard from everyone.	**Wǒmen xīwàng měi gè rén dōu fāyán.**
Does anyone else have a comment or a question?	**Shuí háiyǒu shénme yìjiàn huò wèntí?**
Can we move on to item number 2?	**Wǒmen kěyǐ jìnxíng dì èr xiàng le ma?**
Who will take responsibility for this item?	**Shuí lái fùzé zhè gè xiàngmù?**
Has everyone spoken on this point?	**Shì bu shì měi gè rén dōu duì zhè diǎn fābiǎo le yìjiàn?**
Do we need to vote on this item?	**Wǒmen xūyào duì zhè gè xiàngmù biǎojué ma?**
Those in favor, raise your hand.	**Zàntóng de, qǐng jǔshǒu.**
Those opposed, raise your hand.	**Fǎnduì de, qǐng jǔshǒu.**
The agenda passes.	**Yìchéng tōngguò le.**
The agenda loses.	**Yìchéng méiyǒu tōngguò.**
The motion passes.	Tíyì tōngguò le.
The motion fails.	Tíyì méiyǒu tōngguò.

| Would you like to discuss this topic at a later meeting? | Nǐ xīwàng zài xià cì huì shàng tǎolùn zhège yìtí ma? |
| Let's table discussion on this matter. | Zánmen zhànshí bǎ zhè shì fàng yī biān ba. |

The Closing

Do we need a follow-up meeting?	Wǒmen xūyào zài kāihuì tǎolùn cǐ shì ma?
Before we leave, let's set a date for the next meeting.	Zài líkāi zhīqián, ràng wǒmen bǎ xià cì huìyì de rìqī dìng xià lái.
Thank you for being here today.	Gǎnxiè dàjiā jīntiān chūxí huìyì.

THE PRESENTATION OR SPEECH

How can you tell if the content of your presentation or speech is sound? Perhaps the most successful way is to answer this question: Does it tell a logical story? If it does, people will follow you step-by-step. If not, you will probably confuse your audience, and have questions raised that will sidetrack your main purpose.

Give your presentation or speech ahead of time to those you can count on to provide you with constructive comments. Where do they ask questions? That's where your thoughts may be unclear. Go over each point and make sure you know the information and can articulate it.

One final thought. Assume that there will be something wrong with the physical aspects of the presentation or speech: arrangements, handouts, equipment, or refreshments. Why? Because there usually is.

"Yǎnshì"

ÀOLÌFÓ XIǍOJIE: *Jīntiān wǒmen yǒuxìng qǐng dào le zhōngyāng bàngōngshì de Lín Xiānsheng. Qǐng dàjiā huānyíng Lín Xiānshēng.*

LÍN XIĀNSHENG: *Xièxie gèwèi. Jǐ gè yuè lái, wǒ jiù yīzhí xiǎng lái cāngūan nǐmen de bàngōngshì, zhídào zhè gè xīngqīng cái yǒu le shíjiān. Wǒ shì yī biān jiǎng, yī biān húidá wèntí ne, háishì děng wǒ jiǎng wán yǐhòu cái húidá wèntí?*

ÀOLÌFÓ XIǍOJIE: *Nǐ súibiàn hǎo le.*

"Giving a Presentation"

MS. OLIVER: *We are so fortunate to have Mr. Lin from our central office here today. Please welcome Mr. Lin.*

MR. LIN: *Thank you for having me. I've wanted to come to visit your office for several months, and finally I was able to do so this week. May I take questions during my talk or do you want me to wait until the end?*

MS. OLIVER: *You can do it either way.*

Be sure to prepare the materials for your presentation or speech in both English and Chinese. Put details down on the paper, but keep you presentation or speech general, and leave details or specifics for later negotiation. Your purpose is to explain what your products/services are about, and what the market looks like. Here you can use big words and glowing terms and sound optimistic to describe your products or services, but your focus should always be friendship, cooperation and mutual benefits.

Key Words

Clarification question	*Chǎnmíng wèntí*
Discussion question	*Tǎolùn wèntí*
Discussion	*Tǎolùn*
Introduction	*Jièshào*
Microphone	*Màikèfēng*
Mission	*Shǐmìng*
Point	*Lùndiǎn*
Presentation	*Yǎnshì*
Question	*Wèntí*
Q&A period	*Wèndá shíjiān*
Subject	*Zhǔtí*
Talk	*Tánlùn*
Topic	*Yìtí*
Vision	*Yǔanjiàn/Mùguāng*

Audiovisual Presentation Aids

Here are some common aids you may use . . .

Audio	Lùyīn/Yīn xiǎng zhuāng zhì
Board	Bǎnzi
Chalk	Fěnbǐ
Chart	Biǎogé
Computer	Diànnǎo
Diagram	Túbiāo
Easel	Hùabǎn
Extension cord	Yánshēnxiàn
Folder	Wénjiàn jiá
Handout	Fēnfā
Illustration	Chātú
Marker	Biāoshìqì
Microphone	Màikèfēng
Model	Fànlì/Móxíng/Xínghào
Monitor	Xiǎnshìqì
Notepads	Bǐjìběn
PowerPoint presentation	PowerPoint yǎnshì
Screen	Píngmù

Slide projector	Huàndēngjī
Tape recorder	Lùyīnjī
Television	Diànshì
Transparency	Tòumínghùa/Huàndēngpiàn
Video	Lùxiàng
Video recorder	Lùxiàngjī

Thank you for having me.	**Gǎnxiè nǐmen yāoqǐng wǒ.**
I want to thank Mr. Wang for that nice introduction.	**Wǒ yào gǎnxiè Wáng Xiānshēng de měihǎo jièshào.**
I want to thank Mr. Wang for inviting me to tell you about . . .	Wǒ yào gǎnxiè Wáng Xiānshēng yāoqǐng wǒ wèi nǐmén tántan gūanyú . . .
I want to thank your organization for having me.	**Wǒ yào gǎnxiè nǐmen de zǔzhī yāoqǐng wǒ.**
It's an honor to be with you today.	Jīntiān yǔ nǐmen jùhùi hěn gǎn róngxìng.
It's my pleasure to speak to you today.	**Jīntiān hěn gāoxìng yǔ nǐmen tánhùa.**
I'm grateful for the opportunity to speak with you.	Yǒu jīhùi yǔ nǐ tánhùa, wǒ hěn gǎnjī.

The Subject

The purpose of this presentation/speech/talk is . . .	**Zhè cì shìfàn/yǎnjiǎng/ tánhùa de mùdì shì . . . .**
This morning/afternoon/ evening I'm going to talk about . . .	Jīntiān zǎoshàng/xiàwǔ/ wǎnshàng, wǒ yào tán de shì . . .
The major point of my presentation/speech/talk is . . .	**Wǒ de shìfàn/yǎnjiǎng/ tánhùa de zhǔyào lùndiǎn shì . . .**
In this presentation/ speech/talk, I'd like to . . .	Zài zhè cì shìfàn/yǎnjiǎng/ tánhùa zhōng, wǒ jiāng . . .

49

My topic today is . . .	Wǒ jīntiān de yìtí shì . . .
The subject of my presentation is . . .	Wǒ shìfàn de zhǔtí shì . . .
I'd like to begin by telling you my conclusion.	**Wǒ xiǎng cóng wǒ de jiélùn kāishǐ tán qǐ.**
I'd first like to tell you about the concept behind my presentation/ speech/talk.	Shǒuxiān, wǒ yào gàosu nǐmen wǒ shìfàn/yǎnjiǎng/ tánhùa bèihòu de gàiniàn.
Please feel free to interrupt me with any questions.	**Rú yǒu rènhé wèntí, qǐng súishí dǎdùan wǒ.**

The Major Points

I'd like to begin with a story.	Wǒ xiǎng yòng yī ge gùshì kāishǐ.
There are three issues I would like to cover today.	**Wǒ jīntiān yào tánlun sān ge wèntí.**
There are three points that I would like to make/cover today.	Wǒ jīntiān yào tánlùn de wèntí yǒu sān diǎn.
I want to make several points today.	**Wǒ jīntiān yào tíchū jǐ diǎn.**
First I want to cover . . .	**Shǒuxiān, wǒ yào jiǎng . . .**
Second I want to discuss . . .	**Qǐcì, wǒ yào tǎolùn . . .**
There is a growing need to be aware of . . .	**Yùe lái yùe xūyào liǎojiě . . .**
My/our mission is . . .	**Wǒ/wǒmen de rènwù shì . . .**
My/our vision is . . .	Wǒ/wǒmen de kàn fǎ shì . . .
The following . . .	**Yǐxià . . .**
data	shùjù
financial figures	cáiwù shùzì

findings	fāxiàn
information	xìnxí
results	jiéguǒ
provide support for my central thesis.	wèi wǒ de zhōngxīn lùndiǎn tígòng lùnjù.

Now, on to the second point.	Xiànzài tán dì èr diǎn.
Next, I would like to discuss . . .	Xiàmiàn wǒ xiǎng tǎolùn . . .
Moving along, let's now consider . . .	Jiēzhe, wǒmen lái kǎolǜ . . .

| Before I move on, are there any questions? | Zài wǒ jìxù zhīqián, yǒu shénmen wèntí ma? |

| I hope you'll understand . . . | Wǒ xīwàng nǐmen lǐjiě . . . |
| You should be able to see . . . | Nǐmen kěyǐ kàn dào . . . |

To support my point, I would like to . . .	Wèile jiāqiáng wǒ dc lùndiǎn, wǒ xiǎng . . .
demonstrate . . .	yǎnshì . . .
display . . .	xiǎnshì . . .
distribute . . .	fēnfā . . .
illustrate . . .	tújiě shuōmíng . . .
provide . . .	tígòng . . .
reveal . . .	tòulù . . .
show . . .	biǎolù . . .

The Summary and Conclusion

I would like to review my main points/items/ideas now.	Wǒ xiànzài yào tàntǎo yī xià wǒ de zhǔyào lùndiǎn/ xiàngmù/guāndiǎn.
Finally, I want to say . . .	Zuìhòu, wǒ yào shuō . . .
In summary, I would like to reiterate . . .	Zǒngzhī, wǒ zàicì chóngfù . . .

In conclusion . . .	Zǒngér yánzhī . . .
This concludes my main points.	Zhè jiùshì wǒ de zhǔyào lùndiǎn.
This ends my remarks.	Wǒ de tánhùa dàocǐ jiéshù.
I hope this presentation has convinced you of . . .	Wǒ xīwàng zhècì yǎnshì shǐ nǐmen xiāngxìn . . .
It has been a pleasure talking to you.	Hěn gāoxìng yǔ nǐ jiāotán.
It has been a pleasure being with you today.	Jīntiān hěn gāoxìng yǔ nǐ xiāngjù.
I have enjoyed presenting my . . . to you.	Hěn gāoxìng xiàng nǐ yǎnshì wǒ de . . .
activities	húodòng.
experience(s)	jīnglì/jīng yàn.
ideas	zhǔyì.
paper	wénzhāng.
thesis	lùnwén.
theories	lǐlùn.
I hope you have . . .	Wǒ xīwàng nǐ . . .
enjoyed . . .	xǐhūan wǒ de yǎnshì.
found these ideas helpful from . . .	fāxiàn wǒ yǎnshì de gūandiǎn hěn yǒu bāngzhù.
gained insight from . . .	wǒ de yǎnshì gěi le nǐ qǐfā.
gained knowledge from . . .	cóng wǒ de yǎnshì zhōng hùodé le zhīshi.
learned something from . . .	cóng wǒ de yǎnshì zhōng xúe dào le yīxiē dōngxī.
my presentation.	
Thank you for your attention.	Gǎnxiè nǐ de gūan xīn.

THE SALES CALL OR MEETING

The basis of successful sales is building relationships, i.e., by establishing the trust that allows for the free flow of information. Selling skills also involve the ability to understand and match customer needs with the features of your product or service.

The absolute crucial element of sales, and the most difficult to learn, is the ability to close. To ink the deal. That's where passion and motivation on your part can make a difference.

"Chǎnpǐn Xiāoshòu"

YÙEHÀNXÙN XIĀNSHENG: *Gēnjù nǐmen de wéixiū jìhuà, nǐ dǎ sùan gòumǎi èrshí wǔ hùo wǔshí tái wǒmen de xīn shuǐbàng, shì ma?*

CÁO XIĀNSHENG: *Wǒ bìng méiyǒu shūo wǒ yào mǎi nǐ de shǔibèng.*

YÙEHÀNXÙN XIĀNSHENG: *Xūyào shénme cái kěyǐ shūofú nǐ gòumǎi wǒmen de shuǐbàng ne? Jiàgé, jiāofù, háishì kěkàoxìng?*

CÁO XIĀNSHENG: *Zhǔyào háishì jiàgé.*

YÙEHÀNXÙN XIĀNSHENG: *Nǐ xiànzài yào shì jiù mǎi wǔshí taí, wǒ kěyǐ gěi nǐ bǎifēnzhī shíwǔ de zhékòu.*

CÁO XIĀNSHENG: *Nà wǒmen mǎimai jiù zùo chéng le.*

"Selling Your Products"

MR. JOHNSON: *Then, you would like either 25 or 50 of our new pumps depending on your maintenance schedule?*

MR. CAO: *Well, I haven't said that I would buy your pumps.*

MR. JOHNSON: *What would it take for you to purchase them? Price, delivery, reliability?*

MR. CAO: *Mainly price.*

MR. JOHNSON: *I am prepared to offer you a 15 percent discount if you buy 50 now.*

MR. CAO: *We have a deal.*

It is better to use "soft-sell" tactics in China. A low-key attitude and calmness reap rewards. Pressure sale tactics may not get you anywhere. Refrain from boasting or exaggeration. Try to use another company's recommendations, good remarks, comments, glowing reviews or testimonial letters to help sell your products or service. The most effective way (but also very time-consuming way) to do business in China is to establish your *guānxì* (connections). *Guānxì* is a set of personal relationships based on trust and mutual benefits, and a pervasive network that runs very deep in Chinese society.

Key Words

Brochure	Xiǎocèzi
Buy (to)	Mǎi
Close a deal	Chéngjiāo
Cold call	Diànhùa jiàomài
Deal	Jiāoyì
Delivery	Jiāofù/Jiāohùo
Delivery date	Jiāohùo rìqī
Discount	Zhékòu
Follow-up	Gēnjìn
Option(s)	Xǔanzé
Price	Jiàgé
Product	Chǎnpǐn
Quality	Zhìliàng
Quantity	Shùliàng
Sell (to)	Mài
Service	Fúwù
Shipping	Zhuānghùo/Zhuāng yùn
Specification(s)	Gūigé

| My name is . . . | Wǒ jiào . . . |
| I am from . . . company/ organization. | Wǒ cóng . . . gōngsī/zǔzhī lái. |

Here is a brochure on our product/service.	Zhè shì guānyú wǒmen chǎnpǐn/fúwù de xiǎocèzi.
Here is a folder with information on our firm/company/ organization.	Zhè gè wénjiànjiá yǒu wǒmen shāngháng/gōngsī/ zǔzhī de qíngkuàng.
Here is our company's brochure.	Zhè shì yǒu guān wǒmen gōngsī de xiǎocèzi.

Questions to Ask

Is everything working okay?	Yīqiè dōu yùnzhuǎn zhèngcháng ma?
Would you like to improve your current business?	Nǐ xiǎng gǎishàn nǐ de shēngyì ma?
Would you like to increase your productivity?	Nǐ xiǎng tígāo nǐ de shēngchǎn shuǐpíng ma?
What problems are you having?	Chū le shénme wèntí?
What are your concerns?	Nǐ dānxīn shénme ne?

Your Product or Service

Our product was designed by our engineers with our customers' needs in mind.	Wǒmen de chǎnpǐn shì yóu gōngchéngshī gēnjù wǒmen kèhù de xūyào lái shèjì de.
Our service was designed by our experts.	Wǒmen de fúwù shì yóu wǒmen de zhuānjiā shèjì de.
Our products/services have proved to be highly successful.	Wǒmen de chǎnpǐn/fúwù zhèngmíng shì fēicháng chénggōng de.

We are able to tailor the product/service to your needs.	Wǒmen nénggòu gēnjù nǐ de xūyào lái shèjì chǎnpǐn/fúwù.
We can alter our product/service to your specifications.	Wǒmen kěyǐ gēnjù nǐ de gūigé lái gǎijìn wǒmen de chǎnpǐn/fúwù.
Here are testimonials from our customers.	Zhè shì wǒmen kèhù de jiànzhèng.

Handling Acceptance, Skepticism, and Indifference

Yes, I agree we have an excellent track record.	Wǒ tóngyì wǒmen de yèjī shì fēicháng yōuxiù de.
Yes, we are proud of our product/service.	Wǒmen dùi wǒmen de chǎnpǐn/fúwù gǎndào jiāo'ào.
Our company is very satisfied with our product/service.	Wǒmen gōngsī dùi wǒmen de chǎnpǐn/fúwù hěn mǎnyì.
Thank you for that compliment.	Gǎnxiè nǐ de zànshǎng.
Perhaps you are not aware of the problems in your operations department.	Hùoxǔ nǐ dùi nǐmen yùnzùo bùmén de wèntí bìng bù liǎojiě.
Perhaps you are not aware that our customers find our product/service very effective.	Hùoxù nǐ bù liǎojiě wǒmen de kèhù fāxiàn wǒmen de chǎnpǐn/fúwù xiàolì hěn gāo.
Our product/service has been successful in most companies/organizations.	Wǒmen de chǎnpǐn/fúwù zài dūoshù gōngsī/zǔzhī zhōng dōu shì chénggōng de.
Let me explain what this product/service can do for your company.	Qǐng ràng wǒ jiǎngjiě yī xià zhè gè chǎnpǐn/fúwù hùi gěi gùi gōngsī shénme hǎochù.

Our prices are extremely competitive.	**Wǒmen de jiàgé shì hěn yǒu jìngzhēnglì de.**
Do you realize what this product/service can do for your organization?	Nǐ zhīdào zhè gè chǎnpǐn/fúwù kěyǐ wèi nǐ de zǔzhī dàilái shénme hǎochù ma?
Do you know how much this product/service could save you each year?	Nǐ zhīdào zhè gè chǎnpǐn/fúwù měi nián kěyǐ wèi nǐ jiéyuē duōshǎo qián ma?
Are you aware of what this could do for your company?	Nǐ liǎojiě zhè kěyǐ gěi nǐ gōngsī dàilaí shénme haǒchù ma?

The Close

May I order you this product/service?	**Wǒ kěyǐ gěi nǐ dìnggòu zhè gè chǎnpǐn/**fúwù **ma?**
How many do you want?	**Nǐ yào duōshǎo?**
When would you like it installed?	Nǐ xiǎng zài shénme shíhòu ānzhuāng?
When would you like it delivered?	**Nǐ xūyào zài shénme shíhòu jiāohùo?**

THE NEGOTIATING MEETING

Reading people is key. Who's the decision maker? Is he/she a take charge type, or is he/she looking for you to take the lead? Listening is a critical skill, whether you are leading the negotiations or a member of a negotiating team.

While your Chinese language skills seem still weak to you, pay attention to the body language and make sure you do not miss the heads that nod in agreement. It may just mean that there is, after all, an understanding of what you said. Another piece of advice: Try to be patient because in some cultures, unlike ours, there is often a painstakingly slow process to reach a conclusion or an agreement.

Also, look for the bottom line. What are the key issues, on each side? Is what you are negotiating perceived as a zero-sum game? Turn it into a win-win game.

"Hétóng Tánpàn"

QIÓNGSĪ XIĀNSHENG: *Wǒmen yào zài bǎoxiū dān shàng xiěmíng: "Chú zhè'r shūomíng de yǐwài, bù bāohán rènhé bié de bǎoxiū."*

SÒNG XIǍOJIE: *Wǒmén jiānchí zài bǎo dān shàng xiě míng: "Chù zhè'r shūomíng de bǎoxiū yǐwài, bù chéngdān rènhé bié de bǎoxiū."*

QIÓNGSĪ XIĀNSHENG: *Wǒmen de hétóng yībān dōu shǐyòng bāohán.*

SÒNG XIǍOJIE: *Zài wǒmen gúojiā, wǒmen dōu shǐyòng chéngdān.*

QIÓNGSĪ XIĀNSHENG: *Hǎo ba. Zánmen jiù shǐyòng chéngdān hǎo le.*

"Negotiating the Contract"

MR. JONES: *We would want the warranty to say, "No warranty is "implied" other than what is stated."*

MS. SONG: *We would insist that it says, "No warranty is "assumed" other than what is stated."*

MR. JONES: *Most of our contracts use "implied."*

MS. SONG: *In our country the word "assumed" is used.*

MR. JONES: *Okay. We'll agree to the word "assumed."*

Negotiations in China are always a team game. Send more than one person if you can, so you will have enough staff and energy to handle the marathon negotiations that usually take place in

China. This is the time they get serious about details and specifics. The more details you offer, the better chance you will have for an agreement. Prepare all technical information and supporting materials in both languages. If possible, send or distribute your materials in advance, and give your Chinese partners time to clear their questions and positions among their team members. From the very beginning, you may be pressed to sign a "letter of intent" which is not legally binding in the western sense: it only symbolizes the start of the negotiation process.

Key Words

Accept (to)	Jiēshòu
Acceptable	Kěyǐ jiēshòu de
Agree (to)	Tóngyì
Agreement	Xiéyì
Conflict	Zhēngyì
Contract	Hétóng
Disagree (to)	Bù tóngyì
Guarantee	Bǎozhèng
Issue(s)	Qiānfā
Item(s)	Xiàngmù
Key issues	Gūanjiàn wèntí
Lawyer(s)	Lǜshī
Negotiate (to)	Xiéshang/Tánpàn
Offer	Bàojià
Point(s)	Lùndiǎn
Proposal	Jiànyì
Propose (to)	Tíyì
Reject (to)	Jùjúe
Rejection	Bōhúi
Unacceptable	Bù kě jiēshòu de
Warranty	Bǎoxiū/bǎo dān

I want to introduce my partner.	**Ràng wǒ jièshào yī xià wǒ de héhuǒrén.**
I want to introduce our lawyer.	**Ràng wǒ jièshào yī xià wǒmen de lǜshī.**
Please introduce yourself.	Qǐng jièshào yī xià nǐ zìjǐ.
Please introduce the other people (who are) with you.	Qǐng jièshào yī xìa (gēn nǐ laí de) qítā rén.
Has everyone arrived?	**Dàjiā dōu dào le ma?**
Is everyone here?	**Dàjiā dōu laí le ma?**
Is everyone comfortable?	Dàjiā dōu shūshì ba?
Could we begin?	**Wǒmen kěyǐ kāishǐ le ma?**
May we begin?	Wǒmen kěyǐ kāishǐ ma?
Can we begin?	Kěyǐ kāishǐ ma?
Let's begin.	Zánmen kāishǐ ba.
Are there any questions before we begin?	Kāishǐ zhīqián, yǒu shénme wèntí ma?

Stating the Issues

Let's each of us state the issues.	**Ràng wǒmen měi gè rén dōu chǎnshù yī xià wèntí.**
Let's each of us present our positions.	Ràng wǒmen měi gè rén dōu biǎomíng zìjǐ de lìchǎng.
What are the issues we need to cover in this meeting?	**Wǒmen de hùiyì xūyào tǎolùn shénme wèntí?**
What is the purpose of this meeting?	**Zhè cì hùiyì de mùdì shì shénme?**
What objectives would you like to accomplish in this meeting?	Zhè cì hùiyì xūyào dádào shénme mùdì?
Why is this meeting necessary?	Wèi shénme yǒu bìyào zàokāi zhè cì hùiyì?
What are the key issues as you see them?	Nǐ rènwéi gūanjiàn de wèntí shì shénme?

What is missing?	Yǒu shénme yí lòu ma?
Is anyone confused about our purpose here today?	Hái yǒu rén duì jīntiān lái zhè'r de mùdì bù qīngchǔ ma?
What is it you need us to do?	Nǐ xūyào wǒmen zùo shénme?
Which points are not clear?	Nǎ yī diǎn bù qīngchǔ?
Let's go over the details again.	Ràng wǒmen zài kàn yī biàn xìjié.
Has everything been covered?	Sǔoyǒu shìqíng dōu tán dào le ma?
We have a problem with . . .	Wǒmen zài . . . fāngmiàn yǒu wèntí.
credit and payment.	xìnyòng dàikuǎn hé zhīfù
deadlines.	jiézhǐ qīxiàn
delivery and terms.	jiāohùo hé zhīfù qīxiàn
guarantees.	dānbǎo
licensing.	zhízhào
warranties.	bǎoxiū/bǎodān

Disagreement, Ambivalence, and Reaching an Agreement

We disagree with these points.	Zài zhè jǐ diǎn shàng wǒmen kànfǎ bù tóng.
We don't agree.	Wǒmen bù tóngyì.
That's unacceptable.	Nà shì bù néng jiēshòu de.
Why do you disagree with this provision?	Nǐ wèi shénme bù tóngyì zhè yī tiáokuǎn?
Why do you reject this provision?	Nǐ wèi shénme jùjué zhè yī tiáokuǎn?
There is still too much keeping us apart.	Wǒmen de chājù shízài tài dà le.
We must continue to negotiate.	Wǒmen bìxu jìxù xiéshāng.

We must continue our efforts.	Wǒmen bìxu jìxù nǔlì.
You certainly don't expect us to accept that.	Nǐ dāngrán bù huì xīwàng wǒmen jiēshòu nà ge.
Unfortunately you are not offering enough.	Yíhàn de shì, nǐ de chūjià bù gòu.
We need more.	Wǒmen xūyào tígāo.
Who will pay for delivery?	Shúi fù sònghùo fèi?
Who will pay for insurance?	Shúi fù bǎoxiǎn?
We wish to propose . . .	Wǒmen tíyì . . .
We wish to counter-propose . . .	Wǒmen zài tíyì . . .
What is your counter-offer?	Nǐ húanjià dūoshǎo?
We are prepared to . . .	Wǒmen zhǔnbèi . . .
You should know the following . . .	Nǐ yīnggāi zhīdào yǐxià . . .
Our lawyers have informed us . . .	Wǒmen de lǜshī tōngzhī wǒmen . . .
We expect payment in 30/60/90 days.	Wǒmen xīwàng zhīfù qīxiàn wei sānshí/liùshí/jǐushí tiān.
Is there any discount for early payment?	Tíqián zhīfù yǒu zhékòu ma?
Can you provide us with a letter of credit?	Nǐ néng wèi wǒmen tígòng xìnyòngzhèng ma?
What is your guarantee?	Nǐ yòng shénme zùo dānbǎo?
We are getting close.	Wǒmen chājù bù dà le.
I'm beginning to see your point.	Wǒ kāishǐ míngbái nǐ de kànfǎ le.
Now I understand your point.	Wǒ xiànzài lǐjiě nǐ de gūandiǎn le.
Give us some time to think this over.	Gěi wǒmen yī diǎn shíjiān lái kǎolǜ kǎolǜ.

Let's plan another meeting.	Ràng wǒmen zài ānpaí yī cì huìyì ba.
We agree except for . . .	Chú . . . yǐwài, wǒmen doū tóng yì.
the cost.	chéngběn
the delivery date.	jiāohùo rìqī
the guarantee.	dānbǎo
the legal costs.	fǎlǜ fèiyòng
the price.	jiàgé
the shipping.	zhuāngyùn
We agree with some of your points.	Wǒmen tóngyì nǐmen de yī xiē kànfǎ.
We seem to agree in general.	Wǒmen dàtǐ shàng kàn lái shì tóngyì de.
We agree with your point.	Wǒmen tóngyì ní de kànfǎ.
What is left to discuss?	Hái yǒu shénme méiyǒu tǎolùnde?
This is our final offer.	Zhè shì wǒmen de zùihòu bàojià.
Is that your final offer?	Nà shì nǐmen de zùihòu bàojià ma?

Inking the Deal

Once a deal is reached, you'll want to celebrate, of course. But note that people may celebrate and congratulate each other in different ways in different cultures: bowing, shaking hands, offering a drink or toast, and so forth. If you are not sure of the cultural norms, as usual, the rule of the thumb is to follow your hosts.

We agree.	Wǒmen tóngyì.
We accept your offer.	Wǒmen jiēshòu nǐmen de bàojià.

This point/offer is acceptable.	**Zhè ge kànfǎ/bàojià shì kěyǐ jiēshòu de.**
We have an agreement.	**Wǒmen dáchéng le xiéyì.**
We have the deal.	Wǒmen chéngjiāo le.
We worked hard, let's have an agreement.	Wǒmen gōngzuò zhème xīngkǔ, ràng wǒmen qiān le hétóng ba.
We need a written document by Friday.	**Wǒmen zài xīngqī wǔ yǐqián, yào bǎ wénjiàn xiě hǎo.**
The documents must be signed by all parties.	**Yǒuguān gèfāng bìxū zài wénjiàn shàng qiānzì.**
Who will draft the agreement?	**Shúi lái qǐcǎo xiéyì?**
We will draft/type it.	Wǒmen lái qǐcǎo/dǎ.
We will send you a draft of the agreement.	Wǒmen hùi bǎ xiéyì de chūgǎo jì gěi nǐmen.
We will send a draft of the agreement for your comments.	**Wǒmen hùi bǎ xiéyì de chūgǎo jì gěi nǐmen tí yìjiàn.**
Thank you for your efforts.	Gǎnxiè nǐ de nǔlì.
It was very nice working with you.	**Hěn gāoxìng yǔ nǐ yīdào gōngzuò.**
If you have any questions, please let us know.	**Rú yǒu wèntí, qǐng tōngzhī wǒmen.**
We will be in touch.	**Wǒmen hùi bǎochí liánlùo.**

THE TRAINING SESSION

Are you conducting the session, or are you there to be trained? If you're giving the session, make sure the training is constructed from the participant's point of view. Too often training is organized more for the expert than the learner.

Then again, there may be a cultural aspect to consider when designing training programs. It's important to know how best to provide information to those in other business cultures. Advanced discussions with those in the country, or region of a country, eliminates most of the surprises and difficulties.

You may wish to review two of the sections in this chapter for words and phrases to begin and open the training session with: *The General Business Meeting* and *The Presentation or Speech*.

"Shòuxùn"

SHĬMÌSĪ XIĀNSHENG: *Wǒmen xiànzài tánlùn "Jiànshè Yī Gè Gòngtóng de Yuǎnjǐng Guīhùa." Fān dào èrshí qī yè, nǐ kěyǐ kàn daò zhè yī gàiniàn bèihòu de yúanzé. Sòng Xiǎojiě, nǐ kěyǐ tántan zhè gè chéngxù shì zěnyàng kāishǐ de ma?*

SÒNG XIǍOJIE: *Wǒ rènwéi gòngtóng de yuǎnjǐng guīhùa yīnggāi cóng yī gē zǔzhī gǔanlǐ rényúan zhìdìng shǐmìng xūanyán hé gǔanlǐ mùbiāo kāishǐ, zhèyàng cái kěyǐ dàidòng zhěnggè zǔzhī.*

SHĬMÌSĪ XIĀNSHENG: *Hěn hǎo. Chén Xiānsheng, zěnmeyàng cái kěyǐ shǐ zhígōng yǔ zǔzhī de mùbiāo dáchéng gòngshì?*

CHÉN XIĀNSHENG: *Wǒ xiǎng yīnggāi cǎiqǔ yī gè hùdòng de bànfǎ, bǐrú shèlì xíngdòng xiǎozǔ hùo zhāokāi gōngwěi hùiyì. Zhèyàng zhígōng kěyǐ cānyú júecè, júedìng zěnmeyàng zài jīcéng shíxiàn zhè xiē mùbiāo.*

"Being Trained"

MR. SMITH: *We are now going to talk about "Developing a Shared Vision." If you look in your workbook on page 27, you'll see a list of the prin-*

cipal ideas behind this concept. Ms. Song, could you speculate on how this process begins?

MS. SONG: *Yes. I believe a shared vision starts with the management of the organization establishing a mission statement, a list of management objectives, that will drive the organization.*

MR. SMITH: *Very good. Mr. Chen, how then do you get employees to buy into these organizational objectives?*

MR. CHEN: *I would guess by having some interactive process, like a task force or a series of committee meetings where employees can participate in determining how these objectives can be implemented at the actual work level.*

Speak slowly, be precise, and do not use acronyms or management jargon in training sessions. Try to use encouraging and positive words, and avoid direct criticism. Suggestions, such as "We found this way to be more useful." or "What if we try . . . ?" sit much better with the Chinese. When passing along information or instructions, it is important not to sound arrogant and condescending.

Key Words:	
Ask/have a question (to)	Wèn/yǒu wèntí
Be confused (to)	Bù qīngchǔ
Classroom	Jiàoshì
Course	Kèchéng
Group work	Xiǎozǔ gōngzùo
Notepad	Bǐjìbù
Pencil	Qiānbǐ

Pen	*Gāngbǐ*
Seminar	*Yántǎohùi*
Train (to)	*Péixùn*
Training session	*Péixùn qī*
Understand (to)	*Míngbai/Dǒng*
Workbook	*Shūběn*
Workshop	*Chējiān/Gōngzuòshì*

Today, I'm conducting
   training in . . .
   our policies.
   our procedures.

Jīntiān, wǒ lái jìnxíng . . . de
   péixùn.
   zhèngcè
   chéngxù

The training program
   today covers our
   new . . .
   financial reports.
   marketing reports.
   organization.
   sales reports.
   system(s).
I would like to . . .
   convince you . . .
   discuss . . .
   encourage dialogue
      on . . .
   give feedback
      regarding . . .
   lead a discussion on . . .
   participate in . . .
   provide information
      on . . .

Jīntiān de péixùn xiàngmù
   shì gūanyú wǒmen xīn
   de . . .
   cáiwù bàogào.
   tūixiāo bàogào.
   zǔzhī.
   xiāoshòu bàogào.
   xìtǒng.
Wǒ xiǎng . . .
   shūofú nǐ . . .
   tǎolùn . . .
   gǔlì zài . . . de dùihùa.

   gěi yǒugūan . . . de húankùi.

   yǐndǎo zài . . . de tǎolùn.
   cānyù . . .
   tígòng . . . de xìnxí.

Is there any question
   about the agenda?
Does everyone have all
   the materials?

Dùi hùiyì yìchéng yǒu wèntí
   ma?
Dàjiā dōu yǒu zīliào le ma?

Do you have any questions before we begin?	Zài wǒmen kāishǐ yǐqián, nǐ háiyǒu shénme wèntí ma?
Could you repeat that question?	**Kěyǐ chóngfù yī xià nǐ de wèntí ma?**
Does everyone understand the question?	Dàjiā dōu míngbai zhè gè wèntí ma?
Does everyone understand the issues?	Dàjiā dōu lǐjiě zhè gè wèntí ma?
Let's begin.	Ràng wǒmen kāishǐ ba.
Can I clarify anything?	**Yǒu shénme xūyào wǒ chéngqīng ma?**
What do you think about this?	**Nǐ duì cǐ zěnme kàn?**
Would anyone like to respond?	**Yǒu rén yào húidá ma?**
Are there any other ideas?	Háiyǒu bié de zhǔyì ma?
Let's break out into teams to solve this problem.	**Ràng wǒmen fēnzǔ lái jiějué zhè ge wèntí.**
Who will report on your solutions?	**Shúi lái bàogào yī xià nǐmen de jiějué fāngfǎ?**
That concludes the training on . . .	**Yǒuguān . . . de péixùn jiù dàocǐ jiéshù.**
I'll be happy to answer any questions.	Wǒ hěn lèyì húidá rènhé wèntí.
If you have any further questions, I'll be here for a while.	Nǐ rúgǔo háiyǒu wèntí, wǒ hùi zài dāi yīhūi'r.
Please contact me if you have further questions.	Nǐ rúgǔo yǒu wèntí, qǐng gēn wǒ liánlùo.
Thank you for your attention.	Xièxie nǐ de gūanglín.

Types of Room Setup or Style*

Classroom	Jiàoshì
Conference table	Hùiyì zhūo
Dais	Jiǎngtái
Podium	Zhǐhūitái
Theater	Jùyùan
U-shaped	U zì xíng de

Types of Charts and Graphs

Bar chart	Tiáowén túbiǎo
Display	Xiǎnshì
Dotted line	Xūxiàn
Exponential	Zhǐshù de
Histogram	Zhífāngtú
Horizontal bar chart	Héngtiáo túbiǎo
Line graph	Xiàntiáo túbiǎo
Linear	Xiànxíng de
Logarithmic scale	Dùishù bǐlì
Organization chart	Zǔzhī jiégòutú
Pie chart	Yúanxíngtú
Regression	Yìxíng
Solid line	Shíxiàn
Stacked	Chóngdié de
Table	Zhūozi
3-D chart	Sānwéi túbiǎo
XY scatter	Zònghéng sànbù

Parts of Charts and Graphs

Arc	Hú
Area	Qūyù/Miànjī
Arrow	Jiàntóu
Beginning	Qǐdiǎn

---

*Please refer back to the section *The Presentation or Speech* in this chapter to find the terms for common audio-visual aids.

Bell-shaped	Zhōngxíng de
Box	Hézi
Bullet	Dàntóu/zǐdàn
Circle	Yúanqūan
Column	Yúanzhù
Curve	Wānqū/qūxiàn
Dash	Pòzhéhào
Diagram	Tújiě/tú biǎo
Edge	Biān
Ellipse	Tǔoyúan
End	Zhōngdiǎn
First	Shǒuxiān
Grid	Fānggé
Heading	Biāotí
Label	Biāoqiān
Last	Zùihòu
Layout	Bǎnmiàn
Line	Xiàn
Logo	Biāoshì
Map	Dìtú
Maximum	Zùidà
Middle	Zhōngjiān
Minimum	Zùidī/Zùixiǎo
Numbers	Shùzì
Object	Wùtǐ
Origin	Qǐyúan
Percentage	Bǎifēnbǐ
Polygon	Dūobiānxíng
Right Angle	Zhíjiǎo
Row	Pái
Scale	Chèng/bǐlì
Shadow	Yīnyǐng
Slice	Báopiàn
Space	Kōngjiān
Square	Zhèngfāngxíng
Rectangle	Chángfāngxíng
Text	Zhèngwén
Triangle	Sānjiǎoxíng

| Title | Tímù |
| Values | Jiàzhí |

Positions

Bottom	Dǐdūan
Center	Zhōngyāng
Horizontal	Héng
Inside	Nèibù/Lǐbiān
Left	Zǔo
Outside	Wàibù/wàimiàn
Right	Yòu
Side	Cèmiàn
Top	Dǐngdūan
Touching	Chùmō
Vertical	Chúizhí
X-axis	Héngzhóu
Y-axis	Zòngzhóu
Z-axis	Z zhóu

Other Symbols and Formatting Designs

Asterisk	Xīngbiāo/xīnghào
Blank	Kòngbái
Bold	Hēitǐ
Crosshatched	Wǎngzhùang yīnyǐng/Jiāo chā yīn yǐng
Dash	Pòzhéhào
Pound sign	Jǐngzìhào
Shaded	Sèdù
Solid	Dānsè
Star	Xīngxing
Underlined	Hùa dǐxiàn de

You Can See The Color

Aqua	Shǔisè
Black	Hēisè
Blue	Lánsè

Brown	Zōngsè
Green	Lǜsè
Orange	Chéngsè
Purple	Zǐsè
Red	Hóngsè
Yellow	Húangsè

THE TRADE SHOW

The trade show is a cross between a sales call and a mass presentation. If you are part of the team presenting your company's products or services, you usually have only a brief time to explain them. If you are just attending to learn about what companies are offering, then being organized is helpful. So many exhibits to see, so many people to meet, so many contacts to make.

You might also like to review the section *The Sales Call* in this chapter, and the section on *Presenting Your Business and Department* in Chapter 1.

"Tígòng Xìnxí"

SHǏMÌSĪ XIĀNSHENG: *Nǐ xiǎng yào yī běn xiǎocezi ma?*

CHŪXÍZHĚ: *Shì de. Kěyǐ kànkan nǐmen fúwù de shìfàn ma?*

SHǏMÌSĪ XIĀNSHENG: *Píngmù shàng yǒu xuǎndan. Xuǎnzé dì èr xiàng jiù kěyǐ le.*

CHŪXÍZHĚ: *Nǐmen de xìtǒng yǔ Shìchuāng jiānróng ma?*

"Giving Information"

MS. SMITH: *Would you like a brochure?*

ATTENDEE: *Yes. Can I see a demonstration of your service?*

MS. SMITH: *You can see the menu on the monitor. We'll just select option two.*

ATTENDEE: *Is your system compatible with Windows?*

Make eye contact when communicating with Chinese people. They'll think you are not paying attention to them if you stare away. On the other hand, do not overdo it as some Chinese find constant eye contact to be impolite or overly challenging.

Key Words

Badge	Zhèngzhāng
Booth	Tānwèi
Brochure	Xiǎocèzi
Demonstrate (to)	Shìfàn
Demonstration	Shìfàn
Exhibit	Zhǎnshì
Literature	Wénzì zīliào
Message center	Xìnxí zhōngxīn
Register (to)	Dēngjì
Registration	Zhùcè
Trade show	Màoyì zhǎnxiāohùi

I want to register for the trade show.

Wǒ yào dēngjì cānjiā màoyì zhǎnxiāohùi.

Where do I get my badge?

Zài nǎr lǐngqǔ hùizhāng?

Where is . . .
  the business center?
  check-in?
  the information desk?
  the message center?
  the shipping center?
  ticket sales office?

. . . zài nǎr?
  Shāngyè zhōngxīn
  Bàodàochù
  Wènxún tái
  Xìnxí zhōngxīn
  Yùnhùo zhōngxīn
  Shòupiàochù

I would like to reserve . . .	Wǒ xiǎng yùyūe . . .
a booth.	yī gè tānwèi.
a room at the conference center.	huìyì zhōngxīn de yī gè fángjiān.

I would like to rent . . .	Wǒ xiǎng zūyòng . . .
a color monitor.	yī gè cǎisè xiǎnshìqì.
a computer.	yī tái diànnǎo.
a computer cable.	yī gè diànnǎo diànlǎn.
a microphone.	yī gè màikèfēng.
a slide projector.	yī tí huàndēngjī.
a sound system.	yī tào yīnxiǎng xìtǒng.
a speaker.	yī gè yángshēngqì/yī gè lǎba.
a table.	yī zhāng zhūozi.
a television.	yī tái diànshì.

There is a problem with . . .	. . . yǒu wèntí.
the electrical line.	Diànxiàn
my booth.	Wǒ de tānwèi
the location of my booth.	Wǒ de tānwèi de wèizhi

I need . . .	Wǒ xūyào . . .
chairs.	yǐzi.
display tables.	zhǎnshì zhūozi.
electricity.	diàn.
easels.	huànjià.
extension cords.	yánshēnxiàn.

| My materials have not arrived. | Wǒ de zīliào hái méi dào. |
| Please deliver these to booth number 124. | Qǐng bǎ zhè xiē sòng dào yī bǎi èrshí sì hào tānwèi qù. |

| Hi, my name is . . . | Nǐ hǎo. Wǒ jiào. . . . |
| What's yours? | Nǐ jiào shénme míngzi? |

| My name is . . . | Wǒ jiào . . . |
| My company/ organization is . . . | Wǒ de gōngsī/zǔzhī jiào . . . |

My position is . . .	Wǒ de zhíwèi shì . . .
Are you familiar with our products/services?	**Nǐ shúxī wǒmen de chǎnpǐn/fúwù ma?**
What can I tell you about them?	**Nǐ xiǎng liǎojiě shénme?**
Can I explain anything to you?	**Yǒu shénme xūyào wǒ jiěshì yī xià ma?**
Please take a brochure.	**Qǐng ná yī běn xiǎocèzi.**
Please write your name, address, and phone number.	Qǐng bǎ nǐ de míngzi, dìzhǐ hé diànhùa hàomǎ xiě xià lái.
Do you have any questions?	Nǐ yǒu shénme wèntí?
Can I help you?	Xūyào bāngmáng ma?
May I have your business card?	Kěyǐ yào yì zhāng nǐ de míngpiàn ma?
What is your e-mail address?	Nǐ de diànzi yóujiàn dìzhǐ shì shénme?
You can visit our Web site . . .	**Nǐ kěyǐ qù wǒmen de wǎngzhǐ kànkàn . . .**
Would you like to see . . . a brochure? a demonstration?	**Nǐ yào bu yào kànkan . . .** xiǎocèzi? **shìfàn?**
Do you have a brochure in . . .	**Nǐ yǒu . . . de xiǎocèzi ma?**
English? Chinese? German? Spanish?	yīngyǔ **hànyǔ** déyǔ xībānyáyǔ
What can I tell you about the product/service?	**Yào wǒ gàosu nǐ chǎnpǐn/fúwù de qíngkùang ma?**
My company will be giving a demonstration in the conference room.	**Wǒ gōngsī yào zài hùiyìshì jìnxíng shìfàn cāoyǎn.**

We will be demonstrating the product/service . . .* later.
tomorrow.
at 10:00 A.M.
at 2:00 P.M.

Wǒmen . . . yào duì chǎnpǐn/fúwù jìnxíng shìfàn.
děnghuǐ'r
míngtiān
shàngwǔ shí diǎn
xiàwǔ liǎng diǎn

Can you come back tomorrow at . . .
11:00 A.M.?
3:00 P.M.?

Nǐ kěyǐ zài míngtiān . . . húilái ma?
shàngwǔ shíyī diǎn
xiàwǔ sān diǎn

Can I contact you to keep you informed about our products/services?

Wǒ kěyǐ gēn nǐ bǎochí liánxì, ràng nǐ liǎojiě wǒmen de chǎnpǐn/fúwù de qíngkùang ma?

Can I have . . .
a list of your products/services?
your business card?
your catalog?

Néng gěi wǒ . . .
nǐmen chǎnpǐn/fúwù de mùlù ma?
nǐ de míngpiàn ma?
nǐ de biānmù ma?

Can you tell me more about . . .
the delivery options?
next year's model?
your new system?

Néng bù néng zài gàosu wǒ . . .
sònghuò de xuǎnzé?
míngnían de móxíng?
nǐmen de xīn xìtǒng?

Do you have more information on . . .
your company's history?
your other products?
the system you are developing?

Nǐ yǒu guānyú . . . de xiángxì de zīliào ma?
nǐmen gōngsī de lìshǐ
nǐmen qítā chǎnpǐn
nǐmen zài kāifā de xìtǒng

Please explain your guarantee/warranty.

Qǐng jiěshì yī xià nǐmen de bǎodān/bǎoxiū.

---

*See *Telling Time* in Chapter 6.

Please speak more slowly.	Qǐng shuō màn yì diǎn.
Could you repeat that?	Kěyǐ chóngfù yī xià ma?
I understand.	Wǒ míngbái.
I am not interested.	**Wǒ bù gǎn xìngqù.**
May I give you a call?	Wǒ kěyǐ gěi nǐ dǎ diànhùa ma?
I'll give you a call.	Wǒ hùi gěi nǐ dǎ diànhùa.
Please call me.	Qǐng gěi wǒ dǎ diànhùa.
It was nice meeting you.	Hěn gāoxìng rènshì nǐ.
Perhaps I'll see you later.	Kěnéng děnghǔi'r zàijiàn.
Thank you for stopping by.	Xièxie nǐ de gūanglín.
Thank you for showing me your products.	Gǎnxiè nǐ wèi wǒmen zhǎnshì nǐ de chǎnpǐn.

ATTENDING A CONFERENCE OR SEMINAR

You can accomplish several objectives by attending a conference or seminar. Obviously, you can learn new information, points of view, or better ways of doing something. You can also make important contacts within your industry or field. Also, through questions, you can provide the conference or seminar with your own experiences or information, or express your own or your company's opinions.

Conferences can be large auditorium affairs or small seminars. Taking good notes is key. Also, check with others on information that you weren't sure of. This can also be a way to make interesting and useful contacts.

Remember to write a note to your new contacts as soon as you can after the conference. A personal note, a phone call, or an e-mail goes a long way to continue and solidify a contact.

"Liánlùo"

YŪEHÀNXÙN XIǍOJIE: *Nǐ shì Xīsīkè de, shì ma?*
WǓ XIĀNSHENG: *Shì de. Wǒ lái shì xīwàng liáojiě zěnyàng zài zhè gè gúojiā jìnxíng tūigǔang. Kěyǐ yào yī zhāng nǐ de míngpiàn ma?*
YŪEHÀNXÙN XIǍOJIE: *Dāngrán kěyǐ. Wǒ yě yào yì zhāng nǐ de míngpiàn. Nǐ dùi wǔcānhùi shàng de yǎnjiǎngzhě yǒu shénme kànfǎ?*
WǓ XIĀNSHENG: *Yībān. Tā yàoshì gèng xiángxì de jiǎngjiě tā zěnmeyàng jiějúe jìshù wèntí de hùa, nà jiù gèng hǎo le.*

"Making Contacts"

MS. JOHNSON: *I see you're with Cisco?*
MR. WU: *Yes, I'm attending hoping to learn more about how to market in this country. May I have your business card?*
MS. JOHNSON: *Yes. I would like one of yours as well. How did you like the speaker at lunch?*
MR. WU: *So-so. I would have liked it if she would have been more specific about how she solved the technical problems.*

Humor does not easily cross linguistic and cultural borders. It is rarely a good idea to attempt humor with Chinese people at a conference or a seminar. They might have trouble grasping your joke and will think you are not being serious.

In social gatherings or group situations, body language matters. You should sit upright in your chair. Do not lounge in a chair or slump down. That is regarded as rude and uncaring. Also, do not stand with your hands on your hips. It gives the impression of condescension, especially when explaining or giving instructions.

Key Words

Ballroom	*Wǔtīng*
Business cards	*Míngpiàn*
Conference room	*Huìyìshì*
Cocktail party	*Jīwěijiǔhuì*
Introductions	*Jièshào*
Luncheon	*Wǔcān*
Make contacts (to)	*Liánluò*
Message	*Xìnxí*
Presentation/Talk/	*Yǎnshì/Tánlùn/Yǎnjiǎng*
Speech	

Please introduce yourself.
Qǐng jièshào yī xià nǐ zìjǐ.

Before we begin the meeting, let's introduce ourselves.
Zài kāihuì yǐqián, ràng wǒmén zǔo yī xià zìwǒ jièshào.

Beginning on my left/ right please state your name, company, and position (title).
Cóng wǒ zuǒ/yòu biān kāishǐ, qǐng shuō yī xià nǐ de míngzi, gōngsī hé zhíwèi.

My name is . . .
Wǒ jiào . . .

My company/ organization is . . .
Wǒ de gōngsī/zǔzhī shì . . .

My position is . . .
Wǒ de zhíwèi shì . . .

I hope to get . . .
Wǒ xīwàng cóng zhè cì huìyì/yántǎohuì huòdé . . .

information.
xìnxī.

a better understanding.
gèng hǎo de lǐjiě.

useful data.
yǒuyòng de shùjù.

out of this conference/ seminar.

Questions

Could you please repeat what you just said?
Néng chóngfù yī xià nǐ gāngcái shuō de ma?

| I didn't understand your second point. | **Wǒ bù míngbái nǐ de dì èr diǎn.** |
| Why/How did you reach that conclusion? | **Nǐ wèi shénme/Zěnmeyàng chǔdé zhèyàng de jiélùn?** |

Close

| Could we receive a tape of this conference/seminar? | Kěyǐ gěi wǒmen zhè cì huìyì/yántǎohùi de lùyīndài ma? |
| Thank you for the information. | Xièxie nǐ de xìnxí. |

CONDUCTING AN INTERVIEW

Are you interviewing someone for your own department? Or, are you in human resources and screening people for a position? Getting beyond the details of a resume is the key to a successful interview.

"Miànshì"

SHǏMÌSĪ XIǍOJIE: *Nǐ wèi shénme yào líkāi nǐ xiànzài de gōngzùo?*

HÚANG XIĀNSHENG: *Méiyǒu tíshēng de jīhùi. Wǒ jiù xiàn zhì zài zhè gè zhíwèi shàng. Gēnběn méiyǒu tiǎozhànxing.*

SHǏMÌSĪ XIǍOJIE: *Nǐ xúnqiú shénmeyàng de tiǎozhàn?*

HÚANG XIĀNSHENG: *Wǒ xīwàng néng fùzé zhěnggè rǔantǐ xiàngmù. Wǒ xiànzài jǐnjǐn shì xǔduō chéngxù biānzhìyúan zhī yī.*

"The Interview"

MS. SMITH: *Why do you want to leave your present job?*

MR. HUANG: *There is no advancement for me. I'm stuck in my position. And, there are no challenges for me.*

MS. SMITH: *What kind of challenges are you seeking?*

MR. HUANG: *I would like to be in charge of an entire software project. Now I'm only one of the many programmers.*

Key Words

Ad	Gǔanggào
Benefits	Fúlì
Boss	Lǎobǎn
Career	Zhíyè
Experience	Jīngyàn
Goals	Mùbiāo
Job	Gōngzùo
Interview	Miànshì
Objective	Mùdì
Offer	Gěi
Organization	Zǔzhī
Reference	Dānbǎorén/Zhèng míng rén
Resume	Jiǎnlì
Salary	Gōngzī
Skills	Jìshù

Jiǎn Lì

Xìngmíng:*	Fāng Wén-lín
Gōngzùo dānwèi:	Běijīng Fángdìchǎn Kāifā Gōngsī
Dìzhǐ:	Zhōnggúo Běijīng Dōngchéngqū Shùaifúyúan 5B
Diànhùa:	011–86–01–5124440
Mùdì:	Gúojì zǔzhī de gāojí cáiwù zhíwèi. Rú yǒu bìyào, kěyǐ gǔangfàn lǚyóu.

---

*Xìngmíng means "name," dìzhǐ is "address," and diànhuà is "telephone." It is the Chinese practice to identify each type of information in this way on the resume.

Gōngzùo Jīngyàn: **Běijīng Fángdìchǎn Kāifā Gōngsī,** Zhōngguó Běijīng (1996 zhì jīn)

Cáiwùbù Gāojí Cáiwù Fēnxīshī: fùzé gōngsī jiǎnshǎo chéngběn kāizhī xiàngmù de shèjì yǔ shíshī. Wèi gōngsī jiéyūe 2 bǎiwàn měiyúan.

Shànghǎi Gúojì. Tóuzī Gōngsī, Shànghǎi, Zhōnqgúo (1994–1996)

Cáikùaibù Cáiwù Fēnxīshī. Fùzé gōngsī gěi gǔdōng de rìcháng hé tèshū cáiwù bàobiǎo de fēnxī.

Jiàoyù: Shànghǎi Fùdàn Dàxúe Kùaijì xúeshì.

Dānbǎorén: Miào Tiān-lín, Běijīng Fángdìchǎn Kāifā Gōngsī diànhùa 10–8317502

Fang Wen-lin
Beijing Real Estate Development Company
5B Shuai Fu Yuan
Dongcheng District, Beijing China
011–86–01–5124440

Objective: Seeking a senior financial position at an international organization. Will travel extensively internationally if necessary.

Professional
Experience: **Beijing Real Estate Development Co.,** Beijing, China. 1996–Present

Senior Financial Analyst in the Corporate Finance Department.

Designed and implemented a cost-cutting program company wide. Saved $2 million in inventory.

Shanghai International Investment, Shanghai, China. 1994–1996

Financial Analyst in the Corporate Accounting Department. Handled routine and special analysis of financial reports issued by the company to shareholders.

Education:	B.S. Degree in Accounting, Fudan University, Shanghai.
Professional References:	Miao Tian-lin, Beijing Real Estate Development Co., Tel: 10–8317502

Do you have a resume?	Nǐ yǒu jiǎnlì ma?
Could you review your work experience/history for me?	Gěi wǒ tántan nǐ de gōngzuò jīnglì/lìshǐ, kěyǐ ma?
Please tell me about your education.	Qǐng tántan nǐ de jiàoyù.
Please tell me about your jobs.	Qǐng tántan nǐ de gōngzuò.
What do you feel were your biggest accomplishments at each of your jobs?	Nǐ guòqù měi gè gōngzuò zhōng, nǐ qǔdé de zuì dà chéngjī shì shénme?
What was your salary/compensation at each of your jobs?	Nǐ guòqù de xīn shuǐ/bàochóu shì dūoshǎo?
What is your salary/compensation now?	Nǐ xiànzài de xīn shuǐ/bàochóu shì dūoshǎo?

Do you receive any . . .
bonus?
deferred compensation?
stock options?

**Nǐmen yǒu . . .
hónglì ma?**
yánhuǎn bàochóu ma?
gǔpiào tèquán ma?

Do you have a . . .
401(k) type plan?
pension?

Nǐmen yǒu . . .
401 tùixiū jìhùa ma?
tùixiūjīn ma?

Why did you leave
Dōngfāng Gúojì
Gōngsī and join
Shanghai Fǎngzhì
Kònggǔ Gōngsī?

Nǐ wèi shénme líkāi
Dōngfāng Gúojì Gōngsī
jiārù Shànghǎi Fǎngzhī
Kònggǔ Gōngsī?

Why do you want to
leave Shànghǎi Fǎngzhì
Kònggǔ Gōngsī now?

Nǐ xiànzài wèi shénme yào
líkāi Shànghǎi Fǎngzhī
Kònggǔ Gōngsī?

What position are you
looking for?

**Nǐ yào zhǎo shénme yàng de
zhíwèi?**

What are you looking for
in a position?

Nǐ yào zhǎo shénme yàng de
gōngzùo?

What salary/
compensation are you
looking for?

**Nǐ yāoqiú shénme yàng de
gōngzǐ/bàochóu?**

What were some of the
problems you
experienced?

**Nǐ jīnglì gùo shénme yàng de
wèntí?**

How did you deal with
them?

Nǐ zěnyàng chùlǐ zhèxiē
wèntí?

How well did you get
along with your
boss(es)?

Nǐ gēn lǎobǎn gūanxì rúhé?

How well did you get
along with your peers?

Nǐ gēn tóngshì gūanxì rúhé?

Do you have any
references?

Nǐ yǒu dānbǎorén ma?

Can we check with any

Wǒmen kěyǐ yǔ dañbǎorén

of these references?	cháduì ma?
Do you have any questions for me?	Nǐ yǒu shénme wèntí yaò wèn wǒ?
What questions do you have?	Nǐ yǒu shénme wèntí?
How can we be in touch with you?	**Wǒmen zěnyàng gēn nǐ liánxì?**
Here is my card.	Zhè shì wǒ de míngpiàn.
If you have any questions please call me.	Nǐ rúguǒ yǒu wèntí, qǐng gěi wǒ dǎ diànhuà.
My e-mail address is . . .	Wǒ de diànzǐ yóujiàn dìzhǐ shì . . .
You will hear from us within . . .	**Nǐ huì zài . . . nèi tīng dào wǒmen de xiāoxī.**
We will be in touch with you within . . .	Wǒmen zài. . . . nèi huì tōngzhī nǐ.
two days.	liǎng tiān
one week.	yī gè xīngqī
two weeks.	liǎng gè xīngqī
three weeks.	sān gè xīngqī
one month.	yī gè yuè
Do you have any further questions?	Nǐ háiyǒu bié de wèntí ma?
I enjoyed talking to you.	**Hěn gaōxìng yǔ nǐ jiāotán.**
It was a pleasure talking to you.	Hěn gaōxìng yǔ nǐ jiāotán.
Thank you for seeing us.	**Gǎnxìe nǐ yǔ wǒmen jiànmiàn.**
Good luck to you.	Zhù nǐ yǒu hǎoyùn.

As an international businesswoman, it is in your best interest to understand the position of women in China before setting foot in a Chinese boardroom. Although the government position on women in business officially reads that there is a concentrated effort to push for more female participation in the economy, business circles are still traditional. In order to earn respect, you must establish your rank and expertise from the start. As a foreign businesswoman, you will be given special status, simply because you're a foreigner. Nonetheless, you should retain your respect for the Chinese culture and act according to their rules of politeness and order.

3 GETTING OUT

Dining out, attending a sporting event or going to a movie, or just doing some pleasant sightseeing can offer a welcome break from meetings and conferences. It's a chance to relax after an intense or just busy business day. It's also an opportunity to see and learn about the country, culture and people.

However, when you do these activities with business associates, you have to be as attentive and businesslike as when you are in the office. After all, you are merely extending your selling or negotiating from the office to a more casual setting. Thus, you must be very conscious of crossing the boundary from business to personal. And, if you do cross that line, you do it deliberately.

But this more casual setting can offer the chance to establish or cement relationships that are difficult to do in the office. It offers a chance to better know your business associates or people you are doing business with. This can build trust, the bedrock of successful business relationships.

Thus, getting out can mean different things to different people. We cover a number of different situations:

> **Getting a Taxi**
> **At the Restaurant**
> **Social Conversation**
> **Sporting Events, Movies,**
> **Theater, Clubs**
> **Visiting the Partner's or**
> **Associate's Home**

For most of these activities, we need a taxi. Taxi!

GETTING A TAXI

"Jìchéngchē"

SĪJĪ: *Nǐ yào qù nǎr?*

QIÓNGSĪ XIĀNSHENG: *Wǒ xiǎng qù yí gè hǎo de
Fǎguó cāngǔan. Fùjìn yǒu ma?*

SĪJĪ: *Yǒu, yǒu hǎo jǐ gè. Nǐ yào jiàgé gāo de háishì
zhōngděng jià de?*

QIÓNGSĪ XIĀNSHENG: *Wǒ xiǎng yào zhōngděng jià
de ba.*

"Taking a Taxi"

DRIVER: *Where do you want to go?*

MR. JONES: *I would like to go to a nice French
restaurant. Are there any close by?*

DRIVER: *Yes, there are several. Do you want an
expensive one, or only a moderate one?*

MR. JONES: *A moderate one, I guess.*

Bicycles are still the main transportation for a
lot of Chinese, but taxis are increasingly common in big cities like Beijing and Shanghai. They are
relatively inexpensive and plentiful. Most drivers are
honest; however, if there's no meter you should always negotiate the price before you set off. In any
case, you should write your destination down in Chinese. It's also a good idea to always carry around
your hotel card with its name and address in Chinese.

Taxi!	Jìchéngchē!/Chūzūchē!
I need a taxi.	Wǒ yào jìchéngchē.
Please call a taxi.	Qǐng jiào yī liàng jìchéngchē.
Take me to . . .	Wǒ yào qù . . .
this address . . .	zhè gè dìzhǐ.
the restaurant called . . .	jiào . . . de cānguǎn.
the hotel . . .	zhè gè lǚguǎn.
Please take me to the . . .	Qǐng kāi wǒ qù . . .
concert hall.	yīnyuètīng.
conference center.	huìyì zhōngxīn.
dock/pier.	mǎtóu.
museum.	bówùguǎn.
opera house.	gējùyuàn.
Turn here.	Zài zhè'r guǎiwān.
Stop here.	Tíng zhè'r.
Could you wait ten minutes?	Nǐ kěyǐ děng shí fēn zhōng ma?
How much do I owe?	Wǒ qiàn nǐ dūoshǎo qián?
Keep the change.	Bù yòng zhǎo le.

AT THE RESTAURANT

Here's a chance to learn about the culture you're visiting—through food. If you're adventuresome, you may try a number of dishes indigenous to the country or region. If you are timid, then stay with the foods you know with perhaps one or two dishes that your host may recommend. But even if you don't try too many of the local dishes, you can ask about them and in doing so you will show your interest in the local culture, which will give your host(s) a good impression of you.

"Cāngǔan"

SŪN XIĀNSHENG: *Jīntiān wǎnshàng nǐ xiǎng qù shénme yàng de cāngǔan?*

QIÓNGSĪ XIĀNSHENG: *Fǎgúo hùo Xībānyá cāngǔan dōu xíng.*

SŪN XIĀNSHENG: *Mǎtóu shàng yǒu yī jiā tèbié hǎo de Fǎgúo cāngǔan.*

QIÓNGSĪ XIĀNSHENG: *Hěn yǔan ma?*

SŪN XIĀNSHENG: *Shì de, dàn wǒmen kěyǐ jiào jìchéngchē.*

QIÓNGSĪ XIĀNSHENG: *Tài hǎo le. Zánmen zǒu ba.*

"Finding a Restaurant"

MR. SUN: *So, what kind of restaurant do you want to go to tonight?*

MR. JONES: *Either French or Spanish.*

MR. SUN: *There is a great French restaurant at the wharf.*

MR. JONES: *Isn't that far?*

MR. SUN: *Yes, but we'll take a taxi.*

MR. JONES: *Great. Let's go.*

Food is a central part of Chinese culture. You will be invited to many banquets. They are a means of introducing new people to you, of developing relationships, and of celebrating an event, such as the conclusion of a deal. As a courtesy, you should return the favor by inviting Chinese to a meal at a good restaurant. Ask someone you trust to assist you with the meal arrangements such as the price, guest list and sitting.

Key Words

Coats	Wàitào
Check/Bill	Zhī piào/ Zhàngdān
Drinks	Yǐnliào
Menu	Càidān
Order (to)	Diǎn cài
Restaurant	Cānguǎn
Rest room(s)	Cèsuǒ
Smoking/ Nonsmoking	Xīyān/Bù xīyān (jìnyān)
Table	Zhōuzi
Waiter/Waitress	Fúwùyúan
Wine list	Jiǔdān

Good evening.	Wǎnshàng hǎo.
My name is . . . I have a reservation for two/ three/four/five.	Wǒ jiào . . . Wǒ yǒu liǎng/sān/sì/wǔ gè rén de yùyūe.
Can I/we check our coat(s)?	Wǒ/Wǒmen kěyǐ bǎ wàitào cún zài zhè'r ma?
Could we have a drink at the bar first?	Wǒmen kěyǐ xiān zài jiǔbā hē diǎn yǐnliào ma?
Could we be seated promptly?	Hěn kùai jiù hùi yǒu zùowèi ma?
Could we have a nonsmoking/smoking table/area?	Wǒmen kěyǐ yào bù xīyān/ xīyān de zùowèi/qūwèi ma?
Do you have a table . . . at a window? in a corner?	Nǐ yǒu . . . de zùowèi ma? kào chūang kào jiǎolùo

in a smoking/ nonsmoking area?	xīyān/bùxīyān
in a quiet area?	ānjìng
in the other room?	zài lìng yī gè fángjiān

| Could we have that table there? | **Wǒmen kěyǐ yào méi zhāng zhūozi ma?** |

| We don't have much time, could we order quickly? | **Wǒmen méiyǒu dūoshǎo shíjiān. Kěyǐ hěn kùai jiàocài ma?** |

| Could we have a menu? | **Kěyǐ gěi wǒmen càidān ma?** |
| Do you have a wine list? | Nǐmen yǒu jiǔdān ma? |

| Here is the menu. | Zhè shì càidān. |
| Here is the wine list. | Zhè shì jiǔdān. |

| Do you mind if I have a cocktail/a drink? | Wǒ yào yī bēi jīwěijiǔ/yǐnliào, nǐ bù jièyì ba? |

Ordering Drinks

In some countries, giving a toast is expected. Thus, give some thought ahead of time about what toast you would offer or even write it out. This will greatly impress your hosts, and go a long way to establish you as a world traveler.

I would like to order . . .	**Wǒ yào . . .**
an aperitif.	**yī bēi kāiwèijiǔ.**
a drink.	yī bēi yǐnliào.
a beer.	yī píng píjiǔ.
a cocktail.	yī bēi jīwěijiǔ.
a glass of wine.	yī píng jiǔ.
a juice.	yī bēi gǔozhī.
a Coke.	yī píng kělè.
carbonated mineral water.	qìshǔi.
still mineral water.	bù dài pào de qìshǔi.

What types of wine do you have?	Nǐ yǒu shénme yàng de jiǔ?
Could you recommend a local wine?	**Nǐ kěyǐ tūijiàn yī zhǒng dìfāng jiǔ ma?**
Do you have Beaujolais Nouveau?	Nǐ yǒu Fǎgúo de Beaujolais Nouveau jiǔ ma?
I would like a glass of white/red wine.	**Wǒ yào yī bēi bái/hóng pútáojiǔ.**
I would like to make a toast.	**Wǒ xiǎng jìng yī bēi jiǔ.**

Pace yourself with drinks because the Chinese may serve a very strong spirit called "wine." You do not want to get drunk and lose face in front of the people you are trying to win over. At such gatherings, your host will often make a toast to your honor and ask you to "*gānbēi*" (bottom up). You are expected to empty your glass, and return the favor by proposing a toast to your host. Say something nice and positive, but be careful not to raise business issues at such occasions because with all the food and drink, you may not be able to concentrate. As a result, you may lose your edge.

Ordering Dinner

"*Jiàocài*"

FÚWÙYÚAN: *Nǐ yào diǎn cài le ma?*
SHǏMÌSĪ XIĀNSHENG: *Nǐmen yǒu shénme zhāopáicài ma?*
FÚWÙYÚAN: *Shì de, wǒmen yǒu Běijīng Kǎoyā.*
SŪN XIǍOJIE: *Tài hǎo le. Wǒ jiù yào nà ge hǎo le.*
SHǏMÌSĪ XIĀNSHENG: *Shíjì shàng, wǒ zuìhǎo háishì yào niúpái, liù chéng shú hǎo le.*
FÚWÙYÚAN: *Xièxie.*

"Ordering Dinner"
WAITER: *May I take your order?*
MR. SMITH: *Do you have any local specialties?*
WAITER: *Yes, we have Beijing roasted duck.*
MS. SUN: *That's very good. I think I'll have that.*
MR. SMITH: *Actually, I think I'll have the steak,*
medium rare.
WAITER: *Thank you.*

When you eat in a restaurant or someone's home in China, you are expected to follow certain rules at the table even though not everyone adheres to these traditions. The first thing to learn is how to use chopsticks. Pick up your chopsticks only when your host picks up his or hers and indicates which dish to start with. Always place chopsticks on the rest if provided, or lay them flat on the table. Do not lay chopsticks across your bowl at formal occasions, and never stick chopsticks upright in the rice and leave them standing up as this is only done at funeral ceremonies.

Key Words

Appetizer	Kāiwèi shípǐn
Dessert	Tiándiǎn
Entrée	Zhǔcài
Fruit	Shuǐguǒ
Prix fixe	Kèfàn
Salad	Shālā
Soup	Tāng
Vegetable	Shūcài

Waiter/Waitress!	**Fúwùyúan!***
Do you have any specialties?	**Nǐ yǒu shénme zhāopáicài ma?**
What are your specialties of the day?	**Nǐmen jīntiān de tècān shì shénme?**
I am/We are ready to order.	**Wǒ/Wǒmen kěyǐ diǎncài le.**
Would you like an appetizer?	**Nǐ yào kāiwèi shípǐn ma?**
Yes, I would like an appetizer.	**Shì de, wǒ yào yī gè kāiwèi shípǐn.**
No, I would like just a main course.	**Bù, wǒ zhǐyào zhǔcài.**
I recommend . . .	**Wǒ tuījiàn . . .**
the chicken.	**jī.**
the fish.	**yú.**
the pork.	**zhūròu.**
the steak.	**niúpái.**
the vegetarian platter.	**shūcài pīngpán.**
I would like the prix fixe meal.	**Wǒ yào kèfàn.**
What are you going to order?	**Nǐ yào diǎn shénme cài?**
I'm saving room for dessert.	**Wǒ xiǎng liú xià wèikǒu chī tiándiǎn.**
I would like my meat . . .	**Wǒ de ròu yào. . . .**
medium.	**liù chéng shú.**
medium rare.	**qī chéng shú.**
medium well.	**bā chéng shú.**
rare.	**bàn shú.**
well done.	**zhǔ shú.**
Could we have some . . .	**Kěyǐ gěi wǒmen yī diǎn . . .**
butter?	**niúyóu ma?**
bread?	**miànbāo ma?**

---

*Chinese words do not have gender, so the same word is used for *waiter* and *waitress*.

horseradish?	làgēnjiàng ma?
ketchup?	fānqiéjiàng ma?
lemon?	níngméng ma?
mayonnaise?	dànhuángjiàng ma?
mustard?	jièmòjiàng ma?
pepper?	hújiāo ma?
salt?	yán ma?
sugar?	táng ma?
water?	shuǐ ma?

| Could we have a little more? | Néng zài gěi wǒmen yī diǎn ma? |

Could we have a . . .	Wǒmen kěyǐ yào . . .
cup?	yī gè bēizi ma?
glass?	yī gè bōlíbēi ma?
fork?	yī gè chāzi ma?
knife?	yī bǎ dāozi ma?
napkin?	yī kuài cānjīn ma?
plate?	yī gè pánzi ma?
saucer?	yī gè diézi ma?
spoon?	yī gè tāngshí ma/tāng sháo na?
teaspoon?	yī gè cháshí ma?
toothpick?	yī gēn yáqiān ma?

Appetizers

Antipasto	Kāiwèi shíwù
Bisque	Nóngtāng
Broth	Qīngtāng
Cold cuts	Lěngpán
Pasta	Shēngmiàntuán
Rice	Mǐfàn
Salad	Shālā
Snails (Escargots)	Wōniú
Soup	Tāng

Main Courses

| Chicken | Jī |
| Clams | Bàng/Gélì |

Duck	Yā
Fillet of beef	Ròupiàn
Goose	É
Ham	Huǒtuǐ
Lamb	Xiǎoyángròu
Liver	Gān
Lobster	Lóngxiā
Pork	Zhūròu
Oyster	Mǔlì
Quail	Ānchún
Roast Beef	Kǎoniúròu
Salmon	Guìyú
Sausage	Làcháng
Scallops	Hǎibèi shànbèi
Shrimp	Xiā
Sole	Diéyú
Steak	Niúpái
Tuna	Wèiyú/Chīnqiāngyú
Turkey	Huǒjī
Veal	Xiǎoniúròu
Venison	Lùròu

It can be . . .	Kěyǐ . . .
baked.	hōngkǎo
braised.	wēnhuǒ dùnzhǔ
broiled.	kǎoròu
fried.	yóujiān/yóuzhá
grilled.	kǎojià kǎo
marinated.	jìnpào
roasted.	shāokǎo
poached.	shuǐzhǔ
sautéed.	chǎo
steamed.	zhēng
stewed.	mèn

Vegetables

Artichoke	Yángjì
Asparagus	Lúsǔn

Beans	Dòuzi
Beets	Tiáncài
Cabbage	Jǔanxīncài
Carrots	Húlúobo
Cauliflower	Hūayēcài
Celery	Qíncài
Corn	Yùmǐ
Cucumber	Húanggūa
Eggplant	Qiézi
Leek	Jiǔcài
Lettuce	Wōjù
Lentils	Piándòu/bīngdòu
Mushroom	Mógū
Onion	Yángcōng
Peas	Wāndòu
Potato	Mǎlíngshǔ/Tǔdòu
Spinach	Bōcài
Tomato	Fānqié
Turnip	Báilúobo
Zucchini	Xiǎohúgūa xīhúlu

Herbs and Spices

Anise	Dàhúixiāng
Basil	Jiǔcéngtǎ
Bay leaf	Yùegùi
Capers	Mǎbīngláng
Caraway	Xiāngcài
Chives	Xiāyicōng
Cinnamon	Ròugùi
Dill	Shílúo
Garlic	Dàsùan
Ginger	Jiāng
Marjoram	Móqiào/Mòjiāo lán
Mint	Bòhe
Nutmeg	Ròudòukòu
Oregano	Yúshānshè xiāngcǎo
Parsley	Hélánqín

Pepper	Hújiāo
Pimiento	Gānjiāo
Rosemary	Mǐdiéxiāng
Saffron	Fānhónghūa
Sage	Shūwèicǎo
Tarragon	Lónghāo
Thyme	Bǎilǐxiāng

I would like my potato . . .	Wǒ de mǎlíngshǔ yaò . . .
baked.	hōngkǎo.
boiled.	zhǔ.
creamed.	jiāo nǎiyóu.
french fried.	yóuzhá.
mashed.	dǎosuì.
pureed.	zùo nóngtāng.

Fruits

Apple	Píngguǒ
Apricot	Xìngzi
Banana	Xiāngjiāo
Blueberries	Yùejú
Cherries	Yīngtáo
Dates	Zǎozi
Figs	Wúhūaguǒ
Grapes	Pútáo
Grapefruit	Xīyòu/pútáoyòu
Kiwi	Kèwèiguǒ
Mango	Mángguǒ
Melon	Gūa
Nectarine	Yóutáo
Orange	Chéngzi
Peach	Táozi
Pear	Lí
Pineapple	Bōlúo
Plum	Lǐzi
Prunes	Gānméizi

Raisins	Pútáogān
Raspberries	Shānméi
Strawberries	Căoméi
Watermelon	Xīguā

Nuts

Almonds	Xìngrénguǒ
Cashews	Yāoguǒ
Chestnuts	Bǎnlì
Hazelnuts	Zhēnshí
Peanuts	Huāshēng
Pistachios	Āyùehùizì guǒ

Desserts

"Tiándiǎn"

HŪA XIǍOJIE: *Fúwùyúan. Wǒmen yào lái diǎn tiándiǎn.*

YÙEHÀNXÙN XIǍOJIE: *Nǐmen yǒu shénme tèbíe tiándiǎn ma?*

FÚWÙYÚAN: *Wǒmen yǒu lìzhī he lǜdòugāo.*

YÙEHÀNXÙN XIǍOJIE: *Wǒ yào qiánmian yī gè.*

HŪA XIǍOJIE: *Tīng qǐlái bù cùo. Wǒ yě yào yī gè.*

"Ordering Dessert"

MS. HUA: *Waiter. We would like to order dessert.*

MS. JOHNSON: *Do you have any specialties?*

WAITER: *Yes, we have lichee and mung bean paste cake.*

MS. JOHNSON: *I'll have the first.*

MS. HUA: *Sounds good. I'll have the same.*

 There are some things you should be careful about when at the table with Chinese.

Do not poke through the dish looking for a particular piece you like. Look and make your choice before you pick up the piece.

Refrain from asking for salt, soy sauce or pepper, especially when dining at somebody's home. Chinese may think you are implying that the food is not prepared properly.

Do not ask for a fork and knife if you cannot use chopsticks. Instead, ask for a fork and a spoon. A knife is only used in the kitchen and does not belong on the table since it symbolizes fighting and violence.

Do not settle your bill in front of your guests if you are hosting a group of Chinese in a restaurant. See them off before you pay the bill.

Would you like to order dessert?	Nǐ yào tiándiǎn ma?
No, I think I've had enough.	Bù, wǒ yǐjīng chī tài dūo le.
Yes, do you have a dessert menu?	Shì de, kěyi gěi wǒ kàn yī xià tiándiǎn dān ma?
Yes, I would like to order . . . a piece of cake. a pie. ice cream.	Shì de, wǒ xiǎng yào . . . yī kùai dàngāo. yī kùai shǔigǔopái. bīngqílín.
We have . . . chocolate ice cream. strawberry ice cream. sorbet. vanilla ice cream.	Wǒmen yǒu . . . qiǎokèlì bīngqílín. cǎoméi bīngqílín. gǔozhī bīngshǔi. xiāngcǎo bīngqílín.
Would you like to have some coffee?	Nǐ yào hē kāfēi ma?

No thank you.	Bù, xièxie.
Yes, I would like . . .	Shì de, wǒ yào . . .
coffee.	kāfēi.
espresso.	nóngkāfēi.
cappuccino.	cappuccino kafēi.
tea.	chá.

Would you like your coffee . . .	Nǐ de kāfēi . . .
black?	bù jiā shénme ma?
with cream?	yào jiā nǎiyóu ma?
with milk?	yào jiā niúnǎi ma?

| Do you have decaffeinated coffee? | Nǐ yǒu chúqù kāfēiyīn de kāfēi ma? |

What kind of tea?	Shénme chá?
Black.	Hóngchá.
Earl Grey.	Earl Grey chá.
English breakfast.	Yīngguó zǎocān chá.
Green.	Lǜchá.
Oolong.	Wūlóngchá.

Do you have . . .	Nǐ yǒu . . .
cream?	nǎiyóu ma?
a sweetener?	tángjīng ma?
sugar?	táng ma?

Paying the Bill

| Bill please! | Qǐng jiézhàng! |

| Allow me to pay the bill. | Ràng wǒ lái fù ba. |
| Please be my guest. | Shì wǒ qǐngkè. |

| Is service included? | Fúwùfèi bāokùo zài nèi le ma? |

| Do you take credit cards? | Nǐ jiēshòu xìnyòngkǎ ma? |
| Which credit cards do you take? | Nǐ jiēshòu něizhǒng xìnyòngkǎ? |

| Can I pay by check/ traveler's check? | **Wǒ kěyǐ fù zhīpiào**/lǔxíng zhīpiào **ma?** |

Complaints

I didn't order this.	**Wǒ méiyǒu diǎn zhè gè cài.**
What is this item on the bill?	Zhàngdàn shàng de zhè yī xiàng shì shénme?
This is too cold.	**Zhè tài liáng le.**
This must be some mistake.	**Zhè yīdìng shì nòng cùo le ba.**
May I see the headwaiter please?	Kěyǐ jiàn yī jiàn nǐmen de lǐngbān ma?

The Rest Room

Where is the rest room/ lavatory?	**Cèsuǒ**/xǐshǒujiān **zài nǎr?**
Where is the men's room?	Nán cèsuǒ zài nǎr?
Where is the ladies' room?	Nǔ cèsuǒ zài nǎr?

SOCIAL CONVERSATION

Caution here—in some cultures there is little business discussed during the main part of dinner, only during coffee. In others, there is no prohibition to discussing business at any time. Follow the lead of your hosts or ask if it's proper.

"Lā Jiānchāng"

CHÉN XIǍOJIE: *Lùshàng hái hǎo ma?*

YÙEHÀNXÙN XIǍOJIE: *Hái hǎo le.*

CHÉN XIǍOJIE: *Zài fēijī shàng nǐ shùi le yī hǔi'r ma?*

YÙEHÀNXÙN XIǍOJIE: *Shì de. Fēixíng hěn píngwěn. Nǐmen zhè'r tiānqì tài hǎo le.*

CHÉN XIǍOJIE: *Shì de. Měi nián zhè gè shíhòu dōu hěn hǎo.*

YÙEHÀNXÙN XIǍOJIE: *Zánmen qù chī diǎn dōngxi, hǎo ma?*

CHÉN XIǍOJIE: *Wǒ dōu yào è sǐ le.*

"A Social Conversation"

MS. CHEN: *So, how was your flight?*

MS. JOHNSON: *It was just fine.*

MS. CHEN: *Were you able to sleep on the plane?*

MS. JOHNSON: *Yes. It was a smooth flight. What great weather you have here!*

MS. CHEN: *Yes. We enjoy this time of year.*

MS. CHEN: *Let's go eat, shall we?*

MS. JOHNSON: *I'm starving.*

When they invite you to lunch or dinner, Chinese expect to get to know you better and to establish a more comfortable working relationship. So the conversation at the table, especially at group gatherings, is centered on personal topics. You can safely ask the following questions:

Are you married? Do you have children? How many? Boy or girl? Are they going to school now? How are they doing in school? Which colleges are they going to? What are they studying? When are they going to graduate? What kind of jobs are they interested in?

Have you lived in this area all your life? Where is your hometown? Have you done a lot of traveling? Have you ever visited other counties? Have you been to the United States?

Where did you work before you came to this place? Are you assigned to this job or do you have free choice?

What kind of hobbies do you have? Do you collect stamps? Do you like sports?

Please tell me about your . . .	Qǐng gěi wǒ jiǎngjiang nǐ de . . .
I'd like to hear about your . . .	
child/children.	háizi.*
daughter(s).	nǚ'ér.
son(s).	érzi.
family.	jiātíng.
grandparents.	zǔfùmǔ (wài zǔfùmǔ)*.
husband.	zhàngfū.
parents.	fùmǔ.
wife.	qīzi.
Please give your family my regards.	**Qǐng dài wǒ xiàng nǐ de jiārén wènhǎo.**
How do you spend your weekends?	Nǐ zhōumò zěnme gùo?
Do you like to garden?	Nǐ xǐhūan zhònghūa ma?

Háizi is used for both singular and plural.
Zǔfùmǔ means "grandparents on father's side," *wài zǔfùmǔ* means "grandparents on mother's side."

Do you have pets?	Nǐ yǒu chǒngwù ma?

I have a . . .
  cat.
  dog.
  horse.

Wǒ yǒu . . .
  yī zhī māo.
  yī zhī gǒu.
  yī pī mǎ.

Do you like sports?	Nǐ xǐhuān yùndòng ma?

Yes, I like . . .
  basketball.
  football.
  karate.
  Ping-Pong.
  rugby.
  skiing.
  scuba.
  soccer.

Shì de, wǒ xǐhuān . . .
  lánqiú.
  gǎnlǎnqiú.
  kōngshǒudào.
  pīngpāng.
  Yīngshì gǎnlǎnqiú
  húaxǔe
  qiánshǔi
  zúqiú.

Are you interested in . . .
  art?
  books?
  classical music?
  film?
  history?
  hobbies?
  movies?
  museums?
  music?
  opera?
  philosophy?
  plays?

Nǐ duì . . . yǒu xìngqù ma?
  yìshù
  shū
  gǔdiǎn yīnyuè
  yǐngpiān/diànyǐng
  lìshǐ
  shìhào
  diànyǐng
  bówùguǎn
  yīnyuè
  gējù
  zhéxúe
  xìjù

Saying Good-bye

The food was excellent.	Zhēn hǎo chī.
Will it be difficult to find a taxi?	Jiào jìchéngchē yǒu kùnnán ma?

Please excuse me, but I must go.	Qǐng yúanliàng, wǒ déi zǒu le.
Thank you for a wonderful evening.	Wǎnshàng gùo de hǎo jí le, xièxie nǐ.
I enjoyed very much our conversation.	Wǒ fēicháng xǐhuan wǒmen de tánhùa.
It was nice talking to you.	Hěn gāoxìng yǔ nǐ jiāotán.
I look forward to seeing you . . .	Wǒ qīdài zhe . . . yǔ ni zàijiàn.
at the office.	zài bàngōngshì
tomorrow.	míngtiān
tomorrow morning.	míngtiān shàngwǔ
tomorrow night.	míngtiān wǎnshang
Please be my guest tomorrow night.	Míngtiān wǎnshang ràng wǒ qǐngkè.
It will be my pleasure.	Zhè shì wǒ de lèqù.
Good night.	Wǎn'ān.

SPORTING EVENTS, MOVIES, THEATER, CLUBS

Do you have an evening or weekend free? Then enjoy the country you're visiting. Don't just eat at the hotel restaurant and watch television in your room. Get out.

Part of doing business in another culture is to learn and appreciate what that culture has to offer. What you learn can get you closer to your business contacts.

Finally, seeing a movie, going to the theater, or seeing a sporting event can be a welcome break from an arduous business day.

"Jùyùan"

SŪN XIĀNSHENG: Nǐ huì xǐhūan zhè gè qīnggējù de. Shì àiqíng gùshì.

QIÓNGSĪ XIĀNSHENG: Hěn liúxíng ba?

SŪN XIĀNSHENG: Bù, dàn yīnyùe hěn měi. Xià gè yùe jiùyào tíngyǎn le.

QIÓNGSĪ XIĀNSHENG: Shì zhèyàng de hùa, zànmen qù kàn ba.

"At the Theater"

MR. SUN: You'll like this musical. It's a love story.

MR. JONES: Is it a popular one?

MR. SUN: No, but it has very nice music. It may close next month.

MR. JONES: Well, then, let's go see it.

Key Words

Program	Jiémùdān
Teams	Dùi
Ticket	Piào
What's playing?	Yǎn shénme?
Who's playing?	Shúi yǎn?

I would like to go to a . . .	Wǒ xiǎng qù kàn . . .
basketball game.	lánqiú sài.
boxing match.	quánjī.
soccer game.	zúqiú.
tennis match.	wǎngqiú.
How much do ticket/s cost?	Piào mài dūoshǎo qián?/Piàojià dūoshǎo?
I would like one/two ticket/s.	Wǒ yào yī/liǎng zhāng piào.
When does the match/ play/movie begin?	Qiúsài/xìjù/diànyǐng shénme shíhòu kāishǐ?

Who's playing?	Shúi zhǔyǎn?
What are the teams?	Shúi dùi shúi ya? Nǎ xiē rén yán?
May I buy a program?	Kěyǐ mǎi yi zhāng jiémùdān ma?
I would like to go to the . . .	Wǒ xiǎng qù . . .
ballet.	kàn bāléiwǔ.
cinema.	diànyǐngyuàn.
concert.	yīnyùehùi.
museum.	bówùgǔan.
movies.	kàn diànyǐng.
opera.	gējùyùan.
orchestra.	gǔanxián yùe túan.
theater.	jùyuàn.
I would like a seat in the . . .	Wǒ yào . . . de zùowèi.
balcony.	bāoxiāng
box seats.	bāoxiāng
front row.	qiánpái
gallery.	tèbié xíwèi/lóu zuò
mezzanine.	wǔtái xiàmiàn/zùi dī céng lóu tīng
orchestra.	yùedùi
I would like to see a/ an . . .	Wǒ xiǎng kàn . . .
action movie.	dòngzùopiān.
comedy.	xìjùpiān.
drama.	xìjùpiān
love story.	aìqíng gùshì.
musical.	qīnggējù yin yùe jù.
mystery.	zhēntàn gùshì.
romance.	làngmàn gùshì.
science-fiction movie.	kēhùan piān.
western.	xībù piān.

Does the film have English subtitles?	Diànyǐng pèiyǒu Yīngwén zìmù ma?
May I have a program please?	Kěyǐ yào yì zhāng jiémùdān ma?
What's playing at the opera tonight?	Jīnwǎn gējùyùan shàngyǎn shénme?
Who is the conductor?	Shúi shì zhǐhūi?
I would like to go to a . . .	Wǒ xiǎng qù . . .
disco.	dísīkē.
jazz club.	júeshì jùlèbù.
jazz concert.	júeshì yīnyùehùi.
nightclub.	yèzǒnghùi.
I'd like to go dancing.	Wǒ xiǎng qù tiàowǔ.
Would you like to dance?	Nǐ xiǎng qù tiàowǔ ma?
Is there a cover charge?	Yào rùchǎng fèi ma?
Is there a floor show?	Yǒu Biǎoyǎn jiémù ma?
What time does the floor show start?	Biǎoyǎn jiémù shénme shíhòu kāishǐ?

Participatory Sports

Is there a gym in the hotel?	Lǚgǔan lǐ yǒu jiànshēnfáng ma?
Where is the closest gym?	Nǎr de jiànshēngfáng zùijìn?
Is there a place to jog?	Yǒu dìfāng kěyǐ pǎobù ma?
Where is the pool?	Yóu yǒng chí zài nǎr?
Is it heated?	Shǔi nǔan ma?
Are there towels?	Yǒu yùjīn ma?
I would like to play . . .	Wǒ xiǎng dǎ . . .
golf.	gāo'érfūqiú
racquetball.	páiqiúxì/qiángqíu.
tennis.	wǎngqiú.
volleyball.	páiqiú.

110

I would like to visit a . . .	Wǒ xiǎng kànkan . . .
beach.	hǎitān.
lake.	húbàn/hú pō.

| Is swimming allowed? | Kěyǐ yóuyǒng ma? |
| Are there lifeguards? | Yǒu jiùshēngyúan ma? |

Are there . . .	Yǒu . . .
beach chairs	hǎitān yǐzi
rowboats	húatǐng
sailboats	fānchúan
towels	yùjīn
umbrellas	(tàiyáng) sǎn
for rent?	chūzū ma?

| Are there changing rooms? | Yǒu gēngyīshì ma? |

And don't forget to bring . . .	Bié wàng le dài . . .
sunglasses.	tàiyángjìng.
suntan lotion.	fángshàiyóu.

I would like to go . . .	Wǒ xiǎng qù . . .
ice-skating.	húabīng.
skiing.	húaxǔe.
cross-country skiing.	yùeyě húaxǔe.

VISITING THE PARTNER'S OR ASSOCIATE'S HOME

Here's a chance to get closer to a business host or associate. Check with your contacts or the hotel concierge if flowers or gifts are appropriate. In some cultures, flowers for the wife can be misunderstood. Usually, a gift from home is safe and most welcome. If your host(s) have children, bringing a small present for them is the best move.

"Jiātíng Fǎngwèn"

CHÉN TÀITAI: *Huānyíng lái wǒmen jiā.*
YÙEHÀNXÙN XIǍOJIE: *Xièxie nǐ de yāoqǐng.*
CHÉN TÀITAI: *Zhè shì wǒ de zhàngfū, Zhāo.*
YÙEHÀNXÙN XIǍOJIE: *Hěn gāoxìng rènshì nǐ.*
CHÉN TÀITAI: *Zhè shì wǒmen de liǎng gè háizi, Nán hé Hàn.*
YÙEHÀNXÙN XIǍOJIE: *Zhè shì gěi nǐ háizi de lǐwù.*
CHÉN TÀITAI: *Nǐ xiǎng de zhēn zhōudào. Ràng wǒmen qù kètīng ba.*

"At the Home"

MRS. CHEN: *Welcome to our home.*
MS. JOHNSON: *Thank you for having me.*
MRS. CHEN: *This is my husband, Zhao.*
MS. JOHNSON: *Very nice to meet you.*
MRS. CHEN: *And, here are our two children, Nan and Han.*
MS. JOHNSON: *Here are small gifts for your children.*
MRS. CHEN: *That's very thoughtful of you. Let's move into the living room.*

 You will be greeted at the door when you visit a Chinese home. Some families may expect you to take off your shoes, and will offer you a pair of slippers before you enter the house. Tea will be served on such occasions and it is usually drunk without sugar or milk.

Remember to take a gift for your host, or his or her spouse and child. (As you know, there is usually one child in each household because of the family policy in China.) The gift does not have to be expensive, but it will be more valued if it was made in your home country. Sometimes, you can actually find these small gifts in your hotel shop: fruits, chocolates, imported candies, English books, perfumes, a scarf or a tie, or stamps are all suitable gifts. Avoid knives (symbolizing fighting), cut flowers (symbolizing death), and watches or clocks (symbolizing being sent to the other world). If your gift is wrapped, Chinese may not open it in front of you. This is regarded as good manners in China.

This is my wife/husband.	**Zhè shì wǒ de qīzi/zhàngfū.**
This is our child.	**Zhè shì wǒmen de háizi.**
These are our children.	Zhè xiē shì wǒmen de háizi.
This is our pet cat/dog.	Zhè shì wǒmen de chǒngmāo/gǒu.
Here is a small gift (from the United States).	**Zhè shì (cóng Měigúo dàilái de) yī jiàn xiǎo lǐwù.**
Make yourself at home.	**Qǐng bùyào kèqi.**
Come, let us show you our home.	Lái ba, ràng nǐ kànkàn wǒmen de jiā.
What a pretty house.	**Fángzi hěn piàoliang.**
What a beautiful house you have.	Nǐmen yǒu yī zùo hěn měilì de fángzi.
This is a very nice neighborhood.	Jiēfang línjū hěn hǎo.
Please sit here.	Qǐng zùo zhè'r.
Please take a seat.	Qǐng zùo ba.
Please come in the dinning room.	Qǐng dào fàntīng lái ba.
Would you like a drink before dinner?	**Nǐ fàn qián xiǎng hē diǎn shénme ma?**
Dinner was great.	**Wǎnfàn zhēn hǎo.**
It was a pleasure having you in our home.	Wǒmen hěn gāoxìng nǐ néng lái wǒmen jiā.

113

Thank you for inviting me to your home.

Gǎnxiè nǐmen yāoqíng wǒ lái nǐmen jiā.

SIGHTSEEING

"Lǚguǎn"

QIÓNGSĪ XIĀNSHENG: *Zhèlǐ yǒu shénme dìfang zhídé kàn ma?*

LǙGUǍN FÚWÙYUÁN: *Zhèlǐ yǒu bówùguǎn hé sìmiào kěyǐ kànkan.*

QIÓNGSĪ XIĀNSHENG: *Zài nǎr?*

LǙGUǍN FÚWÙYUÁN: *Bówùguǎn lí zhèlǐ zhǐyǒu sān gè jiēqū, dàn sìmiào zài chéng de lìng yī biān. Nǐ yào chéng jìchéngchē cái néng qù.*

QIÓNGSĪ XIĀNSHENG: *Wǒ xiǎng qù kàn sìmiào. Néng gěi wǒ jiào yí liàng jìchéngchē ma?*

"At the Hotel Reception"

MR. JONES: *What kinds of sites are worthwhile to see here?*

HOTEL CLERK: *There is the museum and the temples.*

MR. JONES: *Where are they?*

HOTEL CLERK: *The museum is only three blocks from here, but the temples are on the other side of the city. You need a taxi to get to them.*

MR. JONES: *I'll go and see the temples. Can you get me a taxi?*

What are the main attractions?	Zùi yǒu xīyǐnlì de dìfāng shì shénme?
Do you have a guide book of the city?	Nǐ yǒu chéngshì zhǐnán ma?
Do you have a map of the city?	Nǐ yǒu chéngshì dìtú ma?

Is there a tour of the city?	Yǒu chéngshì guānguāng húo dòng ma?
Where does it leave from?	Zài nǎr chūfā?
How much is it?	Dūoshǎo qián?
How long is it?	Yào dūoshǎo shíjiān?
I would like to see . . .	Wǒ xiǎng qù kànkàn . . .
an amusement park.	yóulèyúan.
an aquarium.	shǔizúgǔan.
an art gallery.	hùaláng/měishùgǔan.
a botanical garden.	zhíwùyúan.
a castle.	chéngbǎo.
a cathedral.	dàjiàotáng.
a cave.	shāndòng.
a church.	jiàotáng.
a flea market.	jiùhùo shìchǎng.
a library.	túshūgǔan.
a museum.	bówùgǔan.
a park.	gōngyúan.
a planetarium.	tiānwéngǔan.
a synagogue.	yóutài jiàotáng.
a zoo.	dòngwùyúan.
When does the museum open?	Bówùgǔan shenme shíhòu kāimén?
How much is the admission?	Ménpiào dūoshǎo qián?
Do you have an English guide?	Nǐ yǒu Yīngwén zhǐnán ma?
Do you have an audio guide?	Nǐ yǒu lùyīn zhǐnán ma?
May I take photographs?	Kěyǐ zhàoxiàng ma?
I do not use flash bulbs.	Wǒ bù shǐyòng shǎngūangdēng.
I would like to visit the lake.	Wǒ xiǎng qù húbiān kànkan.
Can I take a bus there?	Wǒ kěyǐ zùo qìchē qù ma?

| Which bus do I take? | Wǒ yào zuò něi lù chē? |
| How long is the ride? | Yào zuò dūo cháng shíjiān? |

SHOPPING

I'm looking for a . . .	Wǒ yào zhǎo yī gè . . .
bookstore.	shūdiàn.
camera store.	zhàoxiàngjī shāngdiàn.
clothing store.	fúzhuāngdiàn.
department store.	bǎihùo gōngsī.
flower shop.	hūadiàn.
hardware store.	wǔjīndiàn.
health food store.	jiànkāng shípǐndiàn.
jewelry store.	zhūbǎodiàn.
leather goods store.	píhùodiàn.
liquor store.	jiǔdiàn.
newsstand.	bàotān.
record store.	chàngpiàndiàn.
shoe store.	xiédiàn.
shopping center.	gòuwù zhōngxīn.
souvenir shop.	lǐpǐndiàn.
stationer.	wénjùdiàn.
tobacco store.	yāncǎodiàn.
toy store.	wánjùdiàn.

I would like to find a . . .	Wǒ yào zhǎo yī gè . . .
jeweler.	zhūbǎoshāng.
photographer.	shèyǐngshī.
shoemaker.	xiéjiàng.
tailor.	cáifeng.

| Can you help me? | Kěyǐ bāng wǒ yī xià ma? |
| Can you show me . . . | Nǐ kěyǐ gěi wǒ kànkan . . . |

| I'm just browsing. | Wǒ zhǐshì kànkan. |

| I'd like to buy . . . | Wǒ yào mǎi . . . |

| How much does it cost? | Dūoshǎo qián? |
| How much is this in dollars? | Dūoshǎo měiyúan? |

Can you write down the price?	Nǐ néng bǎ jiàgé xiě xià lái ma?
Do you have a less/more expensive one?	Nǐ yǒu gèng piányi/guì yī diǎn de ma?
Where do I pay?	Zài nǎr fù qián?
Can you gift wrap this?	Nǐ kěyǐ gěi wǒ bāo qǐlái ma?
I'd like to return this.	Wǒ xiǎng tùi hùo.
Here is my receipt.	Zhè shì wǒ de shōujù.

4 GETTING AROUND

This can be a trying time, what with negotiating your flight, getting through customs at your destination, dealing with taxis or rental cars at the airport, getting to your hotel and having to speak in a foreign tongue. Then too, you may need to find a cash machine or a bank, and maybe find a post office or a local Federal Express or UPS center. We're here to help.

Don't underestimate jet lag. The seasoned traveler knows how to best handle this. But, for the first-time business traveler this can be a surprise. The excitement of new places and new contacts may temporarily mask it, but jet lag is the response of the body to a change of daily awake–sleep routine. It manifests itself as tiredness and sometimes disorientation. Best advice is to try to get some sleep on your flight and try not to rush into a meeting just after you land.

In this chapter, we cover:

> **Can You Help Me?**
> **Airplanes, Airports and**
>   **Customs**
> **At the Hotel**
> **Car Rentals**
> **At the Train Station**
> **Barbershop and Beauty Parlor**
> **Cash Machines and Banking**
> **Post Office**
> **In an Emergency: Doctors,**
>   **Dentists, Hospitals,**
>   **Opticians, and Pharmacies**

We hope you'll not need them, but just in case, we list the words you may find useful in an emergency.

CAN YOU HELP ME?

Excuse me.	Duìbuqǐ.
Could you help me?	Néng bāng wǒ yī xià ma?
Yes/No.	Kěyǐ./Bù néng.
I'm sorry.	Hěn bàoqiàn.
Thank you very much.	Fēicháng gǎnxiè.
Do you speak English?	Nǐ shuō Yīngyǔ ma?
Do you understand English?	Nǐ dǒng Yīngyǔ ma?
Do you know where the American Embassy is?	Nǐ zhīdào Měigúo Dàshǐguǎn zài nǎr ma?
I don't speak much Chinese.	Wǒ hùi shuō yī diǎn'r Zhōngwén/Wǒ tīng bù dǒng.
I don't understand.	Wǒ bù dǒng.
Please, repeat.	Qǐng chóngfù yī xià.
Please speak more slowly.	Qǐng shuō màn yī diǎn'r.
Could you write that down please?	Nǐ néng bù néng gěi wǒ xiě xià lái?
Spell it please.	Qǐng pīnxiě yī xià.
Where is the business center?	Shāngwù zhōngxīn zài nǎr?
Where are the telephones?	Diànhùa zài nǎr?
Where are the rest rooms?	Xǐshǒujiān zài nǎr?
Where is the men's bathroom/lavatory?	Nán yùshì/cèsuǒ zài nǎr?
Where is the women's bathroom/laboratory?	Nǚ yùshì/cèsuǒ zài nǎr?

AIRPLANES, AIRPORTS AND CUSTOMS

"Hǎiguān"

HǍIGUĀN GŪANYÚAN: *Zhè shì nǐ de xíngli ma?*
QIÓNGSĪ XIĀNSHENG: *Shì de. Zhè liǎng jiàn shì wǒ de. Yǒu shénme wèntí ma?*

HǍIGŪAN GŪANYÚAN: *Qǐng dǎkāi yī xià.*
QIÓNGSĪ XIĀNSHENG: *Bùguò jiùshì xiē wàitào hé nèiyīkù. Háiyǒu wǒ de kǒuqín. Lǚxíng shí, wǒ xǐhuān zài lǚguǎn fángjiān lǐ chuī kǒuqín.*
HǍIGŪAN GŪANYÚAN: *Nǐ kěyǐ zǒu le.*

"Getting Through Customs"
CUSTOMS OFFICIAL: *Are these your bags?*
MR. JONES: *Yes, these two. Is there a problem?*
CUSTOMS OFFICIAL: *Open them.*
MR. JONES: *Just suits and underwear. Plus my harmonica. I like to play it in the hotel room when I travel.*
CUSTOMS OFFICIAL: *You may go.*

Generally speaking, Chinese will arrange for someone to meet at or send you off to the airport. This is a courtesy that Chinese always extend to their guests. The person that meets you or sends you off at the airport may not be your host himself or herself, but a deputy, a department head or an aide. The rank of the person meeting you shows how they rank you. The level of the person seeing you off shows how well your visit has been received.

Be careful about what you bring into China. Besides drugs, the Chinese customs officers are constantly looking for pornography and weapons. Even magazines, such as *Playboy*™, or books that express negative views about the Chinese society can get you into trouble.

Key Words:

Arrivals	*Dàodá/Dǐdá*
Baggage pickup area	*Qǔ xíngli chù*
Customs	*Hǎiguān*

Departures	*Chūfā/Líkāi*
Domestic flights	*Gúonèi hángbān*
Gate	*Mén/Chūkǒu*
International flights	*Gúojì hángbān*
Make a reservation (to)	*Yùyūe/yù dìng*
Passport	*Hùzhào*
Take a taxi (to)	*Chéng jìchéngchē/Chéng chū zū qì chē*
Ticket	*Piào*

Here is/are my . . .	**Zhè shì wǒ de . . .**
documents.	**wénjiàn.**
identification card.	**shēnfènzhèng.**
passport.	hùzhào.
ticket.	piào.
I need to buy . . .	**Wǒ yào mǎi . . .**
a business-class ticket.	**yī zhāng shāngwùcāng de piào.**
an economy ticket.	yi zhāng jīngjìcāng de piào.
a first-class ticket.	yī zhāng tóudēngcāng de piào.
a roundtrip ticket.	yī zhāng láihúi piào.
a single/one-way ticket.	yī zhāng dānchéng piào.
I'd like to . . . my reservation.	**Wǒ yào . . . wǒ de yùyūe/** yùdìng piào
cancel	**qǔxiāo**
change	gǎibiàn
confirm	quèrèn
I need to change my reservation.	**Wǒ xūyào gǎibiàn wǒ de yùyūe.**
I need to change my seat.	Wǒ xūyào hùan zùowèi.
May I have a smoking/ nonsmoking seat?	**Kěyǐ gěi wǒ xīyān/bù xīyān de zùowèi ma?**

May I have a window/ aisle seat?	Kěyǐ gěi wǒ kào chuāngdào/ guòdào de zuòwèi ma?
Is there a direct flight to . . . ?	Yǒu zhí fēi . . . de hángbān ma?
Is there an earlier/later flight?	Yǒu zǎo/wǎn yī diǎn'r de hángbān ma?

AT THE HOTEL

"Hùan Fángjiān"

ZHĀNMÙSĪ XIǍOJIE: *Wǒ fángjiān de yàoshi dǎ bù kāi mén.*

FÚWÙYÚAN: *Dùibuqǐ, tàitai. Wǒ bǎ yàoshi gěi cùo le. Shìshí shàng, wǒ yào gěi nǐ de shì lìngwài yī gè fángjiān. Nà gè fángjiān yǐjīng yǒu rén le.*

ZHĀNMÙSĪ XIǍOJIE: *Nà nǐ néng gěi wǒ yī gè yǒu jǐnggūan de fángjiān ma?*

FÚWÙYÚAN: *Kěyǐ. Wǒ xiǎng nǐ hùi xǐhuan zhè gè fángjiān. Gěi nǐ tiān máfan le.*

"Getting the Right Room"

MS. JAMES: *This key to my room won't work.*

CLERK: *I'm sorry, madam. I gave you the wrong key. In fact, I have to give you a different room. That one is actually taken.*

MS. JAMES: *Could you then give me a room with a view?*

CLERK: *Yes, I think you will enjoy this room. Sorry for the problem.*

 Tipping used to be illegal in China. In small towns, people do not accept tips even today. However, hotels and restaurants in big cities have adopted this Western concept. Some restaurants actually automatically add a 15% service charge. The usual tipping rate is 10–15% in restaurants. You need small notes for hotel workers, such as porters, cleaners, and room service clerks. They generally prefer American dollars. A one- or two-dollar tip is usually enough.

Key Words

Bag(s)/Luggage	Bāoguǒ/Xíngli
Bath	Yùshì
Confirmation	Qùerèn
Credit card	Xìnyòngkǎ
Hotel	Lǚguǎn
Reservation	Yùyūe/yùdìng
Room	Fángjiān

I have a reservation in the name of . . .	Wǒ yù dìng de míngzi shì . . .
Here is my confirmation.	Wǒ xiànzài qùerèn.
How much are your rooms?	Nǐmen fángjiān de jiàgé zěnyàng?
What is the price for a double room?	Shuāngrén fángjiān dūoshǎo qián?
Do you take credit cards?	Nǐmen jiēshōu xìnyòngkǎ ma?
Which credit cards do you take?	Nǐmen jieshōu něixiē xìnyòngkǎ?
Do you have any rooms available?	Nǐmen háiyǒu fángjiān ma?
Could you recommend any other hotels?	Nǐ kěyǐ tūijiàn bié de lǚguǎn ma?
I'd like . . .	Wǒ yào . . .
a room for one/two night(s).	yī gè fángjiān, zhù yī/liǎng wǎnshang.
a single/double room.	yī gè dānrén/shuāngrén fángjiān.

a room with a private bath.	yī gè dài zìjǐ yùshì de fángjiān.
a room with a queen-/king-size bed.	yī gè yǒu dà/tè dà chuáng de fángjiān.
a suite.	yī gè tàofáng.

I need . . .

Wǒ xūyào . . .

a wake-up call.	**jiào wǒ qǐchuáng.**
a late checkout.	wǎn yī diǎn jiézhàng líkāi.
a fax machine.	yī bù chuánzhēnjī.
a telephone.	yī bù diànhuà.
an Internet connection.	yú guójì wǎnglùo/yīn tè wǎng liánjié.

Is there . . .

Yǒu . . .

a business center?	**shāngwù zhōngxīn ma?**
an Internet connection in my room?	**fángjiān wǎnglùo liánjié ma?**
an exercise room?	jiànshēnfáng ma?
a gym?	tǐyùguǎn ma?
a Jacuzzi?	húiyā ànmōchí ma?
a photocopier?	fùyìnjī ma?
a printer?	dǎyìnjī ma?
a restaurant in the hotel?	lǚguǎn fàndiàn ma?
a swimming pool?	yóuyǒngchí ma?

| Can a porter take my bags up to the room? | **Kěyǐ ràng ménfáng bǎ wǒ de bāoguǒ sòng dào fángjiān qù ma?** |
| May I leave my bags? | **Kěyǐ bǎ wǒ de lǚxíng bāo/bāoguǒ liú xià ma?** |

| Are there any messages for me? | **Yǒu rén gěi wǒ liúyán ma?** |

| May I see the room? | Kěyǐ kàn yī xià fángjiān ma? |
| We want adjacent rooms. | Wǒmen yào āizhe de fángjiān. |

Problems

The room/bathroom needs cleaning.	Fángjiān/yùshì xūyào dǎsǎo.
I need more towels/blankets.	Wǒ xūyào gèngduō de máojīn/tǎnzi.
The room is too small.	Fángjiān tài xiǎo.
I did not receive my paper.	Wǒ méiyǒu shōu dào wǒ de bàozhǐ.
The room is too noisy.	Fángjiān tài chǎo.
The door will not open.	Mén dǎ bù kāi.
The door will not lock.	Mén suǒ bú shàng.
The telephone does not work.	Diànhùa hùai le.
The heating/air-conditioning is not working.	Nuǎnqì/kōngtiáo hùai le.
Can you turn the heat up?	Nǐ néng bǎ nuǎnqì tiáo gāo yī diǎn ma?
How do I make a telephone call?	Zěnyàng dǎ diànhùa?
How do I make a local/international telephone call?	Zěnyàng dǎ shìnèi/gúojì diànhùa?
I need room delivery.	Wǒ xūyào sòng dào fángjiān lái.
I'd like to order dinner to my room.	Wǒ xūyào bǎ wǎncān sòng dào fángjiān lái.
I need laundry service.	Wǒ xūyào xǐyī fúwù.
I need these shirts/suits cleaned overnight.	Zhè xiē chènyī/xīzhuāng jīn yè yào xǐ hǎo.
Can I have these clothes cleaned/laundered today?	Jīntiān kěyǐ bǎ zhè xiē yīfú xǐ hǎo ma?
Can you have this stain removed?	Nǐ néng qùdiào zhè gè wūdiǎn ma?

How much does it cost to have this cleaned/laundered?	Xǐ zhè gè yào dūshǎo qián?
Can I extend my stay one/two day(s)?	Wǒ kěyǐ dūo zhù yī/liǎng tiān ma?
Can I have a late checkout?	Wǒ kěyǐ wǎn yī diǎn jiézhàng líkāi ma?
Can I leave my bags at the reception desk after checkout?	Jiézhàng hòu wǒ kěyǐ bǎ bāogǔo liú zài qiántái ma?
I want to check out.	Wǒ yào jiézhàng líkāi.
May I have my bill?	Kěyǐ gěi wǒ zhàngdān ma?
There is a problem with my bill.	Wǒ de zhàng yǒu wèntí.
What is this charge for?	Zhè shì shénme fèiyòng?
Is there an airport shuttle?	Yǒu qù fēijīchǎng de jiàochē ma?
What time does it leave?	Shénme shíjiān líkāi?
What time is the next one?	Xià yī bān shì shénme shíhòu?
I would like a taxi.	Wǒ yào jiào jìchéngchē.

CAR RENTALS

"Zìpáidǎng"

SĪMÉILÌ XIĀNSHENG: *Zhè chē shì zìpáidǎng ma?*

FÚWÙYÚAN: *Bù shì. Nǐ yào zìpáidǎng ma?*

SĪMÉILÌ XIĀNSHENG: *Shì de. Wǒ zài qùerèn shí tèbié shūomíng liǎo de.*

FÚWÙYÚAN: *Wǒ zhīdào. Dàn yǒu gè xiǎoxiao de wèntí. Yào yī gè xiǎoshí yǐhòu wǒmen cái yǒu zìpái chē.*

SĪMÉILÌ XIĀNSHENG: *Wǒ jiù děng yi děng. Wǒ bù zhīdào zěnyàng kāi shǒupáidǎng.*

"Getting an Automatic Shift"

MR. SMILEY: *Does this car have an automatic shift?*

CLERK: *No. Did you need that?*

MR. SMILEY: *Yes. You can see from my confirmation that I specifically requested it.*

CLERK: *Yes, I see that. However, there is a slight problem. We won't have one for about one hour.*

MR. SMILEY: *I will wait. I don't know how to drive a stick shift.*

You usually cannot rent a car in China because car rental is not yet available in most cities. Unless it is absolutely unavoidable, you should not drive at all because driving conditions are poor, and if you have an accident, the bureaucratic hassle is usually great. Rely on taxis, hire a local driver, or ask your host organization to arrange your transportation. As a courtesy, they will send you a car with a driver for free or a small charge.

Key Words	
Automatic shift	Zìpáidǎng
Car	Chē/Qìchē
Directions	Fāngxiàng
Driver's license	Jiàshǐ zhízhào
Gas	Qìyóu
Gas station	Jiāyóuzhàn
Insurance	Bǎoxiǎn
Map	Dìtú
Stick shift	Shǒupáidǎng

I need to rent a car.	Wǒ yào zū chē.
Here is my reservation number.	Zhè shì wǒ de yùyūe hàomǎ.
Here is my driver's license.	Zhè shì wǒ de jiàshǐ zhízhào.

I need . . .	Wǒ xūyào . . .
air-conditioning.	kōngtiáo.
an automatic shift.	zìpáidǎng.
a compact.	xiǎoxíngchē.
a convertible.	chǎngpéngchē.
an intermediate.	zhōngxíngchē.
a luxury car.	háohúaxíngchē.
a standard shift.	biāozhǔn dǎng.

Is insurance included?	Bāokùo bǎoxiǎn ma?
How much is the insurance?	Bǎoxiǎn dūoshǎo qián?
I want full insurance.	Wǒ yào qúanbǎo.

| How is the mileage charged? | Měi lǐ shōufèi dūoshǎo? |
| Is there unlimited mileage? | Lǐchéng bù shòu xiànzhì ba? |

| Is gas included? | Qìyóu bāokùo zài nèi ma? |
| Do I need to fill the tank when I return? | Húanchē shí, wǒ xūyào jiāmǎn youxiǎng ma? |

| Is there a drop-off charge? | Yào shōu húanchē fèi ma? |

| Which credit cards do you take? | Nǐmen jiēshōu něi zhǒng xìnyòngkǎ? |
| May I pay by check? | Kěyǐ yòng zhīpiào zhīfù ma? |

| I need a map. | Wǒ xūyào dìtú. |
| I need directions. | Wǒ xūyào nǐ zhǐyǐn fāngxiàng. |

Can you help me find . . .	Nǐ kěyǐ bāng wǒ zhǎo . . . ?
How do I get to . . .	Qù . . . zěnme zǒu?
the airport?	jīchǎng
a bank?	yínháng
a gas station?	jiāyóuzhàn
the hotel?	lǚiguǎn
a good restaurant?	hǎo fànguǎn

Is this the road to . . . ? Zhè shì qù . . . de lù ma?

Turn right/left.	Yùo/zǔo zhǔan.
Go straight ahead.	Zhí zǒu.
Turn around.	Zhǔanwān.
Go two traffic lights and	Zǒu dào hónglùdēng shí,
turn right/left.	wàng yòu/zǔo gǔai.

Opposite	Duìmiàn
U-turn	U zìxíng wān
Next to	Kàojìn

Fill it up please.	**Qǐng jiāmǎn.**
I need . . .	Wǒ xūyào . . .
diesel.	cáiyóu.
regular.	pǔtōngyóu.
supreme.	shàngděngyóu.
unleaded.	bù hán qian de yóu.

| Could you check the tire pressure? | Néng jiǎnchá yī xià lúntāi yālì ma? |
| Could you check the water? | Néng jiǎnchá yī xià shǔixiāng ma? |

How much do I owe you? Wǒ qián nǐ dūoshǎo qián?

| Where do I park? | Zài nǎr tíngchē? |
| Is there parking nearby? | Fùjìn yǒu tíngchē de dìfang ma? |

I am having a problem with my car. Wǒ de chē chū máobìng le.

It won't start. Fā bù dòng.

The battery is dead.	Diànchí huài le.
I'm out of gas.	Méiyǒu qìyóu le.
I have a flat tire.	Lúntāi huài le.
The brakes won't work.	Shāchē bù líng.
The lights don't work.	Dēng bù liàng.
May I use the phone?	Kěyǐ yòng yī xià diànhuà ma?
Could you help me?	Néng bāngbang máng ma?
My car has broken down.	Wǒ de chē pāomáo le.
Can you tow it?	Nǐ néng tūo zǒu ma?
Can you repair it?	Nǐ néng xiū hǎo ma?
Do you have . . .	Nǐ yǒu . . .
a flashlight?	shǒudiàn ma?
a jack?	qiānjīndǐng ma?
a screwdriver?	lúosīdāo ma?
tools?	gōngjù ma?
a wrench?	bānshǒu ma?
There's been an accident.	Chū le chēhùo.
I have had an accident.	Wǒ chū le chēhùo.
People are hurt.	Yǒu rén shòushāng le.
It is serious.	Hěn yánzhòng.
It is not serious.	Bù yánzhòng.
Can we exchange driver's license numbers?	Wǒmen kěyǐ jiāohùan jiàshǐ zhízhào hàomǎ ma?
Can we exchange insurance numbers?	Wǒmen kěyi jiāohùan bǎoxiǎn hàomǎ ma?

AT THE TRAIN STATION

Getting around in many countries involves trains. This comes as a surprise to the first-time U.S. business traveler who is not accustomed to using trains in the United States. Often a quick trip to another city involves hopping on a train, which is usually quite punctual and pleasant.

Getting a train ticket can be difficult in China because regular citizens, who cannot afford plane tickets, rely on trains for long-distance travel. That is why the trains are usually jam-packed, especially around Chinese New Year, which usually falls in February. You must book your ticket in advance and be sure to get a "soft sleeper" (a four-berth compartment) or a "soft seat" (first-class seats), which are more comfortable and less crowded, but a little more expensive.

Key Words

Arrival time	Dàodá shíjiān
Departure time	Chūfā shíjiān
Platform	Zhàntái
Reservation	Yùyūe
Sleeping car	Wòchē
Ticket	Chēpiào
Ticket office	Piàofáng
Time	Shíjiān
Time table	Shíjiānbiǎo

Where is the ticket office?	Piàofáng zài nǎr?
I want to go to . . .	Wǒ yàoqù . . .
How much does a ticket cost to . . . ?	Qù . . . de chēpiào yào dūoshǎo qián?
What gate does the train for . . . leave from?	Qù . . . de hǔochē zài něi gè zhàntái chūfā?
Do I need to change trains?	Wǒ xūyào hùan hǔochē ma?
Is there a dining/buffet car?	Yǒu cānchē/zìzhù cānchē ma?
Am I on the right train?	Wǒ méi shàng cùo hǔochē ba?

131

| Is this an open seat? | Zhè zuòwèi yǒu rén ma? |
| What stop is this? | Zhè shì nǎ yī zhàn? |

BARBERSHOP AND BEAUTY PARLOR

"Lǐfàdiàn"

YÙEHÀNXÙN XIǍOJIE: *Nǐ néng bǎ wǒ de tóufa jiǎn diào zhème duō ma?*

LǏFÀSHĪ: *Wǒ rènwéi nà jiǎn de tài duō le.*

YÙEHÀNXÙN XIǍOJIE: *Zhè me duō zěnmeyàng?*

LǏFÀSHĪ: *Hǎo. Zhèyàng kàn qǐlái hǎo duō le.*

"At the Beauty Parlor"

MS. JOHNSON: *Could you cut my hair about this much?*

HAIRDRESSER: *I think that that might be too much.*

MS. JOHNSON: *What about this much?*

HAIRDRESSER: *Yes. I think that will look better.*

Key Words

Blow-dry	Chuīgān
Haircut	Jiǎntóu/lǐfà
Manicure	Xiūjiǎn zhǐjiǎ
Nails	Zhǐjiǎ
Shave	Guāliǎn
Shampoo	Xǐfàjì

| Is there a barbershop/ beauty parlor nearby? | Fùjìn yǒu lǐfàdiàn/ měiróngdiàn ma? |
| Do I need an appointment? | Wǒ xūyào yùyūe ma? |

I need a haircut.	Wǒ yào lǐfà.
I'd like to have . . .	Wǒ xiǎng . . .
a blow-dry.	chūigān.
a cut.	jiǎntóu.
a facial.	xiūliǎn.
a manicure.	xiūjiǎn zhǐjiǎ.
a shampoo.	xǐfàjì.
I'd like a shave.	Wǒ yào xiūmiàn.
Could you trim my mustache/beard?	Nǐ néng gěi wǒ xiūxiu húzi/húxū ma?

CASH MACHINES AND BANKING

Where is the nearest cash machine?	Nǎ gè de tíkuǎnjī zùi jìn?
Where is the nearest bank?	Nǎ gè yínháng zùi jìn?
Is there a money exchange office near here?	Fùjìn yǒu wàibì dùihuàn chù ma?
Do you change money?	Nǐ yào hùan qián ma?
What is the exchange rate?	Dùihuànlǜ shì dūoshǎo?
I'd like to change 100 dollars.	Wǒ yào hùan yī bǎi měiyúan.
I need your passport.	Wǒ xūyào nǐ de hùzhào.

You can exchange money at all banks and western hotels. The exchange rate for U.S. dollars and Chinese currency (*rénmínbì*) is fixed by the government. Of course, you can get a better rate on the black market, but you should not attempt to do so because it is illegal and you do not want to risk your business prospects by being caught and arrested for currency fraud.

POST OFFICE

| Where is the post office/ FedEx office? | Yóujú/Tèkùai Zhúandì zài nǎr? |

Do you have overnight service? — Nǐ yǒu tōngxiāo fúwù ma?

I would like postage for this . . . — Wǒ yào gěi zhè. . . . mǎi yóupiào.
letter. — fēng xìn
package. — ge bāoguǒ
postcard. — zhang míngxīnpiàn

When will the letter/ package arrive? — Zhè fēng xìn/gè bāoguǒ shénme shíhòu dào?

I'd like to send it . . . — Wǒ yào jì . . .
insured. — jiābǎo de.
registered. — gùahào de.
overnight. — lián yè de.

IN AN EMERGENCY: DOCTORS, DENTISTS, HOSPITALS, OPTICIANS, AND PHARMACIES

You should generally pay for these bills with your credit card or by check. When you get home you can submit the expenses to your medical plan for reimbursement.

"Yàofáng"

QIÓNGSĪ XIĀNSHENG: *Wǒ késou hěn xiōng. Néng gěi wǒ diǎn shénme yào ma?*
YÀOJĪSHĪ: *Nǐ shì yào tángjiāng háishì yàopiàn?*
QIÓNGSĪ XIĀNSHENG: *Nǐ yǒu yīngtáowèi de yàopiàn ma?*
YÀOJĪSHĪ: *Méiyǒu, dàn wǒmen yǒu fēngmìwèi de.*

"At the Pharmacy"

MR. JONES: *I have a bad cough. Could you recommend something for it?*

PHARMACIST: *Do you want a syrup or lozenge?*

MR. JONES: *Do you have cherry-flavored lozenges?*

PHARMACIST: *No, but we have these honey-flavored ones.*

It is recommended that you bring plenty of medicine with you for usual illness such as colds or headaches. You can rely on Chinese doctors and try traditional Chinese treatment like acupuncture or herbs, but for serious problems you may want to go to Hong Kong or back to your home country if you are not close to Beijing, Shanghai, or some other big city.

Key Words

Cold	Gănmào
Doctor	Yīshēng
Emergency	Jízhěn
Eye doctor	Yǎnkē yīshēng
Flu	Liúgǎn
Glasses	Yǎnjìng
Headache	Tóutòng
I don't feel well.	Wǒ bù shūfu.
I got hurt.	Wǒ shòu le shāng.
Nurse	Hùshì
Optician	Yǎnjìngshāng/pèijīngshī
Pharmacist	Yàojìshī
Toothache	Yátòng

I want/need to go to . . .	Wǒ yào/xūyào qù . . .
a dentist.	kàn yáyī.
a doctor.	kàn yīshēng.
an eye doctor.	kàn yǎnkē yīshēng.
a hospital.	yīyuàn.
an optician.	yǎnjìngdiàn.
a pharmacy.	yàofáng.

I need to see . . .	Wǒ xūyào kàn . . .
an allergist.	guòmǐn yīshēng.
a general practitioner.	quánkē yīshēng.
a gynecologist.	fùchǎnkē yīshēng.
an internist.	nèikē yīshēng.

Please call an ambulance.	Qǐng jiào jiùhùchē.
Please call a doctor.	Qǐng jiào yīshēng.
Please call the police.	Qǐng jiào jǐngchá.

| There has been an accident. | Chū le shìgù. |
| Someone is hurt. | Yǒu rén shòu shāng. |

| Is there anyone here who speaks English? | Zhèlǐ yǒu rén huì shūo Yīngyǔ ma? |

| Can I have an appointment? | Wǒ kěyǐ yūe gè shíjiān ma? |

| I'm not allergic to penicillin. | Wǒ duì qīngméisù bù guòmǐn. |
| I'm allergic to penicillin. | Wǒ duì qīngméisù guòmǐn. |

| I don't feel well. | Wǒ gǎnjúe bù shūfu. |
| I don't know what I have. | Wǒ bù zhīdao wǒ dé le shénme bìng. |

I think I have a fever.	Wǒ xiǎng wǒ zài fāshāo.
I have asthma.	Wǒ yǒu qìchuǎnbìng.
I have . . .	Wǒ . . .
a backache.	bèi tòng.
a cold.	gǎnmào le.
constipation.	biànmì.

a cough.	késou.
a cut.	gēshāng le.
diarrhea.	xiè dùzi/lā dùzi.
an earache.	ěr tòng.
hay fever.	fāshāo.
a headache.	tóu tòng.
heart trouble.	xīnzàng yǒu máobìng.
a stomachache.	wèi bù hǎo/wèi tòng.
pain.	tòng.

I feel dizzy/sick.   Wǒ gǎnjúe yǎnhūa/ěxin.
I can't sleep.   Wǒ shùi bù hǎo jiào.

Can you fill this   Qǐng gěi wǒ pèi hǎo yàofāng,
prescription for me?   hǎo ma?

Do you have . . .   Nǐ yǒu . . .
    an antacid?   kàngsūanyào ma?
    an antiseptic?   shājùnyào ma?
    aspirin?   āsīpǐlín ma?
    bandages?   bēngdài ma?
    contact-lens solution?   xǐ yǐnxíng yǎnjìng de
        yàoshuǐ ma?
    a disinfectant?   xiāodújì ma?
    eyedrops?   yǎnyàoshuǐ ma?
    sanitary napkins?   wèishēngdài ma?
    sleeping pills?   ānmiányào ma?
    tampons?   miánqiú ma?
    thermometer?   wēndùjì ma/tǐ wēn biǎo ma?
    throat lozenges?   hóutòngwán ma?
    vitamins?   wéitāmìng ma?

I'll wait for it.   Wǒ děng nǐ gěi wǒ.

5 GETTING BUSINESSIZED

In this chapter we cover important business vocabulary that has not yet found a place in previous chapters, such as names for office objects, job titles, and terminology used in different departments of a company.

The chapter is organized as follows:

> **Finding Your Way around the**
> **Office**
> **Office Objects**
> **Titles by Level**
> **Organization Charts**
> **Functional Areas of a Company**

Getting acclimated to the overseas office means getting comfortable so you can concentrate on being effective in your job.

So let's start at the office as you're just settling in. . . .

FINDING YOUR WAY AROUND THE OFFICE

"Bàngōngshì"

FÉNG XIĀNSHENG: *Nǐ zài zhèr de shíhòu kěyǐ shǐyòng zhè zhāng shūzhuō.*

KÈLĀKÈ XIǍOJIE: *Wàixiàn zěnme dǎ?*

FÉNG XIĀNSHENG: *Dǎ wàixiàn yào àn zhè jǐ gè ànniǔ zhōng de yī gè.*

KÈLĀKÈ XIǍOJIE: *Wǒ hái yào fā chuánzhēn.*

FÉNG XIĀNSHENG: *Dàtīng qiánmiàn gùo le fùyìnjī jiùshì.*

"Getting Acclimated to the Office"

MR. FENG: *You can use this desk while you're here.*

MS. CLARK: *How do I dial out?*

MR. FENG: *Press any one of these buttons to get an outside line.*

MS. CLARK: *I also need to send a fax.*

MR. FENG: *Just down the hall past the copier.*

Key Words

Coffee	Kāfēi
Coffee machine	Kāfēijī
Desk	Shūzhūo
Coat	Wàitào
Chair	Yǐzi
Computer	Diànnǎo
Copier	Fùyìnjī
Cubicle	Xiǎoshì/Xiǎogéjiān
Fax	Chúanzhēn
File	Dǎng'àn
Women's room	Nǚcèsǔo
Letter	Xìn
Mail	Yóujiàn
Manual	Shǒucè
Men's room	Náncèsǔo
Office	Bàngōngshì
Pen	Gāngbǐ
Pencil	Qiānbǐ
Phone	Diànhùa
Printer	Dǎyìnjī
Rest room	Xíshǒujiān
Tea	Chá

I'm here to see . . .	Wǒ lái zhèr kàn . . .
Is this the office of . . . ?	Zhè shì . . . de bàngōngshì ma?

Can you tell me how to get there?	Kěyǐ gàosu wǒ zěnme qù nàr ma?
Yes, I can wait.	Shì de, wǒ kěyǐ děng.
Where can I hang my coat?	Nǎr kěyǐ guà wǒ de wàitào?
Is there a rest room?	Yǒu xíshǒujiān ma?
Where is the copier?	Fùyìnjī zài nǎr?
Where can I get some . . .	Shénme dìfang yǒu . . .
coffee?	kāfēi?
tea?	chá?
water?	shuǐ?
Where is the . . .	. . . zài nǎr?
cafeteria?	Zìzhù cāntíng
lunchroom?	Wǔcānshì
women's room?	Nǚcèsuǒ
men's room?	Náncèsuǒ
Where are the rest rooms?	Xíshǒujiān zài nǎr?
How do I get an outside line?	Zěnyàng dǎ wàixiàn?
How can I make a local call?	Shìnèi diànhùa zěnme dǎ?
How can I make a long-distance call?	Chángtú diànhùa zěnme dǎ?
How can I make an overseas call?	Gúojì diànhùa zěnme dǎ?
Do you have . . .	Nǐmen yǒu . . .
a cafeteria?	zìzhù cāntíng ma?
a conference room?	hùiyìshì ma?
a copier?	fùyìnjī ma?
an extra desk?	dūoyú de shūzhūo ma?
an office I can use?	bàngōngshì wǒ kěyǐ yòng ma?

| a phone? | diànhùa ma? |
| a telephone directory? | diànhùabù ma? |

Could you show me/us the . . .	Nǐ néng gěi wǒ/wǒmen zhǐdiǎn yī xià . . .
elevator?	diàntī ma?
exit?	chūkǒu ma?
rest room?	xíshǒujiān ma?
staircase?	lóutī ma?
way out?	zěnme chūqù ma?

Where is the . . .	. . . zài nǎr?
accounting department?	Kùaijìbù
mail room?	Shōufāshì
personnel department?	Rénshìbù
shipping department?	Fāhùobù
warehouse?	Cāngkù

Who is responsible for . . .	Shúi fùzé . . .
arranging my flight?	ānpái wǒ de hángbān?
fixing the copier?	xiūlǐ fùyìnjī?
running the copier?	cāozùo fùyìnjī?
sending mail?	jì yóujiàn?

"Jì Bāogǔo"

SHǏMÌSĪ XIĀNSHENG: *Wǒ yào bǎ zhè ge bāogǔo jì dào Měigúo qù.*

FÚWÙYÚAN: *Nǐ xīwàng shénme shíhòu dào nàr?*

SHǏMÌSĪ XIĀNSHENG: *Liǎng, sān tiān zhīnèi. Yǒu wèntí ma?*

FÚWÙYÚAN: *Méiyǒu, yī diǎn wèntí yě méiyǒu.*

"Shipping a Package"

MR. SMITH: *I would like to ship this package to the United States.*

CLERK: *How soon do you want it to get there?*

MR. SMITH: *In two to three days. Will that be a problem?*
CLERK: *No, not at all.*

OFFICE OBJECTS

Here's a list of office objects in alphabetical order.

Cabinets	Gùichú
Bookcase	Shūchú
File cabinet	Dǎng'àngùi
Hanging cabinets	Xúangùachú
Lateral file	Cègùi
Letter/Legal size	Xìnjiàn (dàxiǎo)/Fǎlǜ xìnjīan (dàxiǎo)
Mobile file	Yídònggùi
Safe	Bǎoxiǎngùi
Steel cabinet	Gānggùi
Storage cabinet	Chǔcángxiāng
Vertical file	Zhílìgùi
Carts and Stands	Shǒutūichē yú jiàzi
Book cart	Shūchē
Computer cart	Diànnǎo tūichē
Mail cart	Yóujiàn tūichē
Printer/Fax stand	Dǎyìnjījià/diàn chúanjī jià
Storage cart	Chǔcáng tūichē
Chairs	Yǐzi
Ergonomic chair	Gōngyì yǐ
Executive chair	Zhǔguǎn yǐ
Folding chair	Zhédié yǐ
Leather chair	Pí yǐ
Manager chair	Jīnglǐ yǐ
Stacking chair	Chóngdié yǐ
Side chair	Cè yǐ
Swivel chair	Zhǔan yǐ

What would we do without computers?
When they are down we are down.

Méiyǒu diànnǎo wǒmen zénme bàn?
Tíng jiù tíng le ba.

Computer Accessories — Diànnǎo fùjiàn

Adapter	Zhuǎnjiēqì
Cables	Diànlǎn
Data cartridge	Shùjù cípán
Diskette or floppy disk	Cípán hùo ruǎncípán
Keyboard	Jiànpán
Monitor	Xiǎnshìqì
Mouse	Húashǔ
Mouse pad	Húashǔdiàn
Power cord	Dònglìxiàn
Surge protector	Diànliú bǎohùqì
Wrist rest	Hùwǎn
Zip® drive	Zip® cídiéjī

Desks — Zhūozi

Computer desk	Diànnǎo zhūo
Steel desk	Bùxiùgāng zhūo
Wood desk	Mù zhūo
Work center	Gōngzhūo tái

Desktop Material — Zhūomiàn Cáiliào

Glass	Bōlí
Leather	Pí
Metal	Jīnshǔ
Plastic	Sùliào
Steel	Gānq
Wood	Mùtou

Furnishings — Shìnèi Chénshè

Business card file	Míngpiànjiā
Bookshelves	Shūjià
Bulletin board	Gàoshìpái
Calendar	Rìlì

Chalkboard	Hēibǎn
Clock	Zhōng
Coat hook or coatrack	Yīgōu hùo yījià
Coffee table	Kāfēi zhuō
Corkboard	Rǔanmùbǎn
Cup	Bēizi
Desk lamp	Táidēng
Doorstop or jamb	Zhìménqì hùo ménsāi
Easel	Hùajià
Floor lamp	Lìdēng
Floor mat	Diànzi
Frame	Kūangjià
Paper clips	Zhǐjiā
Paper cutter	Cáizhǐdāo
Pictures	Hùa
Projection screen	Yǐngmù
Pushpins	Biézhēn
Punch	Dǎkǒngqì
Rubber bands	Xiàngpíjīn
Ruler	Chǐzi
Scissors	Jiǎndāo
Stamps	Yìnzhāng
Stamp pad	Yìndiàn
Stapler	Dìngshūjī
Staple remover	Chāidīngjī
Tacks	Dàtóudīng
Tape dispenser	Jiāodàipán
Telephone book	Diànhùabù
Three-hole punch	Sān yǎn dǎkǒngqì
Wallboard	Qiángbǎn
Wall planner	Qiángshàng gūihùabiǎo
Wastebasket	Fèizhǐlǒu
Organizers	Zǔzhīqì
Appointment Book	Yùyūe dēngjìcè
Basket tray	Gōngwéngé
Binders	Zhūangdìngjī
Bookends	Shūlì

144

Business card holder	Míngpiànjiā
Desk organizer	Táishì jìhuàbiǎo
In/Out box	Jìn/Chū wénjiànxiāng
Hanging wall pocket	Qiángdài
Magazine rack	Qīkānjià
Pencil caddy	Qiānbǐhé
Rolodex® card file	Kǎpiàn hé
Stacking letter tray	Xìnjiàngé
Tray	Gézi
Vertical holder	Zhílìjià

Maybe some day we'll eliminate paperwork, but for now we still need to write things down.

Paper and Forms	Zhǐ yǔ Biǎogé
Bond	Èr hào zhǐ
Business card	Míngpiàn
Business stationery	Shāngyè wénjù
Clipboard	Bǐjiābǎn
Columnar or accounting sheet	Kùaijì yùsùanzhǐ
Continuous computer paper	Diànnǎo liánxù dǎyìnzhǐ
Computer paper	Diànnǎo dǎyìnzhǐ
Construction paper	Jiànzhù gōngchéngzhǐ
Copier paper	Fùyìnzhǐ
Drafting or architecture paper	Hùitúzhǐ
Envelope	Xìnfēng
File folder	Dǎng'ànjiā
Folder	Wénjiànjiā
Form	Biǎogé
Graph paper	Fānggézhǐ
Hanging file folder	Xúangùa dǎng'ànjiā
Labels	Biāoqiān
Large business envelope	Dà shāngyè xìnfēng
Legal-size paper	Lǜshī xìnjiànzhǐ

145

Letterhead	Yǒuxián xìnjiān
Letter opener	Kāixìndāo
Message pad	Liúyánbù
Notebook	Bǐjìběn
Notepad	Bǐjìbù
Post-it® notes	Tiējiān
Report cover	Bàogào fēngmiàn
Reporter notebook	Bàogào bǐjìběn
Ruled writing pad	Yǒugé bǐjìbù
Scratch pad	Cǎogǎoběn
Steno pad	Sùjìběn
Writing pad	Shūxiěběn

Pens and Pencils | Gāngbǐ yú Qiānbǐ

Ballpoint pen	Yúanzhūbǐ
Correction fluid	Gǎizhèngyè
Eraser	Xiàngpícā
Highlighter	Jìhàobǐ
Ink pen	Mòshǔibǐ/Zì làishǔi bǐ
Lead	Qiān
Marker	Biāoshìbǐ
Mechanical pencil	Jīxièbǐ
Pen	Gāngbǐ
Pencil	Qiānbǐ
Pencil sharpener	Qiānbǐdāo
Refills	Bǔchōngyè/Bǐ xīn
Retractable pen	Kěshōushì gāngbǐ/Shēn sūo shì yúanzhù bǐ
Wood pencil	Mùtóu qiānbǐ
Writing pen	Shūxiěbǐ

Printers/Faxes | Dǎyìnjī/Chúanzhēnjī

Cartridge	Cípán
Fax paper	Chúanzhēnzhǐ
Inkjet	Pēnmò
Laser	Léishè
Replacement cartridge	Tìhùandaì
Ribbon	Sèdài

| Toner cartridge | Tànfěnjiā/sèfěnhé |
| Typewriter ribbon | Dǎzìjī sèdài |

| Tables | Zhuōzi |

Computer table	Diànnǎozhuō
Conference table	Hùiyìzhuō
Drafting/Artist table	Hùitúzhuō/Hùihùazhuō
Folding table	Zhédiézhuō
Utility table	Gōngjùzhuō

| Miscellany | Qítā |

Batteries	Diànchí
Broom	Sàozhou
Cleaning supplies	Qīngjié wùpǐn
Cleaning cloth	Qīngjiébù
Duct tape	Jiāodài
Duster	Dǎnzi
Extension cord	Yánchángxiàn
Fan	Shànzi
Flashlight	Shǒudiàn
Floor mat	Dìdiàn
Glue	Jiāoshǔi
Lightbulb	Dēngpào
Lock	Sǔo
Mailer	Yóujiàn fāsòngzhě
Masking tape	Hùtiáo
Postal meter	Yóupiān jìliàngqì
Postal scale	Jìyóuchèng
Scotch® tape	Scotch jiāodài
Shipping tape	Zhūanghùo jiāodaì
Tape	Jiāodài
Trash bags	Lājīdài/lèsèdài

TITLES BY LEVEL

A standardized system of titles has been developed within most U.S. firms. For instance, the term vice president indicates someone at a significant level of management who is usually also an "officer." Officer often designates someone who can approve certain significant expenditures. However, sometimes even within the U.S. titles can differ. For instance, in most companies and organizations the term manager means a person who heads up a subarea of responsibility, like the manager of recruiting or training. But the person in charge of human resources is typically a vice president or director. However, in a few companies the term manager is the equivalent of the title vice president or director.

By contrast, in other countries, titles can be quite dissimilar. For instance, in some countries the term director is often equivalent to president or vice president.

Chairman	Zhǔxí
President	Zǒngcái
Vice President	Fùzǒngcái
Director	Dǒngshì/Zhǔrèn/ Chǎngzhǎng
Manager	Jīnglǐ
Supervisor	Gǔanlǐrén
Senior Analyst	Gāojí Fēnxīshī
Analyst	Fēnxīshī
Junior Analyst	Chūjí Fēnxīshī
Coordinator	Xiétiáorén
Administrative Assistant	Xíngzhèng Zhùlǐ
Secretary	Mìshū
Receptionist	Chúandáyúan

The titles in private enterprises, holding companies and joint ventures usually are parallel to the American system. However, titles in government institutions and state-run enterprises may be confusing. You may run into titles such as *bùzhǎng*, *júzhǎng/tīngzhǎng*, *sīzhǎng/chūzhǎng*, *zhǔrèn*.

These are used to mean directorship of departments, committees or offices at the national, provincial, municipal and county levels, and are listed here according to their order in the hierarchy. These titles are important and may hold the key to the success of your business since you may need these institutions to approve your business documents. Also, many government institutions have formed companies to conduct trade. That is why it is not unusual to find more than one title on business cards in China; for example, one may be a company title like *zǒngcái* (president), and the other one, a government title like *zhǔrèn* (director). In addition, an academic title or a professional title may be added as well.

"Gōngzuò Wèntí"

SHǏMÌSĪ XIĀNSHENG: *Chángwù dǒngshì jìnlái de shíhòu, Wài Bóshì yī xià zǐ jiù húoyùe qǐlái le, nǐ zhùyì dào le ma?*

FÉNG XIĀNSHENG: *Shì ya. Zài zhè zhīqián, tā fēicháng ānjìng, tūrán, tā yào xiǎnshì zhè gē bàogào shì yóu tā fùzé de.*

SHǏMÌSĪ XIĀNSHENG: *Tā méi gàn shénme shì, què xiǎng bǎ gōngláo qūiyú zìjǐ, zhè shǐ rén hěn shēngqì.*

FÉNG XIĀNSHENG: *Zài Měigúo yě yǒu zhèyàng de rén ma?*

"Office Politics"

MR. SMITH: *Did you see Dr. Wye trying to dominate the presentation when the managing director came into the room?*

MR. FENG: *Yes. He was quiet up to then, but he tried to show that he was responsible for the report.*

MR. SMITH: *He made some people angry for taking all the credit for the report when he hardly worked on it.*
MR. FENG: *Do you have people like that in the United States, too?*

Be extremely careful with office politics in China because you may cause someone to lose face. Face is a very important concept in Chinese culture. Causing someone to lose face means that you not only offend that person, but you may also offend a group of people who side with that person. As a result, a whole group of people will stop responding to you positively. It is not always easy to determine what might cause a loss of face, but generally you should avoid: making comments behind someone's back, criticizing someone in public, rejecting a proposal out of hand without at least appearing to consider it, saying no to someone in public, interrupting anyone, or publicly threatening someone.

ORGANIZATION CHARTS

Key Words

Authority	Quánlì
Chart	Túbiǎo
Dotted line	Xūxiàn
Organization	Zǔzhī
Matrix	Jùzhèng
Responsibility	Zérèn
Solid line	Shíxiàn
Title	Zhíchēng

Organization Chart of a U.S. Company

Organization Charts

Organization Chart of a Chinese Company

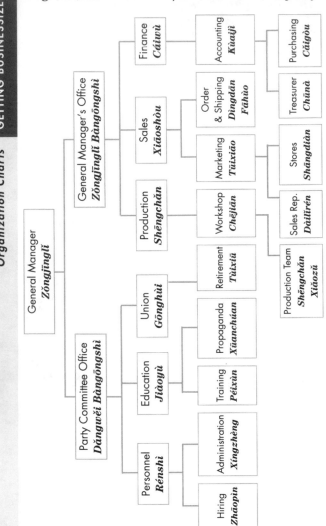

This chart reflects the structure of traditional state-run companies. Even these companies are going through structural changes since China opened to the outside world. Before these changes came about, the Communist Party was the highest power in an organization. Now the Party's power is fading from the business and production fields, but it is still strong. For example, the general manager may be concurrently the Party committee secretary. The private sector is growing very fast in China and companies in that sector, even joint ventures formed between state-run companies and foreign companies, are more likely to assume the organization of western companies.

FUNCTIONAL AREAS OF A COMPANY

Looking for a word in your field of endeavor? You will probably find it below. These are the main areas within a company or organization. Many of these terms, of course, also apply to organizations outside a company. The areas covered are:

> **Accounting and Finance**
> **Computer Systems (Data Processing)**
> **Human Resources (Personnel)**
> **Law and International Law**
> **Manufacturing and Operations**
> **Marketing and Sales**

Accounting and Finance

Kùaijì yǔ Cáiwù

What form do I use to submit my expenses?

Bàozhàng wǒ yīnggāi shǐyòng něi ge biǎogé?

Where are your billing records kept?	Nǐmen de zhàngmù fàng zài nǎr?
Are you on a calendar or fiscal year?	Nǐmen shǐyòng rìlì niándù háishì cáiwù niándù?
When do we close the books?	Zhàngmù shénme shíhòu jiézhǐ?
Is your organization on the accrual or cash method?	Nǐmen zǔzhī shǐyòng yìngjìfǎ háishì xiànjīnfǎ?

Accounting	Kùaijì
Accountant	Kùaijìshī
Accrual method	Yìngjìfǎ
Amortization	Fēnqī zhùxiāo/Fēnqī cháng fù
Assets	Zīchǎn
Audit	Shěnjì
Balance sheet	Zīchǎn fùzhài biǎo
Bankruptcy	Pòchǎn
Billing records	Zhàngmù
Bills	Zhàngdān
Breakeven	Bù yíng bù kūi/Shōu zhī pinghéng
Budget	Yùsùan
Calendar year	Rìlì niándù
Capital	Zīběn
Capital budget	Zīběn yùsùan
Capital improvements	Zīběn gǎishàn
Cash	Xiànjīn
Cash flow	Xiànjīn liúliàng
Cash method	Xiànjīn fāngfǎ
Chart of accounts	Zhàngmùbiǎo
Closing of the books	Jiézhàng
Command	Zhǐlìng
Controller	Shěn jì yúan
Cost	Chéngběn
Cost accounting	Chéngběnzhàng

Credit	Xìnyòng
Debit	Jièfāng
Dcbt	Jièkuǎn
Default	Qiànzhài
Depreciation	Zhéjiù
Disbursement	Zhīfù
Dividends	Gǔxī
Equity	Gǔpiào
Fair market value	Hélǐ shìjià
Financial analyst	Cáiwù fēnxīshī
Financial statement	Cáiwù bàobiǎo
First In—First Out (FIFO)	Xiān jìn—Xiān chū
Fiscal year	Cáiwù niándù
General ledger	Zǒng fēnlèizhàng
Goodwill	Shāngyù
Gross Income	Zǒng shōurù
Gross Sales	Xiāoshòu zǒng'é
Income	Shōurù
Income statement	Shōurùbiǎo
Interest	Lìxi
Inventory	Wùpǐn qīngdān cúnhùo qīngdān
Invoice	Fāpiào
Journal	Rìzhì
Last In—First Out (LIFO)	Hòu Jìn—Xiān Chū
Ledger	Fēnlèizhàng
Liabilities	Zhàiwù
Liquid asset	Liúdòng zīchǎn
Margin	Chā'é
Market value	Shìchǎng jiàzhí
Net earnings	Jìngdé
Net worth	Jìngzhí

Operating expenses	Jīngyíng kāizhī
Overhead	Tōngcháng kāizhī
Payroll	Yuángōng xīnzī
Per diem	Měirì
Profit	Lìrùn
Profit and loss statement	Sǔnyìbiǎo
Requisition	Zhēngshōu
Return on investment	Tóuzī shōuyì
Revenue	Shōurù
Sales	Xiāoshòu
Statement of cash flows	Xiànjīn liúliàngbiǎo
Stock	Gǔpiào
Straight-line depreciation	Zhíxiàn zhéjiù
Trial balance	Shìsuàn biǎo
Voucher	Píngzhèng
Wages	Gōngzī
Zero-based budgeting	Líng yùsuàn

Computer Systems (Data Processing)
Diànnǎo Xìtǒng (Shùjù Chǔlǐ)

(See also Telecommunications in Industry Specific Terms)

What is my password?	Wǒ de mìmǎ shì shénme?
How do I get a password?	Zěnmeyàng dédào mìmǎ?
My printer won't work.	Wǒ de dǎyìnjī huài le.
Who can help me with my computer?	Shúi néng bāngzhù wǒ xiū wǒ de diànnǎo?
Access (to) the Internet	Shàng diànnǎo wǎnglùo
Access code	Xǔkě hàomǎ
Alt key	Alt jiàn
Analog	Mónǐ
Application	Yìngyòng ruǎntǐ

At sign (@)	@ fúhào
Attach a file (to)	Bǎ wénjiàn fùjiā zài . . .
Attachment	Fùjiā wénjiàn
Back slash	Fǎn xiéxiànhào
Backspace key	Tùigéjiàn
Banner ad	Biāotí guǎnggào
BASIC language	BASIC yǔyán
Baud	Bōtè
Beta program	Bèitā chéngxù
Beta test	Bèitā cèshì
Boot (to)	Qǐdòng
Broadband	Kūanpín
Browse (to)	Liúlán
Browser	Liúlánqì
Bug	Cùowù
Byte	Yúanwèizǔ/Èrjìn wèizǔ
CD-ROM	Wéidú guāngdié
CD-ROM drive	Wéidú guāngdiéjī
Cell	Dānyúan
Central Processing Unit (CPU)	Zhōngyāng Chùlǐ Dānyúan
Chip	Jīngpiàn
Click (to)	Jiànrù
Clip art	Diànnǎo hùa
Clock speed	Shímài sùlǜ
Close (to)	Gūanbì
COBOL language	COBAL yǔyán
Command	Zhǐlìng
Communications port	Tōngxùn chūrùkǒu
Compatible	Jiānróng
Compressed file	Yāsūo dǎng'àn
Control key	Kòngzhìjiàn
Copy	Fùzhì
Copy (to)	Fùzhì dào
CPU (Central Processing Unit)	Zhōngyāng Chùlǐ Dānyúan
Crash	Xìtǒng gùzhàng

Cursor	Yóubiāo
Cut (to)	Qiēgē dào
Data	Shùjù
Database	Zīliàokù
Debug (to)	Chúcuò
Delete (to)	Xiāochú
Delete key	Xiāochújiàn
Desktop computer	Zhuōshàngxíng diànnǎo
Desktop publishing	Zhuōshàng chūbǎn
Dialog box	Duìhuàkuāng
Digital	Shùwèi de
Disk	Cídié
Disk drive	Cídiéjī
Diskette	Cípán
Document	Wénjiàn
Double-click (to)	Ànjiàn liǎngcì
Download (to)	Xiàzài
Drag and drop (to)	Tūoyè dào
DRAM—SRAM	Dòngtài súijī jìyìtǐ—Jìngtài súijī jìyìtǐ
DVD	Shùwèi shìpíng diépiàn
E-commerce	Wǎngshàng shāngyè
E-commerce companies	Wǎngshàng shāngyè gōngsī
Educational software	Jiàoyù rǔanjiàn
E-mail	Diànzǐ yóujiàn
E-mail (to)	Fā diànzǐ yóujiàn gěi
Engine	Yǐnqíng
Enter (to)	Jiànrù
Enter key	Jiànrùjiàn/Jìn
Entertainment software	Yúlè rǔanjiàn
Error message	Cùowù xìnxī
Escape (Esc) key	Tùichūjiàn
Field	Lánwéi
File	Dǎng'àn
Flat screen	Píngbǎn píngmù
Folder	Wénjiànkù
Font	Zìxíng

FORTRAN language	FORTRAN yǔyán
Forward an e-mail (to)	Bǎ yóujiàn zhǔan gěi. . . .
Forward slash (/)	Xiéxiànhào
Gigabyte	Qiānzhào wèiyúan/qiānzhào zìjié
Graphics	Túhùa
Go on-line (to)	Shàngwǎng
Hacker	Hēikè
Hard drive	Yìngdié
Hardware	Yìngjiàn
Hertz	Hēzī
Host	Zhǔjī
Host (to)	Zùo . . . zhǔjī
Hypertext	Chāojí wénjiàn
IBM-compatible	IBM jiānróng
Icon	Túfú/túbiāo
Insert (to)	Chārù
Install (to)	Ānzhūang
Instructions	Zhǐshì
Integrated circuit	Jíchéng diànlù
Internet	Wǎngjì wǎnglùo/yin tè wang
Internet address	Wǎngzhǐ
Internet advertising	Wǎngshàng gǔanggào
ISP (Internet Service Provider)	Wǎnglùo tígōngshāng
Key (to)	Jiàn
Keyboard	Jiànpán
Language	Yǔyán
Laptop	xīshàngxíng diànnǎo
Laser printer	Léishè dǎyìnjī
LCD screen	Yèjīng píngmù
Left click (to)	Àn zǔo jiàn
Load (to)	Shàngzài
Log on/off (to)	Qiānrù/qiānchū
Mail merge	Yóujiàn hébìng
Mainframe	Zhǔjī

Maximize (to)	Zùidà jíxiàn
Megahertz	Bǎiwànhēzī
Memory	Jìyìtǐ
Menu	Xǔandān
Minimize (to)	Zùixiǎo jíxiàn
Microprocessor (Intel, Motorola)	Wéichùlǐqì
Modem	Shùjùjī
Monitor	Xiǎnshìqì
Monitor (to)	Xiǎnshì
Mouse	Hùashǔ
Mouse pad	Hùashǔdiàn
Nanosecond	Mòmiǎo (nàdiǎ)
Network	Wǎnglùo
Notebook computer	Bǐjìxíng diànnǎo
Online	Liánxìan
Open (to)	Dǎkāi
Operating system (Windows, Linux, Unix)	Cāozùo xìtǒng (Shìchūang, Linux, Unix)
Palmtop computer	Zhǎngshàng xíng diànnǎo
Page	Yè
Page down/up (to)	Yè xià/shàng
Parallel port	Píngxíngkǒu
Password	Mìmǎ
Paste (to)	Tiēbǔ
PC (Personal Computer)	Gèrén diànnǎo
Plotter	Hùitújī
Portal	Chúansòngmén
Press a button (to)	Ànjiàn dào
Print (to)	Dǎyìn
Printer	Dǎyìnjī
Program	Chéngxù
Program (to)	Biān chéngxù
Programmable logic devices	Chéngxù lúojí shèbèi

Programmer	Chéngxù shèjìshī
Prompt	Tíshìhào
Record	Jìlù
Right click (to)	Àn yòujiàn
Save (to)	Bǎocún
Scan (to)	Sǎomiáo
Scanner	Sǎomiáoqì
Screen	Píngmù
Screen (to)	Píngmù tiáozhěng dào
Scroll (to)	Liánjùan gǔndòng
Search	Sōusuǒ
Search (to)	Sōusuǒ
Search engine	Sōusuǒ yǐnqíng
Serial port	Chùanhángkǒu
Server	Sìfùqì
Shift key	Yíwèijiàn
Software	Rǔanjiàn
Sort (to)	Fénlèi
Space bar	Kòngbáigǎn
Speaker	Lǎba
Spell check (to)	Pīnxiě jiǎnchá
Spell checker	Pīnxiě jiǎncháqì
Surf the Internet (to)	Liúlan wǎnglùo
System	Xìtǒng
Tab key	Lánbiāojiàn
Technical support	Jìshù zhīchí
Telecommuting	Yǔanchéng jiāohùan
Teleconferencing	Diànchúan hùiyì
Use (to)	Shǐyòng
User	Shǐyòngzhě
User-friendly	Shǐyòngzhě qīnhé/yònghù yǒu hǎo
Virus	Bìngdú
Voice recognition	Shēngyīn biànshì
Web	Qúanqiú zīxúnwǎng
Web browser	Wǎnglùo liúlánqì

Web page	Wǎngyè
Web site	Wǎngzhǐ
Wireless	Wúxiàn
Word processor	Wénshū chùlǐ chéngshì/ wénzì chùlǐ jī
World Wide Web (www)	Qúanqiú zīxúnwǎng
Zip® disk	Zip® cípán
Zip® drive	Zip® cípánjī

Human Resources (Personnel)

Rénshì

Where do you keep the personnel files?	Nǐmen de rénshì dǎng'àn fàng zài nǎr?
What do you keep in the personnel files?	Shénme yàng de dōngxī nǐmen fàng zài rénshì dǎng'àn lǐ?
What organization regulates the hiring and firing in your country?	Nǐmen gúojiā shénme jīgòu guǎnlǐ yúangōng de gùyòng hé jiěgù.
How much do you use the Internet for hiring in your country?	Nǐmen shǐyòng gúojì wǎnglùo gùyòng zhígōng de chéngdù rúhé?
How much turnover do you have at this plant?	Zhè gè gōngchǎng de rénshì biàndòng zěnmeyàng?
What benefits do you offer?	Nǐmen yǒu shénmeyàng de fúlì?
How much vacation do you give for a new hire?	Xīn gùyòng de gōngrén yǒu dūoshǎo tiān jiàqī?
What is your normal retirement age?	Nǐmen yībān zài shénme niánlíng tùixiū?
Absent	Qúexí
Advertise a position/job (to)	Gùyòng/gōngzuò gǔanggào

Appraise job performance (to)	Gōngzuò biǎoxiǎn pínggū
Actuary	Gōngzhèngrén
Background	Bèijǐng
Beneficiary	Shòuyìrén
Bonus	Hóngbāo
Career	Zhíyè
Compensation	Bàochóu
Counsel (to)	Quàngào/shōng yì
Counseling	Fúdǎo
Corporate culture	Gōngsī wénhùa
Cross training	Jiāochā péixùn
Deferred compensation	Yánhǔan bàochóu
Disability	Cánzhàng
Dotted-line responsibility	Xūxiàn zérèn
Employee benefits	Zhígōng fúlì
Employee turnover	Yúangōng liúdòng
Employment	Gōngzuò/gùyòng
Expatriate	Wàiqiáo
Flextime	Jīdòng shíjiān
Fringe benefits	Èwài fúlì
Health insurance	Yīliáo bǎoxiǎn
Human resources	Réshì gǔanlǐ
Human relations	Rénjì gūanxì
Interview	Miànshì
Interview (to)	Miànshì
Job	Gōngzuò
Job description	Gōngzuò miáoshù
Job listing/advertisement	Gōngzuò mùlù/gǔanggào
Job skills	Gōngzuò jìshù
Life insurance	Rénshòu bǎoxiǎn
List a job (to)	Dēnglù gōngzuò

Manage (to)	Guǎnlǐ
Management	Guǎnlǐ
Management training	Guǎnlǐ péixùn
Matrix management	Jùzhèn guǎnlǐ
Merit increase	Lùngōng xíngshǎng
Micromanage	Wéiguān guǎnlǐ
Morale	Shìqì
Motivation	Dòngjī
Nepotism	Qúndài guānxī
On-the-job training	Shídì péixùn
Organization	Zǔzhī
Organization chart	Zǔzhītú
Paycheck	Xīnzhǔi zhīpiào
Pension	Yǎnglǎojīn
Performance appraisal	Gōngzuò pínggū
Personnel	Rényúan
Personnel file	Rénshì dǎng'àn
Position	Zhíwèi
Promote (to)	Tíbá
Promotion	Tísheng
Recruiter	Zhēngzhāorén
Relocation	Chóngxīn ānzhì
Resume	Lǚlì
Retire (to)	Tùixiū
Retirement plan	Tùixiū jìhùa
Restructuring	Gǎizǔ
Salary	Xīnshūi
Salary grade	Gōngzī jíbié
Salary survey	Gōngzī diàochá
Seniority	Zīshēn
Skills	Jìshù
Solid-line responsibility	Shíxiàn zérèn
Stock options	Gǔpiào xiàn'é mǎimàiqúan/ yōu xiān rēngǔ qúan
Supervise (to)	Guǎnlǐ
Supervisor	Guǎnlǐrén

Train (to)	Péixùn
Training	Péixùn
Turnover	Rényúan biàndòng
Unemployment	Shīyè
Vacation	Jiàqī
Wages	Gōngzī

China has passed many new laws and adopted international standards in the past few years as it strives to join the international business community. However, not all provinces and local areas actually implement the nation's laws fully. In some cases, they even use the internal regulations to override national laws, and this makes business in China more difficult than in other countries.

Law and International Law
Fǎlǜ yǔ Gúojìfǎ

What is the procedure to apply for a patent, copyright, or trademark in your country?

Zài nǐmen gúojiā shēnqǐng zhuānlì, bǎnquán hùo shāngbiāo de chéngxù rúhé?

Do you recognize a service mark in your country?

Nǐmen gúojiā chéngrèn fúwù biāozhì ma?

What is the procedure to register a prescription drug in your country?

Zài nǐmen gúojiā zhùcè yàowù yǒu shénme shǒuxù?

How much legal work do you do outside the company?

Nǐ zài wàimiàn hái chéngdān dūoshǎo fǎlǜ gōngzùo?

Affidavit	Zhèngcí
Alibi	Bù zài fànzuì xiànchǎng
Appeal	Shàngsù
Appeal (to)	Xiàng . . . shàngsù
Attorney	Lǜshī
Bail	Bǎoshì
Bankruptcy	Pòchǎn
Bar	Fǎyuàn/Lǜshījiè
Barrister	(gāoděng fǎyuàn) lǜshī
Bench	Fǎguān zuòweì
Boilerplate	Yànggǎo
Brief	Gāngyào
Bylaws	Guīzé
Cartel	Qìyè liánhé
Cease and desist order	Tíngzhǐ zhōngduàn mìnglìng
Civil law	Mínshìfǎ
Consideration	Kǎolǜ
Contract	Hétóng
Copyright	Bǎnquán
Copyright (to)	Bǎnqúan
Corpus	Wénjí
Court	Fǎtíng
Covenant	Qìyūe
Crime	Zuìxíng
Crime (to commit)	Fànzuì
Cross-examination	Jiāochā shěnwèn
Cross-examine (to)	Jiāochā shěnwèn
Damages	Sǔnshāng
Defense	Biànhù
Defraud	Qīzhà
Defraud (to)	Zhàpiàn
Discovery	Fāxiàn
Evidence	Zhèngjù
External	Wàibù de
Felony	Zhòngzuì
Fiduciary	Shòutūorén

Find (to)	Xúnzhǎo
Finding	Fāxiàn
Fraud	Qīzhà
Fraud (to)	Qīpiàn
Indict (to)	Qǐshù
Indictment	Kònggào
Internal	Nèibù de
International law	Gúojìfǎ
Judge	Fǎgūan
Judge (to)	Shěnpàn
Judgment	Pànjúe
Jury	Péishěntúan
Law	Fǎlǜ
Law firm	Fǎlǜ shìwùsǔo
Lawsuit	Sùsòng
Lawyer	Lǜshī
Legal	Fǎdìng de
Litigation	Sùsòng
Malpractice	Dúzhí
Motion	Dòngyì
Negligence	Shīzhí
Order (to)	Mìnglìng
Patent	Zhūanlì
Patent (to)	Zhūanlì
Plaintiff	Yúan'gào
Probate	Rènzhèng/yízhu jiǎnyàn
Prosecute (to)	Qǐsù
Prosecutor	Jiǎnchágūan
Restrain (to)	Xiànzhì
Restraining order	Xiànzhìlìng
Service mark	Fúwù biāozhì
Solicitor	Lǜshī
Sue (to)	Kòngsù
Suit	Kònggào

167

Tax	Shùi
Tax (to)	Kēshùi
Tort	Mínshì qīnfàn/qīnquán xíngwéi
Trademark	Shāngbiāo

Manufacturing and Operations
Jiāgōng yú jīngyíng

Where are your main production plants?	Nǐmen de zhǔyào jiāgōngchǎng zài nǎr?
How many shifts do you run?	Nǐmen lún jǐ bān?
Is your plant unionized?	Nǐmen chǎng yǒu gōnghuì ma?
What is your through-put at this plant?	Zhè gè chǎng de chǎnliàng shì dūoshǎo?
How many cars and trucks will you produce at this plant this year?	Zhè gè chǎng jīnnián shēngchǎn de chē hé kǎchē yǒu dūoshǎo?
Where does engineering fit into your organization?	Gōngchéng zài nǐmen zǔzhī zhōng zhàn shénme dìwèi?
What types of engineers to you employ?	Nǐmen gùyòng shénmeyàng de gōngchéngshī?
How many engineers do you employ?	Nǐmen gùyòng dūoshǎo gōngchéngshī?
Accident	Shìgù
Assembly line	Ānzhuāngxiàn
Controls	Kòngzhì
Engineer	Gōngchéngshī
Engineer (to)	Gōngchéng
Earplugs	Ěrsāi

Fabricate	Zhìzào
Factory	Gōngchǎng
Factory floor	Gōngchǎng céngmiàn
Floor	Dìmiàn
Foreperson	Lǐngbān
Forge (to)	Dùanzào
Forklift	Tūigāojī/chǎnchē
Gasket	Chèndiàn
Goggles	Bǎohùjìng/hùmùjìng
Inventory	Wùpǐn qīngdān/cúnhùo gīngdān
Just-in-time inventory	Zùixīn wùpǐn qíngdān
Just-in-time manufacture	Zùixīn jiāgōng
Machinery	Jīxiè
Manufacture (to)	Jiāgōng/zhì zào
Manufacturing plant	Jiāgōngchǎng
Model	Yàngshì
Operate (to)	Jīngyíng
Operations	Jīngyíng
Plant	Gōngchǎng
Plant manager	Gōngchǎng jīnglǐ
Prefabricate	Yùxiān jiànzào
Procurement	Cǎigòu
Purchase (to)	Gòumǎi
Purchasing	Gòumǎi
Quality	Zhìliàng
Quality control	Zhìliàng kòngzhì
Raw materials	Yúan cáiliào
Railroad	Tiělù
Safety	Ānqúan
Safety goggles	Ānqúan bǎohùjìng
Schedule	Jìhùabiǎo

Schedule (to)	Zuò jìhùa
Scheduling	Jìhùa
Shift (first, second, third)	Lúnbān (dì yī bān, dì èr bān, dì sān bān)
Ship (to)	Fāhùo
Shipping	Fāhùo
Specifications	Gūigé
Supervisor	Gǔanlǐrén
Supplier	Gōnghùoshāng
Tank	Yóuxiāng
Total Quality Management (TQM)	Wánqúan zhìliàng gǔanlǐ
Union	Gōnghùi
Union contract	Gōnghùi hétóng
Vat	Dàtǒng
Warehouse	Cāngkù
Workers	Gōngrén

Marketing and Sales

Tūixiāo yú Xiāoshòu

What is your advertising budget for the year?

Nǐmen yī nián de gǔanggào yùsùan shì dūoshǎo?

Which advertising agency do you use?

Nǐmen shǐyòng něi gè gǔanggàoshè?

Which media do you use and why?

Nǐ shǐyòng shénme méitǐ, ér wèishénme shǐyòng zhè gè méitǐ?

Who are your product/ service competitors?

Nǐmen chǎnpǐn/fúwù de jìngzhēng dùishǒu shì shúi?

What is your market share?

Nǐmen de shìchǎng bǐlì shì dūoshǎo?

"Kèhù Bàoyùan"

YÙEHÀNXÙN XIǍOJIE: *Wèi shénme yǒu zhème duo gùkè xiàng nǐmen bàoyùan?*

SÒNG XIĀNSHENG: *Zhè jiùshì wǒmen gùyòng nǐ de yúanyīn.*

YÙEHÀNXÙN XIǍOJIE: *Nà wǒmen ràng gùkè dàibiǎo bǎ zhěnggè xīngqī gùkè de gèzhǒng yìjiàn dōu jì xià lái.*

SÒNG XIĀNSHENG: *Nǐ kěyǐ shèjì yī xià yìjiàn biǎo ma?*

YÙEHÀNXÙN XIǍOJIE: *Wǒ jīntiān xiàwǔ jiù kěyǐ zùo hǎo.*

"Customer Complaints"

MS. JOHNSON: *Why are you getting so many complaints from your customers?*

MR. SONG: *That's why we hired you.*

MS. JOHNSON: *Then let's have the customer representatives keep a log of the various types of complaints for a full week.*

MR. SONG: *Could you design the log?*

MS. JOHNSON: *Yes, I'll have it ready this afternoon.*

Account	Zhànghù
Account executive	Zhànghù gǔanlǐyúan
Ad/Advertisement	Gǔanggào
Ad campaign	Gǔanggào zàoshì/jīng zhēng
Advertising	Dēng gǔanggào
Advertising effectiveness	Gǔanggào xiàoyìng
Advertising manager	Gǔanggào jīnglǐ
Advertising objectives	Gǔanggào mùbiāo
Advertising rates	Gǔanggào shōufèi
Agency	Dàilǐ

Agent	Dàilǐrén
Art director	Měishù zhǐdǎo/yìshù zhǐdǎo
Artwork	Měigōng
Audience	Dúzhě/gūanzhòng
Audience measurement	Dúzhě cèdìng
Audience profile	Dúzhě miànmào
Bait-and-switch advertising	Yǐnyòu gùkè biànhùan de gǔanggào
Banner ad	Biāotí gǔanggào
Bar code	Tiáoxíngmǎ
Barriers to entry	Jìnrù zhàng'ài
Billboard	Gàoshìpái
Billings	Dānjù
Brochure	Xiǎocèzi
Brand	Páizi
Brand loyalty	Zhōngshí yú páizi
Brand name	Míngpái
Broadcast media	Gǔangbō méitǐ
Buyers	Mǎifāng
Campaign	Zàoshì/jìngzhēng
Captive market	Shōuzhī shìchǎng/lǒngduàn shìchǎng
Catalog	Hùowù biānmù
Circular	Chúandān
Circulation	Liútōng
Classified advertising	Fēnlèi gǔanggào
Closing date	Jiézhǐ rìqī
Cold call	Diànhùa tūixiāo
Commercial	Shāngyè/gǔanggào
Commodity product	Rìyòngpǐn
Competition	Jìngzhēng
Competitive advantage	Jìngzhēnglì
Consumer	Xiāofèizhě
Consumer research	Xiāofèi yánjiū
Copy	Fùzhì
Corporate communications	Gōngsī tōngxùn

Creative director	Chùangzùo zhǐdǎo
Creativity	Chùangzùo
Culture	Wénhùa
Customer	Gùkè
Customer complaints	Gùkè bàoyùan
Customer satisfaction	Gùkè mǎnyì
Customer service	Gùkè fúwù
Database	Shùjùkù
Demand	Yāoqiú
Demographics	Rénkǒu tǒngjì
Direct mail	Zhíjíe yóujiàn
Discount	Zhékòu
Distribution	Fēnbù
Economic factors	Jīngjì yīnsù
Elastic demand	Tánxìng yāoqiú
Endorsement	Dānbǎo
Exposure	Bàolù
Expressed warranty	Kùaisù bǎodān
Focus group	Jiāodiǎn qúntǐ
Forecast	Yùbào
Frequency	Pínlù
Fulfillment	Shíxíng
Galley proofs	Chángtiáo jiàoyàng
General sales manager	Xiāoshòu zǒng jīnglǐ
Global marketing	Qúanqiú tūixiāo
Graphic design	Túhùa shèjì
Hard sell	Yìngxìng tūixiāo
Illustration	Yǎnshì/lì zhèng
Image	Xíngxiàng
Implied warranty	Mòshì bǎodān
Impulse buying	Chōngdòng gòumǎi
Incentive	Cìjī
Inelastic demand	Fēitánxìng yāoqiú
Infomercial	Xìnxí gǔangào
Insert (to)	Chārù
Institutional marketing	Túantǐ shìchǎng

Inventory	Wùpǐn qīngdān/cúnhuò qīngdōn
Island display	Dǎoshàng zhǎnshì
Jobber	Línggōng
Junk mail	Lèsè yóujiàn/lā jī yònjian
Kiosk	Tíngzi
Label	Biāoqiān
Layout	Hùa bǎnmìan
Lead(s)	Yǐnxìan/yǐndǎo
Licensing	Zhízhào
Lifestyle	Shēnghuó fāngshì
List price	Jiàmùbiǎo jiàgé
Logo	Túbiāo
Magazine	Zázhì
Mailing list	Yóujì míngdān
Mail order	Yóugòu
Margin	Zhùantóu
Markdown	Jiǎnjià
Market(s)	Shìchǎng
Market (to)	Xiāo wáng
Marketing	Tūixiāo
Marketing budget	Tūixiāo yùsùan
Marketing director	Tūixiāo zhǔrèn
Marketing manager	Tūixiāo jīnglí
Marketing plan	Tūixiāo jìhùa
Market niche	Shìchǎng dìwèi
Market penetration	Shìchǎng chuāntoù
Market research	Shìchǎng yánjiū
Market share	Shìchǎng bǐlì
Mass marketing	Dàzhòng tūixiāo
Mass media	Dàzhòng chuánbō méitǐ
Media	Méitǐ
Media buyer	Méitǐ goùmǎizhě
Media research	Méitǐ yánjiū
Merchandise	Shāngpǐn
Merchandizing	Shāngpǐn gǔanggào tūixiāo

Message	Xìnxí
National account	Quánguó zhànghù
Need(s)	Xūyào/xūqiú
New product development	Xīn chǎnpǐn kāifā
News conference	Jìzhě zhāodàihùi
Newspaper	Bàozhǐ
News release	Xīnwéngǎo/xīnwén fābū
Niche	Dìwèi
Niche marketing	Dìwèi tūixiāo
Opinion research	Yúlùn yánjiū
Order form	Dìngdān
Outdoor advertising	Shìwài gǔanggào
Outdoor billboards	Shìwài gàoshìpái
Packaging	Bāozhūang
PMS colors (Pantone® Matching System)	PMS yánsè
Point-of-sale advertising	Xiāoshòu diǎn gǔanggào
Premium	Chóujīn
Price	Jiàgé
Price (to)	Biāojia
Pricing	Biāojià
Product(s)	Chǎnpǐn
Product design	Chǎnpǐn shèjì
Product liability	Chǎnpǐn zérèn
Product life cycle	Chǎnpǐn zhòuqī
Product launch	Chǎnpǐn tūichū
Product mix	Chǎnpǐn hùnhé
Promotion	Cùxiāo
Prospect	Zhǎnwàng
Publicity	Xūanchúan
Public relations	Gōngguān
Publication	Chūbǎn
Qualified lead	Yǒuyòng de xiànsǔo
Radio	Shōuyīnjī
Rate(s)	Fèiyòng

Rate card	Fèiyòngkǎ
Reach	Chùjí
Readership	Dúzhě
Rebate	Húikòu
Recall	Zhàohúi
Repetition	Chóngfù
Research	Yánjiū
Research report	Yánjiū bàogào
Response(s)	Dáfù
Returns and allowances	Tùihùo yú zhékòu
Rollout	Shǒucì tūichū
Sales	Xiāoshòu
Sales analysis	Xiāoshòu fēnxī
Sales contest	Xiāoshòu jìngsài
Sales force	Xiāoshòu dùiwǔ
Sales manager	Xiāoshòu jinglǐ
Salesperson	Xiāoshòuyúan
Sales report	Xiāoshòu bàogào
Sales representative	Xiāoshòu dàibiǎo
Segmentation	Fēngē
Sell (to)	Mài
Selling	Mài
Service	Fúwù
Share of market	Shìchǎng bǐlì
Shelf life	Jiàshàng zhòuqī
Slogan	Kǒuhào
Specialty product	Tèchǎn
Sponsor	Zànzhùrén
Sponsor (to)	Zànzhù
Spot (radio and TV)	Chābō
Storyboard	Gùshì biānpáibǎn
Strategy	Zhànlùe
Subliminal advertising	Qiányìshì gǔanggào
Supplier	Gōngyìngshāng
Supply and demand	Gōng yǔ qiú
Target audience	Mùbiāo gūanzhòng
Target marketing	Yǒu mùbiāo de tūixiāo

Television	Diànshì
Test group	Cèshìqún
Test market	Cèshì shìchǎng
Trade magazine	Màoyì zázhì
Trade show	Màoyì zhǎnxiāohùi
Trail offer	Gēnzhōng chūshòu
Unit pricing	Dānjià
Universal product code system	Wàngúo chǎnpǐn biānmǎ xìtǒng
Vendor	Chūshòushāng
Wants	Xūqiú
Warehouse	Cāngkù
Warranty	Bǎodān
Web site	Wǎngzhǐ
Word-of-mouth advertising	Kǒuchúan gǔanggào

6 REFERENCE

Here's a place to find words and phrases for everything we missed in other chapters. For example, this chapter contains some critical information to keep you on schedule, such as expressions used to tell time or words for numbers.

We'll start with words and phrases we hope you'll never have to use, but in an emergency they're critical.

EMERGENCY EXPRESSIONS

Help!	Jiùmìng a!
Fire!	Zháohǔo la!
Hurry!	Gǎnkùai!
Call an ambulance!	Jiào jiùhùchē!
Call the police!	Jiào jǐngchá!
Call the fire department!	Jiào xiāofángdùi!
Stop, thief!	Zhūa zéi ya!
Stop him/her!	Lán zhù tā/tā!

Someone/he/she/they stole my . . .	Yǒu rén/tā/tā/tāmen tōu le wǒ de . . .
bag!	tíbāo!
briefcase!	gōngshìbāo!
wallet!	qiánbāo!
watch!	shǒubiǎo!
Leave me alone!	Bié pèng wǒ!
Can you help me please!	Qǐng nǐ jiùjiu wǒ!
Where's the police station?	Jǐngchájú zài nǎr?
I need a lawyer.	Wǒ xūyào lüshī.
Can I make a telephone call?	Wǒ kěyǐ dǎ gè diànhùa ma?
Do you speak English?	Nǐ shūo Yīngwén ma?
Can you tell me where the U.S. Embassy is?	Néng gàosu wǒ Měigúo Dàshǐguǎn zài nǎr ma?

TELLING TIME

In the United States, most offices use *A.M.* and *P.M.* after the number to distinguish between morning, and afternoon hours, for instance 9:00 A.M. and 9:00 P.M. Elsewhere, however, the 24-hour system is often used in offices and for other official purposes. For instance, following noon, the hours are 13, 14, etc. as opposed to 1, 2, etc. An easy way to keep this straight is to subtract or add 12 to the hours you're accustomed to. For instance, if someone says 15:00 hours (spoken as 15 hundred hours), you know that it's 3:00 P.M. Likewise, if it's 2:00 P.M. you add 12 to get 14:00 hours. The U.S. army adopted this system to make sure there would be no misunderstanding what time was meant. But for business there is little confusion. When we say we'll meet for at 4, we know that it's P.M. not A.M.

What time is it?	**Xiànzài jǐdiǎn zhōng?**
It's 10:30 A.M.	**Shàngwǔ shí diǎn sānshí.**
It's exactly 9:00 A.M.	Shàngwǔ jiǔ diǎn zhěng.
Shortly after 10:00 A.M.	Shàngwǔ shídiǎn gùo yì diǎn.
Around noon.	**Zhōngwǔ shíhòu.**
What year is it?	**Xiànzài shì něi yì nián?**
It's year 2002.	**Shì èr líng líng èr nián.**
What time do we begin?	**Wǒmen shénme shíjiān kāishǐ?**
We begin at 10:30 sharp.	**Wǒmen shí diǎn sānshí kāishǐ.**
The meeting will start at . . .	**Hùiyì jiāng zài . . . kāishǐ.**
The meeting will end at . . .	**Hùiyì jiāng zài . . . jiéshù.**
It's break time.	**Xiànzài shì xiūxí shíjiān.**
We will have a coffee break at . . .	Wǒmen zài . . . xiūxi hē kāfēi.
Lunch will be served at . . .	Wǔfàn zài . . . kāishǐ.
Lunch will last . . .	Wǔfàn yào . . . de shíjiān.
I'm early./It's early.	**Wǒ lái zǎo le./**Hái zǎo.
I'm on time./It's on time.	**Wǒ ànshí lái le./**Ànshí.
I'm late./It's late.	**Wǒ lái chí le./**Wǎn le.
I'm too late./It's too late.	**Wǒ lái de tài chí le./**Tài chí le.
Is this clock right?	**Zhè ge zhōng zhǔn ma?**
It's running slow/fast.	**Zhè ge màn/**kùai le.
It's five minutes slow/ fast.	Màn/kùai le wǔ fēn zhōng.
When will it start?	**Shénme shíjiān kāishǐ?**
In about two minutes.	**Dàgài liǎng fēn zhōng nèi.**
In five minutes.	Wǔ fēn zhōng nèi.
In one hour.	Yì gè xiǎoshí nèi.
In a half hour.	Bàn gè xiǎoshí nèi.

In a quarter hour.	**Shíwǔ fēn zhōng nèi.**
In an hour and a half.	**Yī gè bàn xiǎoshí nèi.**
Tomorrow/after tomorrow/in three days.	**Míngtiān.**/Hòutiān./Sān tiān yǐnèi.
Next week/month/year.	Xià zhōu/yuè/(míng)nián.
Soon.	Hěn kuài.
When did it happen?	**Fāshēng shénme shì le?**
Five minutes ago.	Wǔ fēn zhōng yǐqián.
A half hour ago.	Bàn xiǎoshí yǐqián.
An hour ago.	Yī ge xiǎoshí yǐqián.
Yesterday/the day before yesterday.	**Zuótiān/**Qiántiān.
Last month/year.	**Shàng ge yuè/**qùnián.
Hours/days/months/ years ago.	Jǐ xiǎoshí/tiān/yuè/nián qián.
In the middle of the night/day.	Bànyè/zhōngwǔ shífēn.
Recently.	Zuìjìn.
A long time ago.	Hěn jiǔ yǐqián.
How long did it last?	**Chíxù le duōcháng shíjiān?**
A long time.	**Hěn cháng de shíjiān.**
A short time.	Hěn duǎn de shíjiān.
A half hour.	Bàn gè xiǎoshí.
An hour.	Yī gè xiǎoshí.
For hours.	Hǎo jǐ gè xiǎoshí.
All day long.	Zhěngtiān.
All night long.	Zhěngyè.
All month.	Zhěngyuè.

For the Specific Time

It is . . .	Xiànzài shì . . .
one o'clock.	yī diǎn (zhōng).
one A.M.	shàngwǔ yī diǎn.
one P.M.	xiàwǔ yī diǎn.

one-fifteen.	yī diǎn shíwǔ fēn.
one-thirty/half past one.	**yī diǎn sānshí fēn/bàn.**
one-thirty-five/quarter to two.	yī diǎn sānshíwǔ/liǎng diǎn chà yī kè.
one-ten/ten minutes after one.	yī diǎn shí fēn/yī diǎn gùo shí fēn.
one-fifty/ten to two.	yī diǎn wǔshí/liǎng diǎn chà shí fēn.

"Shíqū"

YÚAN XIĀNSHENG: *Měigúo de shíjiān xiāngchà dūoshao?*

KÈLĀKÈ XIǍOJIE: *Wǎn shí'èr ge xiǎoshí.*

YUÁN XIĀNSHENG: *Hùan jù hùa shūo, zhèlǐ de xiàwǔ liǎng diǎn, zài . . .*

KÈLĀKÈ XIǍOJIE: *Zài jiā jiùshì zǎoshàng liǎng diǎn.*

"Getting the Time Zone Right"

MR. YUAN: *How many hours is the time difference between China and the United States?*

MS. CLARK: *China is twelve hours later than the United States.*

MR. YUAN: *In other words, when it is 2 in the afternoon here, it is . . .*

MS. CLARK: *Two in the morning back home.*

What time of day is it?	**Xiànzài shì shénme shíhòu?**
It's . . .	**Shì . . .**
dawn.	límíng shífèn.
early morning.	qīngchén.
morning.	**shàngwǔ.**
midmorning.	shàngwǔ shífèn.
late morning.	jìn zhōngwǔ.
noon.	**zhōngwǔ.**
early afternoon.	zhōngwǔ gùohòu.
midafternoon.	**xiàwǔ shífèn.**

late afternoon.	bàngwǎn shíhòu.
dusk.	húanghūn.
early evening.	cāhēi shífèn.
evening.	**wǎnshang.**
late evening.	jìn bànyè.
midnight.	**bànyè.**

DAYS OF THE WEEK

| What day of the week is it? | Jīntiān xīngqī jǐ? |
| It's . . . | Jīntiān shì . . . |

Monday.	xīngqī yī.
Tuesday.	xīngqī èr.
Wednesday.	xīngqī sān.
Thursday.	xīngqī sì.
Friday.	xīngqī wǔ.
Saturday.	xīngqī liù.
Sunday.	xīngqī tiān.

Weekday	**Zhōurì**
Weeknight	**Zhōuyè**
Weekend	**Zhōumò**

Yesterday	**Zuótiān**
The day before yesterday	**Qiántiān**
Today	**Jīntiān**
Tomorrow	**Míngtiān**
The day after tomorrow.	**Hòutiān**

Last week	**Shàngzhōu**
This week	**Běnzhōu**
Next week	**Xiàzhōu**

| On Tuesday | **Xīngqī èr** |
| Next Thursday | **Xià xīngqī sì** |

| When does it take place? | Shénme shíhòu fāshēng de? |

| Every Tuesday/Tuesdays. | **Měi gè xīngqī èr.** |
| Once/twice/three times a week/month/year. | **Měi zhōu/yuè/nián yī/èr/ sān cì.** |

MONTHS OF THE YEAR

| What month is it? | Xiànzài shì jǐ yuè . . . ? |
| It's . . . | Shì . . . |

January.	yī yuè.
February.	èr yuè.
March.	sān yuè.
April.	sì yuè.
May.	wǔ yuè.
June.	liù yuè.
July.	qī yuè.
August.	bā yuè.
September.	jiǔ yuè.
October.	shí yuè.
November.	shíyī yuè.
December.	shí'èr yuè.

Last month	Shàngyuè
This month	Běnyuè
Next month	Xiàyuè

| Two months ago | Liǎng gè yuè qián |
| In a month | Yī gè yuè nèi |

SEASONS OF THE YEAR

| What season is it? | Zhè shì shénme jìjié? |
| It's . . . | Shì . . . |

spring.	chūntiān.
summer.	xiàtiān.
fall.	qiūtiān.
winter.	dōngtiān.

last year.	qùnián.
this year.	jīnnián.
next year.	míngnián.

| two years ago. | liǎng nián qián. |
| in two years. | liǎng nián nèi. |

ORDINAL NUMBERS

What position is it?	Shénme wèizhì?
It's . . .	Shì . . .
first.	dì yī.
second.	dì èr.
third.	dì sān.
fourth.	dì sì.
fifth.	dì wǔ.
sixth.	dì liù.
seventh.	dì qī.
eighth.	dì bā.
ninth.	dì jiǔ.
tenth.	dì shí.

CARDINAL NUMBERS

0 líng	
1 yī	21 èrshí yī
2 èr	22 èrshí èr
3 sān	23 èrshí sān
4 sì	24 èrshí sì
5 wǔ	25 èrshí wǔ
6 liu	26 èrshí liù
7 qī	27 èrshí qī
8 bā	28 èrshí bā
9 jiǔ	29 èrshí jiǔ
10 shí	30 sānshí
11 shíyī	40 sìshí
12 shí'èr	50 wǔshí
13 shísān	60 liùshí
14 shísì	70 qīshí
15 shíwǔ	80 bāshí
16 shíliù	90 jiǔshí
17 shíqī	100 yī bǎi
18 shíbā	200 èr bǎi
19 shíjiǔ	210 èr bǎi yīshí
20 èrshí	

1,000	yī qiān
10,000	yī wàn
100,000	shí wàn
1,000,000	bǎi wàn
100,000,000	yī yì/yī wànwan
½	èr fēn zhī yī
⅓	sān fēn zhī yī
¼	sì fēn zhī yī
⅕	wǔ fēn zhī yī
⅒	shí fēn zhī yī
⅟₁₀₀	bǎi fēn zhī yī
0.1	líng diǎn yī
0.2	líng diǎn èr
0.25	líng diǎn wǔ
0.5	líng diǎn èr wǔ
0.75	líng diǎn qī wǔ

BASIC MATHEMATICAL TERMS

Absolute value	Júedùi zhí
Acute angle	Rùijiǎo
Add (to)	Jiā
Addition	Jiā
Algebra	Dàishù
Algorithm	Sùanfǎ
Amortize	Tānhúan
Angle	Jiǎo
Approximation	Jìnsì zhí
Area	Miànjī
Asymptote	Jiàn jìn xiàn
Average	Píngjūn
Axis (horizontal/vertical)	Zhóu (héng/zòng)/Zhóu xiàn

Bell-curve	Língxíng qūxiàn
Binary	Èr jìn wèi zhì
Bimodal distribution	Shūangfēng fēnbù
Binomial	Èrxiàngshì
Boolean algebra	Lúojì dàishù
Breakeven analysis	Píngzhí fēnxī

Calculate (to)	Jìsùan
Calculator	Jìsùanqì
Calculus	Wēijīfēnxué
Cardinal number	Jīshù
Chaos theory	Wú zhìxù lǐlùn
Chi-square test	Chi píngfāng cèshì
Circumference	Yúanzhōu
Coefficient	Xìshù
Compound interest	Fùlì
Concave	Āomiàntǐ
Count (to)	Jìshù
Cone	Yúanzhūitǐ
Congruent	Héshì de
Constant	Héngshù
Convex	Tūmiàntǐ
Correlation	Guanliánshù
Cube	Lìfāng
Cubed root	Lìfānggēn
Cylinder	Yúanzhùtǐ
Decimal	Xiǎoshù
Delta	Sānjiǎo
Denominator	Fēnmǔ
Dependent variable	Yìngbiànliàng
Depth	Shēndù
Derivative	Yánshēngshù
Diameter	Zhíjìng
Difference	Chā'é
Differentiation	Qūbié
Digit	Shùwèi
Dispersion	Fēnsàn
Divide (to)	Chúyǐ
Division	Chú
Ellipsis	Shěnglüèfǎ
Elliptical	Tǔoyúan de
Equation	Děngshì
Exponent	Zhǐshù

Factor	Yīnzi
Factorial	Jiēchéng
F distribution	F fēnbù
Formula	Gōngshì
Fraction	Fēnshù
Future value	Wèilái zhí
Geometry	Jǐhéxúe
Geometric figure	Jǐhé túxíng
Geometric progression	Jǐhé jìshù
Geometric shape	Jǐhé xíngzhùang
Height	Gāodù
Histogram	Jǔxíngtú
Hyperbola	Shūangqūxiàn
Hypotenuse	Zhíjiǎo xiébiān
Hypothesis	Jiǎdìng
Imaginary number	Xūshù
Independent variable	Zìbiànliàng
Inequalities	Bùděngshì
Infinity	Wúqióngdà
Inflection point	Gǔaidiǎn
Integer	Zhěngshù
Integral	Jīfēn
Integration	Jīfēnfǎ
Interest	Lìxí
Interval	Qūjiān
Inverse	Fǎn de
Irrational number	Wúlǐshù
Length	Chángdù
Linear	Xiànxíng
Linear programming	Xiànxíng chéngxù
Logarithm	Dùishù
Matrix	Jǔzhèng
Mean	Píngjūn
Median (value)	Zhōng (zhí)
Multiple	Bèishù
Multiplication	Chéngfǎ
Multiply (to)	Chéngyǐ

Net present value	Shízhí
Nominal	Èdìng de/míngyì shàngde
Null hypothesis	Líng shèdìng
Numerator	Fēnzǐ
Obtuse angle	Dùnjiǎo
Octagon	Bābiānxíng
Optimization	Yōuhùa
Ordinal number	Xùshù
Origin	Yúandiǎn
Outline	Wàixíng
Parabola	Pāowùxiàn
Parameter	Cānshù
Parallel	Píngxíng
Parallelogram	Píngxíng sìbiānxíng
Pascal's triangle	Pāsīkǎ sānjiǎoxíng
Pentagon	Wǔjiǎoxíng
Percent	Bǎifēnlù
Percentage	Bǎifēnbǐ
Perpendicular	Chéng zhíjiǎo de
Pi	Yúanzhōu fúhào
Plain	Píngmiàn
Polygon	Dūobiānxíng
Polynomial	Dūoxiàngshì
Power	Gōnglù
Prism	Léngzhù
Present value	Cúnzàizhí
Probability	Gàilù
Proportion	Bǐlì
Pyramid	Jiǎozhūi
Quadratic equation	Èr cì fāngchéngshì
Quotient	Shāng
R squared	R fāngzhèn
Radical sign	Gēnhào
Radius	Bànjìng
Random	Súiyì de
Random number	Súijīshù
Range	Qūyù

Rational number	Yǒulǐshù
Ratio	Bǐlì
Real	Shíshù
Reciprocal	Hùfǎnde
Rectangular	Chángfāngxíng de
Regression line	Húiguīxiàn
Rhomboid	Cháng líng xíng
Rhombus	Língxíng
Right angle	Zhíjiǎo
Sample	Chōuyàng
Scientific notation	Kēxúe jìlù
Sigma	Sìgémǎ
Significance	Yǒuxiàoshù
Six sigma	Liù cì sìgémǎ
Skewed distribution	Biànxíng fēnbù/piānxié fēnbù
Sphere	Qiúmiàn
Square	Píngfāng
Square of a number	Shù de píngfāng
Square root	Píngfānggēn
Standard deviation	Biāozhǔn piānchā
Statistics	Tǒngjìshù
Student's t	Xúeshēng de t
Subtract (to)	Jiǎn
Subtraction	Jiǎnfǎ
Sum	Jiā
T-test	t cèshì
Tridimensional	Sān wèi tǐ
Variable	Biànshù
Vector	Xiàngliàng
Volume	Tǐjī
Weight	Zhòngliàng
Weighted average	Jiāquán píngjūn
Width	Kūandù
Zero	Líng

ACRONYMS AND ABBREVIATIONS

ABA American Bankers Association — Měiguó Yínhángjiā Xiéhùi

AD&D accidental death and dismemberment — chēhùo sǐwáng yǔ shānghài

ADEA Age Discrimination in Employment Act — Zhígōng Niánlíng Qíshì Fǎ

ADP automated data processing — zìdòng shùjù chùlǐ

AFL-CIO American Federation of Labor–Congress of Industrial Organizations — Měiguó láogōng liánhé hùi–Chǎnyè gōnghùi liánhé hùi

AI artificial intelligence — Réngōng zhìnéng

AICPA American Institute of Certified Public Accountants — Měiguó Yǒuzhèng Kùaijì Xiéhùi

AMA American Management Association — Měiguó Gǔanlǐ Xiéhùi

AMEX American Stock Exchange — Měiguó Gǔpiào Jiāoyì Sǔo

APB Accounting Principles Board — Kùaijì Gūizé Wěiyúanhùi

APR annual percentage rate — nián lìlǜ

ARM adjustable rate mortgage — kě tiáo xìng dǐyā lǜ

ASAP as soon as possible — jìnkùai

ASTD American Society for Training and Development — Měiguó Péixùn Kāifā Wěiyúanhùi

ATM automated teller machine	zìdòng tíkuǎnjī
BBB Better Business Bureau	Shāngwù Guǎnlí Wěiyuánhuì
BBS bulletin board system	gōnggào diànnǎo xìtǒng
BLS Bureau of Labor Statistics	Láogōng Tǒngjìjú
bps bits per second	měi miǎo . . . wèiyuán
BOL or B/L bill of lading	tídān
CAD/CAM computer-aided design/computer-aided manufacturing	diànnǎo xiézhù shèjì yǔ jiāgōng/zhì zào
CAI computer-aided instruction	diànnǎo fǔzhù zhǐdǎo
CAPM capital asset pricing model	zīchǎn dìngjià móshì
cc copy	fùyìn
CD Compact disc or certificate of deposit	léishè chàngpiān huò dìngqī cúnkuǎn
CD-ROM compact disc, read-only memory	wéidú guāngdié
CEO chief executive officer	zuìgāo jīngyíng zhǎngguān
CERN Conseil Européen pour la Recherche Nucléaire	Ōuzhōu Hézi Yánjiū Gùwèn Wěiyuánhuì
CFO chief financial officer	zuìgāo cáiwù zhǎngguān
CIF cost, insurance, and freight	daò'ànjià

CIS Commonwealth of Independent States	Dúlì guóxié
CISC Complex Instruction Set Computer	Fùshù Zhǐlìng Xìtǒng Diànnǎo
c/o care of	yóu . . . zhuǎnjiāo
CO certificate of occupancy	zhànyǒu zhèngmíngshū
COBOL Common Business Oriented Language	pǔtōng shāngyòng yǔyán
COD cash on delivery or collect on delivery	huò dào jí fù
COLA cost-of-living allowance	shēnghuò feìyòng tiáozhěng
COO chief operating officer	zùigāo yùnzùo guǎnlǐyuán
CPA certified public accountant	yǒuzhèng kùaijìshī/zhí zhào kùaijìshī
CPI Consumer Price Index	xiaofèi wùjià zhǐshù
cpi characters per inch	měi cùn zìshù
CPM Cost per thousand	měi qiān chéngběn
CPS characters per second	měi miǎo zìshù
CPU central processing unit	zhōngyāng chǔlǐ dānyuán
CRT cathode ray tube	yīnjí xiàngǔan
CUSIP Committee on Uniform Securities Identification Procedures	Tǒngyī Gǔpiào Rènzhèng Chéngxù Wěiyúanhùi
D&B Dun & Bradstreet report (credit report on a company)	D&B gōngsī xìnyòng bàogào

DDB double-declining-balance depreciation — shuāngchóng jiǎndī jiéyú zhéjiù

DJIA Dow-Jones Industrial Average — Dàoqióng Gōngyè Zhǐshù

DOS disk operating system — cídié cāozuò xìtǒng

DOT Department of Transportation *or* designated order turnaround — Yùnshūbù huò zhǐdìng dìngdān huíshōu

DP data processing — shùjù chǔlǐ

DTP desktop publishing — zhuōshàng chūbǎn

EAFE Europe, Australia, Far East — Ōuzhōu, Āodàlìyà, Yuǎndōng

EAP employee assistance program — zhígōng fǔzhù xiàngmù

EC European Community — Ōuméng Gòngtóngtǐ

EEC European Economic Community — Ōuzhōu Jīngjì Gòngtóngtǐ

EFT electronic funds transfer — diànhuì

EIB Export-Import Bank — Jìnchūkǒu Yínháng

EMU European Economic and Monetary Union — Ōuzhōu Jīngjì Huòbì Liánméng

EOQ economic order quantity — jīngjì dìngdān shùliàng

EU European Union — Ōuzhōu Liánméng

FAA Federal Aviation Administration — Liánbāng Fēixíng Guǎnlǐ Wěiyúanhuì

FAQ frequently asked question — wèndálán

194

FAS free alongside (ship)	chúanbiān miǎnfèi/chúan biān jiāohùo
FASB Financial Accounting Standards Board	Cáikùai Biāozhǔn Wěiyúanhùi
fax facsimile	chúanzhēn
FDA Food and Drug Administration	Shípǐn Yàowù Gǎunlǐ Jú
Fed Federal Reserve System	Liánchǔhùi
FedEx Federal Express	Liánbāng Kùaidì Gōngsī
FIFO first in, first out	xiānjìn, xiānchū
FMV fair market value	shìchǎng hélǐ jiàgé
FOB free on board	lǐ'ànjià
FORTRAN Formula Translation	gōngshì fānyì chéngxù yǔyán
FTP file transfer protocol	wénjiàn chúansòng xiéyì
FV future value	wèilái jiàzhí
FYI for your information	gòng nǐ cānkǎo
G or GB gigabyte	qiān zhào wèiyúan
G-7 Group of Seven nations	qī gúo jítúan
G-10 Group of Ten nations	shí gúo jítúan
GAAP generally accepted accounting principles	gúojì gōngrèn kùaijì yúanzé
GATT General Agreement on Tariffs and Trade	Gūanmào Zǔzhī/gūanshùi jí màoyì zǒngxiédìng
GDP Gross Domestic Product	gúomín shēngchǎn zǒngzhí

GIM gross income multiplier	zǒng shōurù zēngzhí
GRM gross rent multiplier	zǒng zūjīn zēngzhí
GTC good till canceled	bǎoliú zhídào qǔxiāo
GUI graphical user interface	túxíng shǐyòng jièmiàn
HDTV high-definition television	gāo mìdù diànshì
HMO health maintenance organization	yīliǎo jiànkāng zǔzhī
HR human resources	rénshì guǎnlǐ
HTML hypertext markup language	chāowénběn biāojì yǔyán
HTTP hypertext transfer protocol	chāo wénjiàn chuánshū xiédìng
Hz hertz	hézī
IMF International Monetary Fund	Gúojì Hùobì Jījīnhùi
Inc. Incorporated	zǔchéng gōngsī/gǔfèn yǒuxiànde
I/O input/output	shūrù shūchū
IP Internet protocol	wǎngjì xiédìng
IPO initial public offering	xīngǔ
IRC Internet Relay Chat	wǎngjì chuánsòng dùihùa
IRR internal rate of return	nèibù húishōu lǜ
ISBN International Standard Book Number	Gúojì Biāozhǔn Shūhào

ISDN Integrated Services Digital Network	zhěngtǐ fúwù shùwèi wǎnglùo
ISSN International Standard Serial Number	Gúojì Biāozhǔn Biān Hào
ITC International Trade Commission	Gúojì Màoyì Wěiyúanhùi
ITO International Trade Organization	Gúojì Màoyì Zǔzhī
JIT just-in-time inventory *or* just-in-time manufacturing	zùixīn wùpǐn qīngdān zuìxīn jiāgōng
K or KB kilobyte	qiānzìjié
LAN local area network	quyù wǎnglúo
LAWN local area wireless network	qūyù wúxiàn wǎnglúo
LBO leveraged buyout	jièdài mǎixìa/jǔzhài shōumǎi
L/C letter of credit	xìnyòngzhèng
LCD liquid crystal display	yèjīng xiǎnshì
LED light-emitting diode	gūang èr jí jǔan
LIBOR London Interbank Offer Rate	Lúndūn Yínháng Bàojià
LIFO last in, first out	zùihòu jìn, zùi xiān chū
LTC less than carload	dī yú zhūangzài liàng
LTV loan to value ratio	dàikǔan jiàzhí bǐlì
MB or Megs megabyte	bǎiwàn wèiyúanzǔ/zhào szìjié
MBO management by objective	mùdì gǔanlǐ fāngshì
MFN most favored nation	yōuhùi gúo

MHz megahertz	bǎiwànhè
MICR magnetic ink character recognition	címò zìfú shìbié
MIPS million instructions per second	měi miǎo bǎiwàn zhǐlìng
MIS management information systems	xìnxī guǎnlǐ xìtǒng
MLM multilevel marketing	dūo céngcì tūixiāo
MPT Modern Portfolio Theory	xiàndài gǔpiào zǔhé lǐlùn
NAFTA North American Free Trade Agreement	Běiměi Zìyóu Màoyì Xiédìng
NASA National Aeronautics and Space Administration	Gúojiā Hángtiān Jú
NASD National Association of Securities Dealers	Gúojiā Zhèngqùan Jīngjìrén Xiéhùi
NASDAQ National Association of Securities Dealers Automated Quotation	Gúojiā Zhèngqùan Jīngjìrén Xiéhùi Zìdòng Bàojià Xìtǒng
NAV net asset value	zīchǎn jìngzhí
NOI net operating income	yíngyè jìng shōurù
NOL net operating loss	yíngyè jìng sǔnshī
NPV net present value	jìng xiànzhí
ns nanosecond	háowēimiǎo
NYSE New York Stock Exchange	Nǐuyūe Zhèngqùan Jiāoyìsǔo

OBL ocean bill of lading	hǎiyùn tídān
OCR optical character recognition	guāngfú shìbié
OECD Organization for Economic Cooperation and Development	Jīngjì Hézùo Kāifā Zǔzhī
OEM original equipment manufacturer	yúan shèbèi shēngchǎn chǎngjiā
OJT on-the-job training	xiànchǎng péixùn
OPEC Organization of Petroleum Exporting Countries	Shíyóu Shūchūgúo Zǔzhī
OPM other people's money	tārén de qián
P&L profit and loss	sǔnyìbiǎo
PBX private branch exchange	sīrén jiāohùan
PC personal computer	gèrén diànnǎo
PCS personal communications services	gèrén tōngxùn fúwù
PDA personal digital assistant	xiǎoxíng shùzì diànnǎo
P/E price/earnings	jiàgé yǔ sǔodé de bǐlǜ
PERT Program Evaluation Review Technique	Xiàngmù Píngshěn Jìqiǎo
PGIM potential gross income multiplier	zēngjiā zǒng shōurù de qiánlì
PIN personal identification number	gèrén shēnfèn hàomǎ
PMS Pantone® matching system	pèisè xìtǒng

POP point-of-purchase	màidiǎn xiǎnshì
PPP purchasing power parity	gòumǎilì bǐzhí
prefab prefabricated house	yùzhìfáng
PV present value	xiànzhí
R&D research and development	yánjiū yú kāifā
RAM random-access memory	súijī cúnqǔ jìyìtǐ
RFP request for proposal	sǔoqǔ jiànyì
RGB red, green, and blue	hóng, lǜ, lán
RIF reduction in force	jiǎnshǎo shìlì
ROI return on investment	tóuzī húibào
ROM read-only memory	wéidú jìyìtǐ
SDRs special drawing rights	tèshū tíkǔan qúanlì
SIG special interest group	tèshū lìyì qún
SKU stock-keeping unit	gǔpiào bǎocún dānyúan
SLIP Serial Line Internet Protocol	chùanxiàn wǎngjì xiédìng
SMSA Standard Metropolitan Statistical Area	Biāozhǔn Dūshì Tǒngjì Qūyù
SOP standard operating procedure	biāozhǔn jīngyíng chéngxù
spec on speculation	tūixiǎng
SYD sum-of-the-year's-digits depreciation	niándù shùwèi zhéjiù shù
T or TB terabyte	zhàozhàowèi

T&E travel and entertainment expense	lǚxíng yǔ yúlè fèiyòng
TIN taxpayer identification number	fùshùi shēnfèn hàomǎ
TQM Total Quality Management	zhílìang gǔanlǐ
UPC Universal Product Code	Tǒngyī Chǎnpǐn Biānmǎ
URL uniform resource locator	jūnyún zīyúan dìngwèi
VAT value-added tax	zēngzhí shùi
VGA video graphic array	túxíng shùzǔ
VP vice president	fù zǒngcái
WAIS Wide Area Information Server	Gǔangyù Wǎnglùo Xìnxī Sìfùqì
WWW World Wide Web	Qúanqiú Zīxùnwǎng
WYSIWYG what you see is what you get	shì shénme jiù xiǎnshì shénmc
YTD year-to-date	qùnlǎn qijm
ZBB zero based budgeting	língjī yùsùan

COUNTRIES, CONTINENTS AND LANGUAGES

Countries

Argentina	Āgēntíng
Australia	Àodàlìyà
Bolivia	Bōlíwěiyà
Brazil	Bāxī
Canada	Jiānádà
Chile	Zhìlì
China	Zhōnggúo

Colombia	Gēlúnbǐyà
Costa Rica	Gēsīdálíjiā
Cuba	Gǔbā
Dominican Republic	Duōmíníjiā gònghéguó
Ecuador	Èguāduō'ér
Egypt	Āijí
El Salvador	Sā'rwǎduō
England	Yīngguó
Finland	Fēnlán
France	Fǎguó
Germany	Déguó
Great Britain	Dàbùlièdiān
Greece	Xīlà
Guatemala	Guādìmǎlā
Haiti	Hǎidì
Holland	Hèlán
Honduras	Hóngdūlāsī
Hungary	Xiōngyàlì
Iceland	Bīngdǎo
Iran	Yīláng
Iraq	Yīlākè
Ireland	Ài'ěrlán
Israel	Yǐsèlìe
Italy	Yìdàlì
Japan	Rìběn
Malaysia	Mǎláixīyà
Mexico	Mòxīgē
Morocco	Móluógē
Nicaragua	Níjiālāguā
Norway	Nuówēi
Panama	Bānámǎ
Paraguay	Bālāguī
Peru	Mìlǔ
Poland	Bōlán
Portugal	Pútáoyá
Puerto Rico	Bōduōlígē
Romania	Lúomǎníyà
Russia	Égúo

Saudi Arabia	Shātè ālābó
South Africa	Nánfēi
Spain	Xībānyá
Sweden	Ruìdiǎn
Switzerland	Ruìshì
Thailand	Tàiguó
Taiwan	Táiwān
Turkey	Tú'ěrqí
Ukraine	Wūkèlán
United States of America	Měiguó
Uruguay	Wūlāguī
Venezuela	Wěinèiruìlā

Continents

Africa	Fēizhōu
North America	Běiměizhōu
South America	Nánměizhōu
Asia	Yàzhōu
Australia	Àodàlìyà
Antarctica	Nánjí
Europe	Ōuzhōu

Languages

Arabic	Ālābóyǔ
Bengali	Mèngjiālāyǔ
Chinese	Hànyǔ
English	Yīngyǔ
Finnish	Fēnlányǔ
French	Fǎyǔ
Greek	Xīlàyǔ
German	Déyǔ
Hebrew	Xībóláiyǔ
Hungarian	Xiōngyàlìyǔ
Hindi	Yìndùyǔ
Italian	Yìdàlìyǔ
Japanese	Rìyǔ
Korean	Hángúoyǔ

Malay	Mǎláiyǔ
Polish	Bōlányǔ
Portuguese	Pútāoyáyǔ
Russian	Éyǔ
Spanish	Xībānyáyǔ
Swedish	Rùidiǎnyǔ
Thai	Tàigúoyǔ
Turkish	Tú'ěrqíyǔ
Ukranian	Wūkèlányǔ

APPENDIX A: Measurements

MILES/KILOMETERS

1 kilometer (km) = 0.62 miles

1 mile = 1.61 km (1,61 km)

Kilometers	1	5	8	10	15	20	50	75	100	150	200
Miles	0.62	3.1	5	6.2	9.3	12.4	31	46.5	62	93	124

GALLONS/LITERS

1 liter (l) = 0.26 gallon

1 gallon = 3.75 liters (3,75 l)

Liters	10	15	20	30	40	50	60	70
Gallons	2.6	3.9	5.2	7.8	10.4	13	15.6	18.2

WOMEN'S CLOTHING SIZES

Coats, dresses, suits, skirts, slacks

U.S.	4	6	8	10	12	14	16
Europe	36	38	40	42	44	46	48
China	32	34	36	38	40	42	44

Blouses/Sweaters

U.S.	32/6	34/8	36/10	38/12	40/14	42/16
Europe	38/2	40/3	42/4	44/5	46/6	48/7
China	34	36	38	40	42	44

Shoes

U.S.	4	$4^{1/2}$	5	$5^{1/2}$	6	$6^{1/2}$	7	$7^{1/2}$	8	$8^{1/2}$	9	$9^{1/2}$	10	11
Europe	35	35	36	36	37	37	38	38	39	39	40	40	41	42
China	$34^{1/2}$	35	$35^{1/2}$	36	$36^{1/2}$	37	$37^{1/2}$	38	$38^{1/2}$	39	$39^{1/2}$	40	$40^{1/2}$	41

MEN'S CLOTHING SIZES

Suits/Coats

U.S.	34	36	38	40	42	44	46	48
Europe	44	46	48	50	52	54	56	58
China	44	46	48	50	52	54	56	58

Slacks

U.S.	30	31	32	33	34	35	36	37	38	39
Europe	38	39–40	41	42	43	44–45	46	47	48–49	50
China	38	39–40	41	42	43	44–45	46	47	48–49	50

Shirts

U.S.	14	$14^{1/2}$	15	$15^{1/2}$	16	$16^{1/2}$	17	$17^{1/2}$	18
Europe	36	37	38	39	40	41	42	43	44
China	35/36	37	38	39	40	41	42	43	44

Sweaters

U.S.	XS/36	S/38	M/40	L/42	XL/44
Europe	42/2	44/3	46–48/4	50/5	52–54/6
China	42/2	44/3	46–48/4	50/5	52–54/6

Shoes

U.S.	7	$7^{1/2}$	8	$8^{1/2}$	9	$9^{1/2}$	10	$10^{1/2}$	11
Europe	39	40	41	42	43	43	44	44	45
China	$39^{1/2}$	40	41	$41^{1/2}$	42	$42^{1/2}$	43	$43^{1/2}$	44

WEIGHTS AND MEASURES

Weight

Metric

1 gram (g) = 0.035 ounce
100 g = 3.5 ounces
1 kilogram (kg) = 2.2 pounds

U.S.

1 ounce = 28.35 g
1 pound = 454 g
100 pounds = 45.4 kg

Liquid

Metric

1 liter (l) = 4.226 cups
1 l = 2.113 pints
1 l = 1.056 quarts
1 l = 0.264 gallon

U.S.

1 cup = 0.236 liter
1 pint = 0.473 l
1 quart = 0.947 l
1 gallon = 3.785 l

TEMPERATURE CONVERSIONS

**To Convert
Celsius to Fahrenheit**

$(9/5)$ C° + 32 = F°
1. Divide by 5
2. Multiply by 9
3. Add 32

**To Convert
Fahrenheit to Celsius**

$(F° - 32)$ $5/9$ = C°
1. Subtract 32
2. Divide by 9
3. Multiply by 5

Celsius	-17.8	0	10	15.6	23.9	30	37	100
Fahrenheit	0	32	50	60	75	86	98.6	212

APPENDIX B:
Useful Addresses, Telephone Numbers and Web Sites

Emergency Telephone Numbers in China

Ambulance	120
Fire	119
Information	114
Police	110

Embassies and Consulates

Chinese Embassies and Consulates:

The Embassy of the People's Republic of China	2300 Connecticut Ave., N.W. Washington, DC 20008 Tel.: (202) 328–2517 Fax: (202) 328–2564
The Consulate General of the People's Republic of China New York	520 12th Ave. New York, NY 10036 Tel.: (212) 330–7409 Fax: (212) 502–0245
The Consulate General of the People's Republic of China Chicago	104 S. Michigan Ave., Suite 900 Chicago, IL 60603 Tel.: (312) 803–0097 Fax: (312) 803–0122
The Consulate General of the People's Republic of China Los Angeles	443 Shatto Place Los Angeles, CA 90020 Tel.: (213) 380–2506 Fax: (213) 380–1961

U.S. Embassy in China:

| U.S. Embassy in
Beijing | 3 Xiu Shui Bei Jie
Beijing
China 100600
Tel.: (86–10) 6532–3431 |

Chambers of Commerce

| United States
of America–
China Chamber
of Commerce | 200 West Madison Street,
Suite 2000
Chicago, IL 60606
Tel.: (312) 368–0430
Fax: (312) 368–0418
info@usccc.org
www.usccc.org |

| Chinese Chamber of
Commerce of
Los Angeles | 977 N. Broadway, G/F., #E
Los Angeles, CA 90012
Tel.: (213) 617–0396
Fax: (213) 617–2128
info@lachinesechamber.org
www.lachinesechamber.org |

| American Chamber of
Commerce in Beijing | China Resources Building,
Suite 1903
No. 8, Jianguomenbei Avenue
Beijing 100005
Tel.: (86–10) 8519–1920
Fax: (86–10) 8519–1910
mjf@amcham-china.org.cn
www.amcham-china.org.cn |

| American Chamber of
Commerce in Shanghai | The Portman Ritz-Carlton
Hotel, Suite 435 East
1376 Nanjing Road West
Shanghai 200040 |

Tel.: (86–21) 6279–7108,
6279–7119
Fax: (86–21) 6279–7643
info@amcham-shanghai.org
www.amcham-shanghai.org

Major Airlines

In the United States:

Air China
45 East 49th Street
New York, NY 10017
Tel.: (212) 371–9898, (800) 982–8802

Air China
222 N. Sepulveda Blvd., #1500
El Segundo, CA 90245
Tel.: (800) 882–8122

China Eastern Airlines
55 S. Lake Ave. #120
Pasadena, CA 91101
Tel.: (626) 583–1500

China Southern Airlines
6300 Wilshire Blvd., #101
Los Angeles, CA 90048
Tel.: (888) 338–8988

In China:

Air China
15 Chang'an Ave. West
Beijing
Domestic Reservations: (86–10) 6601–3336
Int'l Reservations: (86–10) 6601–6667
www.airchina.com.cn

China Eastern Airlines
200 West Wan An Road
Shanghai
Tel.: (86–21) 6247–5953 or (86–21) 6247–2255
www.cea.online.sh.cn

China Southern Airlines (Group)
181 Huang Shi Road
Guangzhon 510010
China
Tel.: (86–020) 8668–2000
www.cs-air.com

For more information on travel in China, contact the following offices:

China National Tourist Office, New York
350 Fifth Avenue, Suite 6413
Empire State Building
New York, NY 10118
Tel.: (212) 760–9700
Fax: (212) 760–8809

China National Tourist Office, Los Angeles
333 West Broadway, Suite 201
Glendale, CA 91204
Tel.: (818) 545–7504, 545–7505
Fax: (818) 545–7506

Useful Sites
on the Internet

CHINAONLINE, LLC
www.chinaonline.com
US-Based Web site for China Business News and Information with industry channels, daily updates, statistics and company profiles.

CHINABIG YELLOW PAGES
www.chinabig.com
This giant bilingual online business directory covers all of China and has regional and industry categories.

CHINA ENTERPRISES INFORMATION NETWORK
www.cen.com.cn
Brief introductions to selected major Chinese enterprises. Covers Chinese companies by industry category.

CHINA SECURITIES
www.chinasecurites.com.cn
Daily News and reports on selected Chinese listed companies.

MEET CHINA
www.meetchina.com
Helps Chinese and Western companies find business counterparts on-line.

SINO SOURCE
www.sinosourcc.com
Helps small to medium-size foreign businesses communicate directly with businesses in China.

TRADE EASY INTERNATIONAL
www.tradeeasy.com
A trade directory of manufacturers and exporters from China and Hong Kong.

APPENDIX C:
Chinese National Holidays

New Year's Day   January 1
Spring Festival   Usually in February
                        (follows lunar calendar)
Women's Day   March 8
Labor Day   May 1
Children's Day   June 1
The Party's Day   July 1
Army Day   August 1
National Day   October 1

APPENDIX D:
Chinese Grammar Summary

A. *Types of Questions*

1. QUESTION WORD QUESTIONS

shéi (who, whom)
Nǐ qǐng shéi chīfàn?
   Whom did you invite to dinner?

shénme (what)
Nǐmen zùo shénme?
   What are you doing?

zěnme (how, why)
Nǐ zěnme dǎ tàijíqúan?
   How do you do tai chi?

zěnme-yàng (how)
Tā de háizi zěnmeyàng?
   How is his child?

wèishénme (why)
Nǐ wèishénme bú shàngbān?
   Why aren't you going to work?

dūoshǎo (how much)
Nèi jiàn chènshān dūoshǎo qián?
   How much does this shirt cost?

jǐ (how many)
Nǐ yǒu jǐ zhī bǐ?
   How many pens do you have?

nǎr (where)
Nǐ de lǎojiā zài nǎr?
   Where is your hometown?

něi (which)
Nǐ xǐhuan něi wèi lǎoshī?
   Which teacher do you like?

2. ALTERNATIVE QUESTIONS

Nǐ xǐhuan bù xǐhuan tā de chènshān?
   Do you like her shirt?

Nǐ māma yǒu méiyǒu zìxíngchē?
   Does your mother have a bicycle?

3. QUESTIONS WITH PARTICLES

Nǐ hǎo <u>ma</u>?
   How are you?

Wǒ hǎo, nǐ <u>ne</u>?
   I'm fine, and you?

4. TAG QUESTIONS

Wǒmen qù chīfàn, hǎo bù hǎo?
   Let's go eat, okay?

Tā zhèngzài dǎ diànhuà, shì bú shì?
   He's on the phone, right?

B. Adverbs

běnlái	originally
cóng	again
cónglái	since
dōu	all
gāng (cái)	just
gēnběn	basically
hái	still
mǎshàng	at once, immediately
qǐmǎ	at least
yě	also
yīdiǎn	a little
yǐjīng	already
yòu	again
zài	again
zài	at

| **zhǐ** | only |
| **zhǐhǎo** | had better |

C. *Particles*

1. QUESTIONS PARTICLES

   ma
   Nǐ è ma?
     Are you hungry?

   ne
   Wǒ hǎo. Nǐ ne?
     I'm fine. And you?

2. SUGGESTION PARTICLES

   ba
   Wǒmen huíjiā ba.
     Let's go home.

   bié
   Nǐ bié shūohùa.
     Don't speak.

3. NEGATION PARTICLES

   bù
   Wǒ bù xǐhuan chī niúròu.
     I don't like to eat beef.

   méi
   Wǒ méiyǒu hěn dūo qián.
     I don't have much money.

4. POSSESSION PARTICLE

   de
   Nà shì wǒ de shū.
     That's my book.

5. Resultative Verb Particle

de

Nǐ shūo Zhōngwén shūo de hěn hǎo.
You speak Chinese very well.

6. "Tense" Particles

le

Tài lèi le!
Too exhausting!

Wǒ xúele sānbǎi ge zì.
I studied 300 characters.

Yínháng gūanmén le.
The bank just closed.

Hǔochē kùai zǒu le.
The train is about to leave.

gùo

Wǒ qùgùo Zhōnggúo.
I have been to China.

zhe

Chūanghu kāizhe.
The window is open.

APPENDIX E:
Essential Chinese Signs

Doctor	医生	Yīshēng
Entrance	大门	Dàmén
Exit	出口	Chūkǒu
Gas station	加油站	Jiāyóuzhàn
Hospital	医院	Yīyùan
Hotel	旅馆	Lǚgǔan
Parking	停车场	Tíngchēchǎng
Police	警察	Jǐnchá
Rent-a-car	租车场	Zūchēchǎng
Restaurant	餐馆	Cāngǔan
Rest rooms	厕所	Cèsǔo
Taxi	出租车	Chūzūchē

GLOSSARY OF
INDUSTRY-SPECIFIC TERMS

Here are various areas of commerce, government, and nongovernmental activities. Each has its particular terminology and we've offered some of the more common terms. The areas we cover are:*

Advertising and Public Relations	*Gǔanggào yǔ gōngguān*
Agriculture	*Nóngyè*
Architecture and Construction	*Jiànzhù yǔ jiànzào*
Automotive	*Qìchē*
Banking and Finance	*Yínháng yǔ cáiwù*
Computer Systems	*diànnǎo xìtǒng*
Engineering	*Gōngchéng*
Entertainment, Journalism and Media	*Yúlè, xīnwén yǔ méitǐ*
Fashion	*Shízhūang*
Government and ~~Government~~ Agencies	*Zhèngfǔ jīgòu*
Insurance	*Bǎoxiǎn*
Management Consulting	*Gǔanlǐ zīxún*
Mining and Petroleum	*Cǎikùang yú shíyóu*
Nongovernmental Agencies	*Fēi zhèngfǔ*
Perfume and Fragrance	*Xiāngshǔi yǔ xiāngwèi*
Pharmaceutical, Medical and Dental	*Zhìyào, yīliáo, yákē*
Publishing	*Chūbǎn*
Real Estate	*Fángdìchǎn*
Shipping and Distribution	*Yùnhùo yǔ fēnfā*

---

*For the terminology related to computers and computer industry see *Functional Areas of a Company* in Chapter 5.

Telecommunications (See Computer and Systems in Functional Area)	*Diànxùn*
Textile	*Fǎngzhī*
Toys	*Wánjù*
Watches, Scales and Precision Instruments	*Zhōngbiǎo, Chèng, Jīngmì Yíbiǎo*
Wine	*Jiǔ*

ADVERTISING AND PUBLIC RELATIONS

(See Marketing and Sales in *Functional Areas of Company* in Chapter 5)

Account executive	*Zhànghù zhǔguǎn*
Ad	*Guǎnggào*
Ad agency	*Guǎnggàoshè*
Ad style	*Guǎnggào fēnggé*
Ad time	*Guǎnggào shíjiān*
Advertise (to)	*Dēng guǎnggào*
Advertisement	*Guǎnggào*
Advertising	*Guǎnggào*
Advertising	*Guǎnggào*
agency	*shè*
budget	*yùsùan*
campaign	*xūanchúan/yùn dòng*
message	*xìnxí*
papers	*wénjiàn*
space	*kōngjiān*
strategy	*zhànlüè*
vehicle	*méijiè*
Air (to)/broadcast (to)	*Guǎngbō*
Audience	*Gūanzhòng*
Baseline	*Dǐxiàn*
Block of commercials	*Yī zǔ guǎnggào*
Brand-name promotion	*Pǐnpái tūiguǎng*

Broadcast times	*Gǔangbō shíjiān*
Brochure	*Xiǎocezǐ*
Campaign	*Xūanchúan/Yùn dòng*
Catalog	*Chǎnpǐn biānmù*
Commercial	*Shāngyè gǔanggào*
Commodity	*Shāngpǐn*
Competition	*Jìngzhēng*
Consumer research	*Xiāofèi yánjiū*
Cooperative advertising	*Liánhé gǔanggào*
Cost per thousand	*Měi qiān chéngběn*
Coupon(s)	*Zèngqùan*
Cover	*Fēngmiàn*
Daily (newspaper)	*Rìbào*
Depth of coverage	*Bàodào shēndù*
Direct marketing	*Zhíjiē tūixiāo*
Early adopters	*Shǒuxiān cǎiyòngzhě*
Effectiveness	*Xiàoyì*
Endorsements	*Chéngzhèny/Bèishū/ Rènkě*
Focus group	*Jiāodiǎnqún*
Free shoppers' papers	*Miǎnfèi gùkè bàozhǐ*
Infomercial	*Xìnxí gǔanggào*
In-house	*Nèibù*
Insert (to)	*Chārù*
In-store campaign	*Diànnèi xūanchúan*
Introductory campaign	*Jièshào xūanchúan*
Jingle	*Dīngdāng*
Layout	*Zhìbǎn*
Leaflet	*Chúandān*
Listenership	*Tīngzhòng*
Listening rate	*Tīngzhònglù*

Logo	*Túbiāo*
Madison Avenue	*Màidìshēn dàjiē*
Mail/Letter campaign	*Yóujiàn/Shūxìn xuānchúan*
Market	*Shìchǎng*
Market (to)	*Tūixiāo gěi*
Marketing	*Tūixiāo*
Market research	*Shìchǎng yánjiū*
Mass marketing	*Dàzhòng shìchǎng*
Media	*Méitǐ*
Media agent	*Méitǐ dàilǐ*
Media plan	*Méitǐ jìhùa*
Merchandise	*Shāngpǐn*
Merchandise (to)	*Jīngshāng*
Merchandising	*Shāngpǐn tūixiāo*
Misleading advertising	*Bùshí gǔanggào*
Niche	*Dìwèi*
Opener	*Kāi de gōngjù*
Packaging	*Bāozhūang*
Periodicals	*Qīkān*
Point-of-sale advertising	*Shòudiǎn gǔanggào*
Positioning	*Zhǎo . . . wèizhì*
Poster advertising	*Hǎibào gǔanggào*
Premium	*Èwài fèiyòng*
Presentation	*Zhǎnshì*
Press officer	*Xīnwén gūanyúan*
Press release	*Jìzhě zhāodàihùi*
Prime time	*Húangjīn shídùan*
Product	*Chǎnpǐn*
Product information	*Chǎnpǐn xìnxí*
Product life cycle	*Chǎnpǐn zhōuqī*
Professional publications	*Zhūanyè chūbǎn*
Promote (to)	*Cùjìn*
Promotion	*Cùjìn*

Public relations	*Gōngguān*
Publicity	*Gōnggào*
Readership	*Dúzhě*
Sales	*Xiāoshòu*
Sales promotion	*Cùxiāo*
Sample	*Yàngběn/Yàngpǐn*
Sample products	*Yàngpǐn*
Selection	*Tiāoxuǎn*
Share	*Gǔfèn*
Slogan	*Kǒuhào*
Space	*Kōngjiān*
Special offers	*Tèshū bàojià*
Sponsor	*Zànzhùrén*
Sponsor (to)	*Zànzhù*
Sponsorship	*Zànzhù*
Spot radio and TV ads	*Chābō yú diànshì guǎnggào*
Storyboard	*Gùshì xùshùbǎn*
Survey	*Diàochá*
Target	*Mùbiāo*
Target group	*Mùbiāoqún*
Target market	*Mùbiāo shìchǎng*
Telemarketing	*Diànhùa tūixiāo*
Test market	*Cèshì shìchǎng*
Trade show	*Màoyì zhǎnxiāohùi*
Trial	*Cèshì*
White space	*Kòngbái*
Word-of-mouth advertising	*Kǒuchúan guǎnggào*

AGRICULTURE

Acre	*Yīngmǔ*
Agronomy	*Nóngyìxúe*
Area	*Miànjī*

Arid	*Gānhàn de*
Chemicals	*Huàxúe yàopǐn*
Cotton	*Mián*
Crop(s)	*Nóngzùowù*
Cropland	*Zhūangjiadì*
Cultivate (to)	*Gēngzhòng*
Cultivation	*Gēngzhòng*
Drought	*Gānhàn*
Export	*Chūkǒu*
Farm	*Nóngchǎng*
Farm (to)	*Zhòngtián*
Farmers	*Nóngfū*
Farm income	*Nóngyè shōurù*
Farming	*Nóngyè*
Feedstock	*Sìyǎng shēngchù*
Fertilize (to)	*Shīféi*
Fertilizer(s)	*Féiliào*
Grow (to)	*Zhòngzhí*
Harvest	*Shōuhùo*
Harvest (to)	*Shōugē*
Herbicides	*Chúcǎojī*
Husbandry	*Nónyshì*
Insecticides	*Shāchóngjī*
Irrigate (to)	*Gùangài*
Irrigation	*Gùangài*
Irrigation system	*Gùangài xìtǒng*
Land	*Tǔdì*
Livestock	*Shēngchù*
Machinery	*Jīxiè*
Pesticides	*Shāchóngyào*
Plant	*Zhíwù*

Plant (to)	*Zhòngzhí*
Planting	*Zāipéi*
Plow (to)	*Lítdì*
Potatoes	*Mǎlíngshǔ/Tǔ dòu*
Price	*Jiàgé*
Price supports	*Jiàgé zhīchí*
Produce (to)	*Shēngchǎn*
Production	*Shēngchǎn*
Rice	*Dàomǐ*
Seed (to)	*Bōzhǒng*
Seeds	*Zhǒngzi*
Seed stock	*Zhǒngliào/Zhǒngzi chǔbèi*
Soil	*Tǔrǎng*
Soil conservation	*Tǔrǎng bǎohù*
Store	*Chǔbèi*
Subsidy	*Bǔzhùjīn*
Surplus	*Shèngyú*
Tariff	*Gūanshùi*
Till (to)	*Gēngzùo*
Tobacco	*Yāncǎo*
Vegetables	*Shūcài*
Wheat	*Màizǐ*
Yields	*Chǎnliàng*

ARCHITECTURE AND CONSTRUCTION

Aluminum	*Lǚ*
Architect	*Jiànzhùshī*
Art	*Yìshù*
Asphalt	*Bǎiyóu*
Blueprint	*Lántú*
Brick	*Zhūan*

Brick layer	*Zhuāngōng*
Build (to)	*Xiūjiàn*
Builder	*Jiànzhù gōngrén*
Building	*Jiànzhù*
Building materials	*Jiànzhù cáiliào*
Carpenter (master/apprentice)	*Mùgōng (shīfu/xúetú)*
Cement	*Shŭiní*
Cement (to)	*Yòng shuĭní*
Chart (to)	*Zhìtú*
Cinder block	*Kōngxīnzhūan*
Computer design	*Diànnăo shèjì*
Concrete	*Hùnníngtŭ*
Construct (to)	*Jiànshè*
Construction	*Jiànshè*
Cool (to)	*Lěngqùe*
Demolish (to)	*Tūidăo*
Design	*Shèjì*
Design (to)	*Shèjì*
Designer	*Shèjìshī*
Destroy (to)	*Chāichú*
Develop (to)	*Kāifā*
Developer	*Kāifāshāng*
Dig (to)	*Wājúe*
Draft	*Căotú*
Draft (to)	*Qĭcăotú*
Drafting	*Qĭcăo*
Draw (to)	*Hùa tú*
Drawing	*Hùa*
Elevators	*Diàntī*
Engineer	*Gōngchéngshī*
Excavate (to)	*Wājúe*
Excavation	*Wājúe*

Fix (to)	*Gùdìng*
Fixture	*Gùdìngwù*
Glass	*Bōlí*
Fiber	*Xiānwéi bōlí*
Frosted	*Shūang bōlí*
Insulated	*Júeyúan bōlí*
Plexi	*Shùzhī bōlí*
See-through	*Tòumíng bōlí*
Safety	*Ānqúan bōlí*
Gravel	*Sùishí*
Heat	*Nǔanqì*
Heat (to)	*Jiārè*
Heating and Ventilation	*Nǔanqì yǔ tōngfēng*
Implement (to)	*Shíshī*
Iron	*Tiě*
Ironworks	*Tiězhìpǐn*
Joiner	*Jiéhézhě*
Joint	*Jiétóu*
Joist	*Xiǎoliáng*
Land	*Tǔdì*
Lay (to)	*Fàngzhì*
Light	*Dēnggūang*
Lighting	*Zhàomíng*
Material	*Cáiliào*
Metal	*Jīnshǔ*
Measure (to)	*Dùliàng*
Model	*Móxíng*
Mortar	*Níjiāng*
Office layout	*Bàngōngshì píng miàntú*
Paint	*Yóuqī*

Paint (to)	*Yóuqī*
Painter	*Yóuqījiàng*
Parking	*Tíngchē*
Plan (to)	*Jìhùa*
Plans	*Jìhùa*
Plasterer	*Níshǔijiàng*
Plastic	*Sùjiāo/Sùliào*
Plumber	*Shǔigǔangōng*
Refurbish (to)	*Hùanxīn*
Renovate (to)	*Shūaxīn/Zhūangxiū*
Repair (to)	*Xiūfù*
Replace (to)	*Gēnghùan*
Rock	*Yánshí*
Steel	*Gāng*
Stone	*Shítou*
Structure	*Jiégòu*
Survey	*Diàochá*
Survey (to)	*Diàochá*
Surveyor	*Diàocháyúan*
Tile (to)	*Pūwǎ/pū cízhūan*
Tiles	*Wǎ/cízhūan*
Weather (to)	*Fēnggān*
Welder	*Hànjiēgōng*
Windows	*Chūanghù*
Wire (to)	*Ānzhūang diànxiàn*
Wood	*Mùtou*
Ebony	*Wūmù*
Cedar	*Xīyángshān/xǔe sōng*
Mahogany	*Hóngmù*
Oak	*Xiàngmù*
Pecan	*Hútáomù*
Pine	*Sōngmù*
Redwood	*Měigúo shānshù/Hóng shān shù*

AUTOMOTIVE

ABS brakes	*Fánghùa shāchē xìtǒng*
Air bag(s)	*Ānqúan qìdài*
Air cleaner	*Kōngqì qīngjiéqì*
Air filter	*Kōngqì lùqīngqì*
Air vent	*Chūqìkǒng*
Antilock brakes	*Fánghùa shāchē*
Ashtray	*Yānhūigāng*
Assembly line	*Zhūangpèixìan*
Automatic shift	*Zìdòng lúnhùan*
Automobile	*Qìchē*
Auto show	*Qìchē zhǎnxiāohùi*
Axle	*Lúnzhóu*
Backlog	*Wèi jiāofù de dìnghùo*
Bearing	*Zhóuchéng*
Belt	*Lúndài/Jiāndài/ Anqúandàí*
Blinker	*Jǐngshìdēng*
Body	*Chēshēn*
Body panel	*Chēbǎn*
Body shop	*Bǎnjīn xiūlǐdiàn/ Chē shēn xiūlǐdiàn*
Bonnet	*Bǎohùmào*
Brake	*Shāchē*
Brake (to)	*Shāchē*
Brake cylinder	*Shāchē gǔntǒng*
Bucket seat	*Āobèi zhéyǐ*
Bumper	*Hǔanchōngdǎng*
Bushing	*Zhóuchèn*
Buy (to)	*Mǎi*
Camshaft	*Tūlúnzhóu*
Car	*Jiàochē*
Carburetor	*Qìhùaqì*
Car dealer	*Qìchē jīngxiāoshāng*
Car maintenance	*Qìchē yǎnghù*

Carpet	*Dìtǎn*
Catalytic converter	*Cūihùajì zhǔanhùanqì*
CD player	*Léishè chàngpiànjī*
Chassis	*Dǐpán*
Child seat	*Értóngyǐ*
Cigarette lighter	*Xiāngyān diǎnhǔoqì/ dǎhǔojī*
Climate control	*Qūyù kōngtiáo kòngzhì*
Clock	*Zhōng*
Cockpit	*Zùocāng*
Component	*Gòujiàn*
Component stage	*Gòuzhì jiēdùan*
Computer chip	*Diànnǎo jīngpiàn*
Connecting rod	*Liánjiēgǎn*
Console	*Yíbiǎobǎn*
Consolidation	*Jiāgù*
Convertible	*Chǎngpéngchē*
Cooling system	*Lěngqùe xìtǒng*
Cooling and heating system	*Lěngnǔan xìtǒng*
Corporate average fuel economy (CAFE)	*Gōngsī píngjūn rányóu jīngjì*
Chrome	*Dùgè*
Competition	*Jìngzhēng*
Coolant	*Lěngqùejī*
Cost competitiveness	*Chéngběn jìngzhēng*
Crankshaft	*Jīzhóu*
Cream puff	*Yóugāo*
Cross member	*Héngliáng*
Cruise control	*Chēsù kòngzhì zhūangzhì*
Cup holder	*Bēijià*
Customer support	*Gùkè fúwù*
Custom made	*Dìngzùo de*
Cylinder	*Qìgāng*
Cylinder lining	*Qìgāng chèntào*

Cylinder head	*Qìgāng gài*
Dashboard	*Yíqìbǎn*
Dealers	*Jīngxiāoshāng*
Defog (to)	*Chúwù*
Defogger	*Chúwùqì*
Design	*Shèjì*
Designer	*Shèjìshī*
Diesel	*Cháiyóu*
Differential	*Chābié*
Dimmer switch	*Jiǎnguāng kāiguān*
Displacement	*Huànzhì*
Distributor	*Fēnpèiqì*
Door	*Chēmén*
Door handle	*Mén bǎshǒu*
Door lock	*Ménsǔo*
Door panel	*Chēmén miànbǎn*
Drive (to)	*Kāichē*
Driver's seat	*Jiàshǐyúan zùoyǐ*
Driver training	*Jiàshǐ péixùn*
Electrical harness	*Diàndòng mǎjù*
Electrical system	*Diànlì xìtǒng*
Electronic systems	*Diànzǐ xìtǒng*
Emergency flasher	*Jǐnjí shǎnliàngdēng*
Emission system	*Páiqì xìtǒng*
Engine	*Yǐnqíng*
Engine block	*Yǐnqíng qìgāngtǐ*
Engine cradle	*Yǐnqínglán*
Engineer	*Gōngchéngshī*
Engineering	*Gōngchéng*
Environmental protection agency	*Húanbǎo jīgòu*
Exhaust	*Páiqì*
Exhaust manifold	*Páiqì qígǔan*
Exhaust system	*Páiqì xìtǒng*

Experimental design	*Shìyàn shèjì*
Exterior	*Wàibiǎo*
Fabricate (to)	*Zhìzùo*
Fabrication	*Zhìzùo*
Fan	*Fēngshàn*
Fiberglass	*Xiānwéi bōlí*
Fill (to)	*Jiāmǎn*
Finish	*Wánchéng*
Four-door	*Sì mén de*
Frame	*Chējià*
Fuel	*Rányóu*
Fuel gage	*Rányóubiǎo*
Fuel pump	*Rányóubèng*
Fuel tank	*Rányóuxiāng*
Fuse	*Bǎoxiǎnsī*
Fuse box	*Bǎoxiǎnsī hé*
Garage	*Chēkù*
Gasket	*Diànqūan*
Gas	*Qìyóu*
Gas cap	*Qìyóuxiāng gài*
Gas tank	*Qìyóuxiāng*
Gauge	*Liánggūi*
Gear	*Chǐlín*
Gear shift	*Hùandǎng jīgòu*
Glove compartment	*Shǒugōngjùxiāng*
Headlight	*Dàdēng/Qiándōng*
Headrest	*Tóuzhěn/Tánxìng tóudiàn*
Heating system	*Nǔanqì xìtǒng*
High beam	*Yǔangūangdēng*
Hood	*Yǐnqínggài*
Hood ornament	*Jīzhào zhūangshìpǐn*
Hubcaps	*Lúngǔzhào*

Indicator lights	*Zhǐshìdēng*
Interior	*Nèibù*
Instrument panel	*Yíbiǎobǎn*
Intake manifold	*Jìnqì qígǔan*
Inventory	*Wùpǐn qīngdān*
Jack	*Qiānjīndǐng*
Jobber	*Línggōng*
Key	*Yàoshi*
Labor	*Láogōng*
Leather	*Pígé*
Lemon	*Níngméng*
Lights	*Dēng*
Light truck	*Qīngxíng kǎchē*
Light vehicle	*Qīngxíng chē*
Lock	*Sǔo*
Lock (to)	*Sǔo*
Look (to)	*Kàn*
Lot	*Dìpǐ*
Machine shop	*Jīqì chējiān*
Machining	*Jīxiè*
Maintenance	*Wéixiū*
Make (to)	*Zhìzùo*
Manual	*Shǒucè*
Miles per hour/ Kilometers per hour	*Měi xiǎoshí yīnglǐ/ Měi xiǎoshí gōnglǐ*
Miles per gallon/ Kilometers per gallon	*Měi jiālún yīnglǐ/ Měi jiālún gōnglǐ*
Mint condition	*Qúanxīn de*
Mirror	*Jìngzi*
Model	*Xínghào*
New Model	*Xīn chēxíng*
Noise	*Zàoyīn*

Odometer	*Chēchéngbiǎo*
Oil gauge	*Jìyóubiǎo*
Oil pressure	*Yóuyā*
Open (to)	*Dǎkāi*
Overhead cam	*Dǐngzhìshì tūlúnzhóu*
Paint	*Yóuqī*
Park	*Tíngchēchǎng*
Park (to)	*Tíngchē*
Parking brake	*Tíngchē zhìdòng*
Parts	*Bùjiàn*
Parts distribution	*Bùjiàn fēnfā*
Parts manufacturer	*Bùjiàn shēngchǎnshāng*
Passenger car	*Kèchē*
Passenger's seat	*Kèzuò*
Pedal	*Tàbǎn*
Pickup truck	*Xiǎoxíng zàihùo kǎchē*
Piston	*Húosāi*
Piston ring	*Huósāihúan*
Platform	*Píngtái*
Power brakes	*Dònglì shāchē*
Power windows	*Diàndòng chēchūang*
Price	*Jiàgé*
Price tag	*Jiàgé biāoqiān*
Radio	*Shōuyīnjī*
Rear suspension	*Hòuxúan*
Rearview mirror	*Hòushìjìng*
Repair shop	*Xiūlǐ chējiān*
Replacement part	*Tìhùanjiàn*
Reverse (to)	*Dàotùi*
Robot	*Jīqìrén*
Rocker arm	*Yáobèi*
Run (to)	*Pǎo*

Seal	*Fēngbì*
Seat	*Zuòyǐ*
Seat belt	*Zuòyǐ ānqúandài*
Sedan	*Sì mén jiàochē*
Service	*Fúwù*
Service station	*Fúwùzhàn*
Shift (to)	*Hùandǎng*
Shop (to)	*Chējiān*
Showroom	*Chén liè shì/Zhǎnshì*
Side mirror	*Cèshìjìng*
Signal	*Xìnhào*
Signal (to)	*Dǎ xìnhào*
Sound system	*Yīnxiǎng xìtǒng*
Sparc tire	*Bèiyòngtāi*
Spark plug	*Hǔohūasāi*
Speedometer	*Chēsùbiǎo*
Sports car	*Yùndòngchē*
Stall (to)	*Shīsù/tíng chē*
Stamping	*Dǎ jìhào*
Start (to)	*Qǐdòng*
Starter	*Qǐdòngjī*
Startup	*Qǐdòng*
Station wagon	*Lǚxíngchē*
Steer (to)	*Zhǔanxiàng*
Steering wheel	*Zhǔanxiàngpǎn*
Stick shift	*Shǒupáidǎng*
Strut	*Zhīzhù*
Sun roof	*Zhēyáng dǐngpéng*
Supplier	*Gōngyìngshāng*
Suspension	*Xúanjià*
SUV (sports utility vehicle)	*Dūoyòngtú yùndòngchē*
Switch	*Kāigūan*
System	*Xìtǒng*

Tachometer	*Zhuǎnsùbiǎo*
Tire	*Lúntāi*
Tool	*Gōngjù*
Tool kit	*Gōngjùxiāng*
Torque	*Niǔjù*
Transmission	*Chúandòng zhūangzhì*
Truck	*Kǎchē*
Trunk	*Xínglǐxiāng*
Turn (to)	*Zhuǎnwān*
Turn over (to)	*Zhuǎn shàng*
Turn signal	*Zhuǎnxiàng xìnhào*
Twin cap	*Shūanggài*
Two-door	*Liǎng mén*
Union	*Gōnghùi*
Valve	*Qìmén*
Van	*Xiāngshì hùochē*
Vanity mirror	*Xūróngjìng*
Vehicle	*Chē*
Vent	*Tōngfēng*
Vibration	*Zhèndòng*
Wagon	*Yùnhùochē*
Warning light	*Jǐnggàodēng*
Wheel	*Lúnzi*
Window	*Chūanghù*
Wipers	*Gūashuǐqì*
Windshield	*Dǎngfēng bōlí*

BANKING AND FINANCE

Account	*Zhànghù*
Accrue (to)	*Yìngjì/zēng zhí*
Acquire (to)	*Qǔdé*
Acquisition	*Shōugòu*
Asset	*Zīchǎn*

Assets under management	*Shòu guǎn zīchǎn*
Automatic teller machine (ATM)	*Zìdòng tíkuǎnjī*
Back office	*Hòumiàn bàngōngshì*
Bailout	*Jǐnjí róngzī*
Bond	*Zhàiquàn*
Bond market	*Zhàiquàn shìchǎng*
Borrow (to)	*Jièdài*
Borrowing	*Jiè*
Bottom line	*Dǐxiàn*
Branch	*Fēnháng*
Branch manager	*Fēnháng jīnglǐ*
Capital	*Zīběn*
Cash	*Xiànjīn*
Cash (to)	*Xiànjīn*
Cashier	*Chūnàyúan*
Central bank	*Zhōngxīn yínháng*
Certificate of Deposit (CD)	*Dìng cúnkuǎn*
Check	*Zhīpiào*
Checking account	*Zhīpiào zhànghù*
Close (to)	*Gūanbì*
Commercial bank	*Shāngyè yínháng*
Commercial banking	*Shāngyè yínháng*
Commission	*Yòngjīn*
Commodities	*Shāngpǐn*
Corporate bond	*Fǎrén zhàiquàn*
Correspondent banking	*Wǎnglái yínháng*
Cost of funds	*Jījīn chéngběn*
Credit	*Xìnyòng*
Credit card	*Xìnyòngkǎ*
Credit limit	*Xìnyòng xiàn'é*
Credit line	*Shēzhàng de zùi gāo é*

Currency	*Huòbì*
Day-trader	*Dāngrì gǔpiào jīngjìrén*
Debt (short-term, long-term)	*Zhàiwù (duǎnqī, chángqī)*
Deficit	*Chìzì*
Deflation	*Tōnghuò jǐnsūo*
Delinquency rate	*Qiànzhàilǜ*
Deposit	*Cúnkuǎn*
Deposit (to)	*Cúnkuǎn*
Derivatives	*Dǎoshù*
Down payment	*Tóukuǎn*
Due date	*Jiāofù rìqī*
Earnings	*Suǒdé*
Economy	*Jīngjì*
Efficiency ratio	*Xiàolǜ*
Exchange rate	*Duìhuànlǜ*
Fee	*Fèiyòng*
Financial adviser	*Cáiwù gùwèn*
Fiscal policy	*Cáiwù zhèngcè*
Foreign exchange	*Wàihuì duìhuàn*
Futures contract	*Qīhuò hétóng*
Go long/short (to)	*Chángxiàn/duǎnxiàn*
Hedge	*Tàotóu jiāoyì*
Hedge (to)	*Xiànmǎixiànmài*
Hedge fund	*Tàotóu jījīn*
Hedging	*Tàotóu jiāoyì*
Inflation	*Tōnghuò péngzhàng*
Institutional investor	*Jīgòu tóuzī*
Interest	*Lìxí*
Interest rate (fixed, floating)	*Lìlǜ*

Invest (to)	*Jìnxíng tóuzī*
Investment	*Tóuzī*
Investment bank	*Tóuzī yínháng*
Investment banking	*Tóuzī yínháng*
Investment services	*Tóuzī fúwù*
Letter of credit (L/C)	*Xìnyòngzhèng*
Liability	*Zhàiwù*
Liquid	*Liúdòng de*
Liquidate (to)	*Qīngsùan*
Lend (to)	*Jiè gěi*
Loan (short-term, long-term, secured)	*Dàikuǎn (dǔanqī, chángqī, dānbǎo de)*
Loan (to)	*Dài gěi*
Loan officer	*Dàikuǎnyúan*
Loan volume	*Dàikuǎn dìnglìang*
Loss	*Kūisǔn*
Merchant bank	*Shāngyè yínháng*
Merchant banking	*Shāngyè yínháng*
Merge (to)	*Hébìng*
Merger	*Hébìng*
Monetary policy	*Hùobì zhèngcè*
Money	*Hùobì/Qián*
Mortgage	*Dǐyā*
Mortgage (to)	*Dǐyā*
Mutual fund	*Hùzhù jījīn*
Net	*Jìngzhí*
Net interest margin	*Jìngzhí lìlǜ zhùantóu*
Nonrevolving credit	*Fēi xúnhúi xìnyòng/ Fēi zhōu zhǔanxíng xìnyòng*
Open an account (to)	*Kāihù*
Open a letter of credit (to)	*Kāi xìnyòngzhèng*
Overdraft	*Tòuzhī*

Overdrawn	*Tòuzhī*
Pay (to)	*Zhīfù*
Payment	*Fùkuǎn*
Percent	*Bǎifēnbǐ*
Portfolio	*Gǔpiào zǔhé*
Portfolio manager	*Gǔpiào zǔhé jīnglǐ*
Price	*Jiàgé*
Price (to)	*Biāojià*
Price/Earnings (P/E) ratio	*Jiàgé yǔ suǒdé de bǐlǜ*
Private banking	*Sīyǒu yínháng*
Profit	*Yínglì*
Profit (to)	*Yínglì*
Profit margin	*Yínglì bǐlǜ*
Recession	*Jīngjì shūaitùi*
Repayment	*Chánghúan*
Retail banking	*Língshòu yínháng*
Revolving credit	*Xúnhúan xìnyòng/ Zhōu zhǔan xìnyòng*
Safe-deposit box	*Bǎoguǎnxiāng*
Save (to)	*Chǔxù*
Savings account	*Chǔxù zhànghù*
Security	*Zhèngqùan*
Securitization	*Zhèngqùanhùa*
Share price	*Gǔpiào jiàgé*
Spread	*Chājià*
Stock market	*Gǔpiào shìchǎng*
Stockholders	*Gǔdōng*
Stocks	*Gǔpiào*
Surplus	*Yíngyú*
Syndicate	*Xīndíjiā*
Syndicated loan	*Zǔhé dàikuǎn*
Takeover	*Shōugòu*
Tax	*Shùi*

Tax (to)	*Nàshùi*
Teller	*Chūnàyúan*
Trade (to)	*Jiāoyì*
Trader	*Jīngjìrén*
Transact (to)	*Bànlí*
Transaction	*Jiāoyì*
Transaction costs	*Jiāoyì chéngběn*
Transfer (to)	*Zhǔanzhàng*
Traveler's check	*Lǚxíng zhīpiào*
Treasury bonds	*Gúokù zhèngqúan*
Trust	*Tūolāsī*
Trust (to)	*Xìntūo/xìntūo*
Trust officer	*Tūogǔanrén*
Underwrite (to)	*Zhèngqùan bāoxiāo*
Underwriter	*Zhèngqùan jīngjìrén*
Wire	*Diànhùi*
Wire (to)	*Diànhùi*
Wholesale banking	*Pīfā yínháng*
Withdraw (to)	*Tíkǔan*
Withdrawal	*Tíkùan*

ENGINEERING

Calculus	*Wēijīfen*
Chemical	*Hùaxúe de*
Civil	*Mínshì de*
Design	*Shèjì*
Develop	*Kāifā*
Engineer	*Gōngchéngshī*
Instruments	*Yíbiǎo*
Mathematics	*Shùxúe*
Mechanical	*Jīxiè*

Nuclear	*Hézǐ de*
Science	*Kēxúe*
Structural	*Jiégòu de*
Technology	*Jìshù*
Test	*Cèshì*

ENTERTAINMENT, JOURNALISM AND MEDIA
(See also Publishing, Advertising and Public Relations)

Actor	*Yǎnyúan*
Artist	*Yìshùjiā*
Choreographer	*Biānwǔ*
Cinema	*Diànyǐngyùan*
Column	*Zhūanlán*
Columnist	*Zhūanlán zùojiā*
Commentary	*Pínglùn*
Contact	*Liánxì*
Correspondent	*Tōngxùn*
Dancer	*Wǔdǎojiā*
Director	*Dǎoyǎn*
Edit (to)	*Jiǎnjiē*
Edition	*Jiǎnjiē*
Editor	*Biānjí*
Editorial	*Shèlùn*
Editor-in-Chief	*Zǒngbiānjí*
Feature story	*Gùshìpiān*
Headline	*Xīnwén tíyào*
Interpreter	*Fānyì*
Journalism	*Xīnwénxúe*
Journalist	*Jìzhě*

Music	*Yīnyùe*
Musician	*Yīnyùejiā*
News (story)	*Xīnwén*
Perform (to)	*Bànyǎn*
Performance	*Biǎoyǎn*
Photographer	*Shèyǐngshī*
Postproduction	*Hòuqī zhìzùo*
Producer	*Zhìpiānrén*
Production	*Zhìzùo*
Radio	*Shōuyīnjī/Wú xiàn diàn*
Recording	*Lùyīn*
Rehearsal	*Páiliàn*
Report (to)	*Bàodào*
Reporter	*Jìzhě*
Review	*Pínglùn*
Score	*Yùepǔ*
Script	*Jùběn*
Technician	*Jìshī*
Television	*Diànshì*
Translator	*Fānyì*
Writer	*Zùojiā*

FASHION
(See also Textile)

Accessories	*Fúshì*
Accessorize	*Pèi fúshì*
Appearance	*Wàigūan*
Beauty	*Měilì*
Bell-bottom	*Lǎbakù*
Belt	*Pídài*
Bias cut	*Xiécái*

Blazer	*Yùndòngyī*
Blouse	*Shàngyī*
Boots	*Tǒngxuē*
Boutiques	*Zhuāngshìdiàn/Fú shìdiàn*
Bow tie	*Lǐngjié*
Bra	*Xiōngzhào*
Buzz	*Wēngwēngshēng*
Cap	*Màozi*
Collar	*Lǐngzi*
Collection	*Shōují*
Corset	*Jǐnshēnyī*
Couturier	*Nǚ zhuāng nán cáifeng*
Cover (to)	*Zhēgài*
Cravat	*Jiùshì lǐngdài*
Design	*Shèjì*
Design (to)	*Shèjì*
Designer	*Shèjìshī*
Dinner jacket	*Wǎnlǐfú*
Double-breasted suit	*Shuāngpáikòu tàozhuāng*
Dress	*Nǚzhuāng*
Dressing room	*Gēngyīshì*
Earmuffs	*Ěrhù*
Etiquette	*Lǐyí*
Fabric	*Miànliào*
Fake fur	*Jiǎ pímáo*
Fashion	*Shízhuāng*
Fashion show	*Shízhuāng zhǎnshìhùi*
Fur (clothing)	*Pímáo*
Garment	*Fúzhuāng*
Girdle	*Shùyāoyī/Jǐn shēn dā*

Gloves	*Shǒutào*
Hat	*Màozi*
Haute couture	*Shízhuāng nǚfú*
Haute couturier	*Shízhuāng nǚfú shèjìshī*
Heels	*Hòugēn*
Hem	*Féngbiān*
Hem (to)	*Féngbiān*
Hemline	*Dǐbiān*
Image	*Xíngxiàng*
Jacket	*Wàitào*
Lapel	*Fānlǐng*
Length	*Chángdù*
Lingerie	*Fùnǚ tiēshēn nèiyī*
Metallics	*Hánjīn de*
Midi	*Zhōngchángqún*
Miniskirt	*Chāoduǎnqún*
Model	*Mótè'ěr*
Model (to)	*Zuò mótè*
Muff	*Pí shǒutào*
Necktie	*Lǐngdài*
Nightgown	*Nǚ shùiyī*
Noncrease	*Kàngzhòu*
Overcoat	*Dàyī*
Pad	*Hùdiàn*
Padded	*Jiā hùdiàn*
Pajamas	*Shùiyī*
Pants	*Chángkù*
Plastics	*Sùjiāo/Sùliào*
Platform shoes	*Miànbāoxié*
Pleat	*Zhěhén*
Proportions	*Dùichèn*

Raincoat	*Yǔyī*
Ready-to-wear	*Chéngyī/Xiànchéng fúzhūang*
Relaxed	*Fàngsōng de*
Robe	*Chángpáo*
Runway	*Tōngdào*
Sash	*Shìdài*
Scarf	*Pījīn/Wéijīn*
Seam (finished, unfinished)	*Jiēfèng (wánchéng de, wèi wánchéng de)*
Season	*Jìjié*
Separates	*Fēnlí*
Shawl	*Pījiān*
Sheath	*Hùtào*
Shirt	*Chènshān*
Shoe	*Xié*
Shoulder pads	*Jiāndiàn*
Show	*Zhǎnxiāohùi*
Show (to)	*Zhǎnshì*
Showroom	*Zhǎntīng*
Skirt	*Qúnzi*
Sleeve	*Xiùzi*
Socks	*Dǔanwà*
Stiletto heel	*Zhūiliáo/Xìgāogēn*
Stitch (to)	*Féngrèn*
Stitching	*Zhēnfǎ*
Stockings	*Chángwà*
Straight-leg	*Zhítǔi*
Style	*Fēnggé*
Suit	*Tàozhūang*
Sweater	*Máoyī*
Tailor	*Cáifeng*
Tailor (to)	*Jiǎncái*
Tailored	*Jiǎncái jiǎngjiu de*

INDUSTRY-SPECIFIC TERMS

Tailoring	*Chéngyī yè*
Tank top	*Bèixīn*
Three-piece suit	*Sānjiàntào*
Tie	*Lǐngdài*
Trousers	*Kùzi*
T-shirt	*Duǎnxiù hànshān/* *T xù shān*
Undergarment	*Nèiyī*
Underwear	*Nèiyī nèikù*
Vest	*Hànshān*
Waist	*Yāo*
Wardrobe	*Yīguì*
Wedge	*Xiēzi*

GOVERNMENT AND GOVERNMENT AGENCIES

Administration	*Xíngzhèng*
Agency	*Jīgòu*
Arts	*Yìshù*
Associations	*Xiéhùi*
Citizen	*Gōngmín*
Citizenship	*Gōngmín*
College	*Xúeyùan*
Commission	*Wěituō*
Committee	*Wěiyúanhùi*
Community	*Shèqū*
Cultural	*Wénhùa de*
Delegation	*Dàibiǎotúan*
Department	*Bùmén*
Development	*Kāifā*
Economic	*Jīngjì de*
Education	*Jiàoyù*

Environment	*Húanjìng*
Forms	*Biǎogé*
Government	*Zhèngfǔ*
Governmental	*Zhèngfǔ de*
Grant (to)	*Xǔkě*
Highways	*Gōnglù*
Housing	*Fángwū*
Industrial part	*Gōngyè bùjiàn*
Information	*Xìnxí*
Institute	*Xúehùi*
International	*Gúojì*
Legislation	*Lìfǎ*
Long range	*Chángqī*
Military	*Jūnshì de*
Negotiate	*Tánpàn*
Negotiations	*Tánpàn*
Nongovernmental agency	*Fēi gūanfāng jīgòu*
Nonprofit	*Fēi yínglì*
Office	*Bàngōngshì*
Park	*Gōngyúan*
Plan	*Jìhùa*
Plan (to)	*Jìhùa*
Planner	*Jìhùarén*
Policy	*Zhèngcè*
Political	*Zhèngzhì de*
Politics	*Zhèngzhì*
Population	*Rénkǒu*
Procedures	*Chéngxù*
Proposal	*Tíyì*
Public	*Gōnggòng*

Public service	*Gōnggòng fúwù*
Recommendation	*Tūijìan*
Region	*Dìqū*
Regional	*Dìqū de*
Regional office	*Dìqū bàngōngshì*
Regulation	*Gūidìng*
Regulatory agency	*Fǎgūi jīgòu*
Report	*Bàogào*
Representative	*Dàibiǎo*
Research	*Yánjiū*
Resources	*Zīyúan*
Road	*Dàolù*
Rural	*Nóngcūn de*
Services	*Fúwù*
Social	*Shèhùi de*
Society	*Shèhùi*
Suburb	*Jiāoqū*
Transportation	*Yùnshū*
University	*Dàxúe*
Urban	*Dūshì de*

INSURANCE

Actuary	*Baǒxiǎn tónggìyúan*
Agent	*Dàilǐ*
Annuity	*Niánjīn/Yǎnglǎojīn*
Broker	*Jīngjìrén*
Casualty	*Shāngwáng shìgù*
Claim	*Sǔopéi*
Commission	*Yòngjīn*
Coverage	*Bǎoxiǎn fànwéi*
Death benefit	*Sǐwáng jīntiē*

Deductible	*Kě jiǎnqù de*
Endowment	*Jūanzèng*
Face value	*Miànzhí*
Health	*Jiànkāng*
Insure (to)	*Bǎoxiǎn*
Life	*Rénshòu*
Life expectancy	*Píngjūn shòumìng*
Mortality rate	*Sǐwánglǜ*
Peril	*Wēixiǎn*
Policy	*Zhèngcè*
Policy owner	*Bǎoxiǎn kèhù*
Premium	*Èwài fèiyòng*
Property	*Cáichǎn*
Reinsurance	*Zàibǎoxiǎn*
Reserve	*Bǎolíu/chǔbèi*
Risk	*Fēngxiǎn*
Risk management	*Fēngxiǎn guǎnlǐ*
Term	*Qīxiàn*
Underwriter	*Bǎoxiǎn yè zhě*
Universal	*Pǔbiàn de*
Variable annuity	*Kěbiàn xìng niánjīn*
Viatical settlement	*Bùdìng qīngcháng*
Whole life	*Zhěnggè shēngmìng/ Zhěnggè yīshēng*

MANAGEMENT CONSULTING

Account	*Zhànghù*
Accounting executive	*Zhànghù guǎnlǐrén*

Bill	*Zhàngdān*
Bill (to)	*Shōuzhàng*
Entrepreneur	*Qǐyèjiā*
Expert	*Zhūanjiā*
Fee	*Fèiyòng*
Implement (to)	*Zhíxíng*
Implementation	*Zhíxíng*
Manage (to)	*Gǔanlǐ*
Management	*Gǔanlǐ*
Organize (to)	*Zǔzhī*
Organization	*Zǔzhī*
Organizational development	*Zǔzhī de fāzhǎn*
Presentation	*Zhǎnshì*
Project	*Xiàngmù*
Proposal	*Tíyì*
Recommend (to)	*Tūijiàn*
Recommendation	*Tūijiàn*
Report	*Bàogào*
Report (to)	*Bàogào*
Specialize (to)	*Zhūanmén cóngshì*
Specialist	*Zhūanjiā*
Team build (to)	*Túandùi jiànshè*
Team building	*Túandùi jiànshè*
Time sheet	*Shíjiān biǎo*
Train (to)	*Shòuxùn*
Training	*Péixùn*
Value	*Jiàzhí*
Value added	*Zēngzhí*

MINING AND PETROLEUM

Blasting	*Bàopò*
Chemical	*Hùaxúepǐn*
Coal	*Méi*
Conveyor	*Chúansòngdài*
Cooling	*Lěngqùe*
Copper	*Tóng*
Crosscut	*Héngqiē*
Crush (to)	*Yāsùi*
Crusher	*Yāsuìjī*
Crystal	*Shuǐjīng*
Deposit	*Kuàngchuáng*
Diamonds	*Zuànshí*
Dig (to)	*Wājué*
Digging	*Wājué*
Dredge (to)	*Lāoqǔ/wājué*
Dredging	*Lāoqǔ/wājué*
Drilling	*Zuānkǒng*
Earth	*Tǔrǎng*
Engineer	*Gōngchéngshī*
Engineering	*Gōngchéng*
Excavating	*Wāchū*
Extraction	*Tíqǔ*
Gas	*Qìyǒu*
Gems	*Bǎoshí*
Geologist	*Dìzhì xué zhě*
Gold	*Huángjīn*
Hydraulic	*Shuǐlì de*
Iron	*Tiě*
Lead	*Qiān*

Metal	*Jīnshǔ*
Metallurgist	*Yějīnxué jiā*
Mine	*Kuàng*
Mine (to)	*Cǎikuàng*
Minerals	*Kuàngwù*
Natural gas	*Tiānránqì*
Natural resources	*Zìrán zīyuán*
Oil	*Shíyóu*
Open-pit	*Lùtiān kuàng*
Ore	*Kuàngshí*
Outcrop	*Lùtóu*
Pit	*Cǎijúechǎng*
Platform	*Píngtái*
Power	*Dònglì*
Processing	*Chǔlǐ*
Pump	*Bèng*
Pump (to)	*Chōu shuǐ*
Pumping	*Chōu chū*
Quarry	*Cǎikùangchǎng*
Quarry (to)	*Cǎikùang*
Refine (to)	*Túliàn*
Refinery	*Jīngliànchǎng*
Resources	*Zīyúan*
Safety	*Ānqúan*
Shaft	*Jiàngān*
Silver	*Báiyín*
Sluice	*Xǐkùangcáo*
Sluicing	*Xǐkùang*
Smelting	*Róngliàn*
Strip-mining	*Tiáozhùang cǎikùang*
Surface	*Biǎopí*

Mining and Petroleum

INDUSTRY-SPECIFIC TERMS

Tin	*Xī*
Ton	*Dūn*
Truck	*Kǎchē*
Tunnel	*Suìdào*
Tunnel (to)	*Dǎ suìdào*
Tunneling	*Dǎ suìdào*
Vein	*Kùangmài*
Uranium	*Yóu*
Water	*Shǔi*
Waste	*Fèiwù*
Well	*Yóujǐng*
Zinc	*Xīn*

NONGOVERNMENTAL AGENCIES

Academic	*Xúeshù de*
Analyst	*Fēnxīshī*
Associate	*Hùiyúan*
Association	*Xiéhùi*
Center	*Zhōngxīn*
Charity	*Císhàn*
College	*Xúeyùan*
Consult (to)	*Zīxún*
Consulting	*Zīxún*
Contract	*Hétóng*
Contract (to)	*Qiān hétóng*
Coordinate	*Xiétiáo*
Council	*Yìhùi*
Cultural arts	*Wénhùa yìshù*
Database	*Shùjùkù*
Develop (to)	*Kāifā*
Development	*Fāzhǎn*

Directory	*Zhǐnán*
Donation	*Jūanzèng*
Educate (to)	*Jiàoyù*
Education	*Jiàoyù*
Educational	*Jiàoyù de*
Enterprise	*Qǐyè*
Fellowship	*Jiǎngxúejīn*
Foundation	*Jījīnhùi*
Fund-raiser	*Chóukǔanrén*
Fund-raising	*Chóukǔan*
Gifts	*Lǐwù*
Grant (to)	*Xǔkě/Zhùxúejīn*
Information	*Xìnxī*
Institute	*Xúehùi*
Institute (to)	*Shèlì*
Institution	*Jīgūan túantǐ*
Interest group	*Lìyìqún/lì yì jítían*
International	*Gúojì*
Issue (to)	*Fāchū*
Laboratory	*Shíyànshì*
Library	*Túshūgǔan*
Lobbying	*Yóushùi*
Museum	*Bówùgǔan*
Nonprofit group/ not-for-profit group	*Fēi yínglì zǔzhī*
Organization	*Zǔzhī*
Philanthropy	*Bó'ài/Cí shàn*
Professional association	*Zhūanyè xiéhùi*
Program	*Jiémù*
Publish (to)	*Chūbǎn*

Raise funds (to)	*Jízī/Chóu kuǎn*
Report	*Bàogào*
Report (to)	*Bàogào*
Research	*Yánjiū*
Research (to)	*Yánjiū*

School	*Xúexiào*
Society	*Shèhùi*
Statistics	*Tǒngjìxúe*
Strategy	*Zhànlùe*
Study	*Xúexí*
Survey	*Diàochá*
Survey (to)	*Diàochá*

| University | *Dàxúe* |

PERFUME AND FRAGRANCE

Aerosol	*Yèhùejī*
Aftershave	*Xiūmiànyóu*
Air freshener	*Kōngqì qīngxīnjì*
Alcohol	*Jiǔjīng*
Aloe	*Lúhùiyóu*
Aroma	*Fāngxiāng*

Base note	*Jīdiào*
Bath	*Mùyù*
Bath oil	*Yùshìyóu*
Blush	*Liǎnhóng*

Citrus	*Gānjú*
Cologne	*Gǔlóng xiāngshǔi*
Compact	*Xiǎofěnhé*
Cosmetics	*Hùazhūangpǐn*
Cream	*Xǔehūagāo*

| Deodorant | *Chúchòuyào* |

Essential oils	*Jīnghùayóu*
Eyeliner	*Yǎnxiàngāo*
Eye shadow	*Yǎnyǐnggāo*
Floral	*Hūa sì de*
Fragrance	*Xiāngwèi*
Fresh	*Qīngxīn*
Freshener	*Qīngxīnjì*
Herbal	*Cǎoběn de*
Lemon	*Níngméng*
Lipstick	*Kǒuhóng*
Mascara	*Rǎnméijì*
Middle note	*Zhōngdiào*
Nose	*Bízi*
Oil	*Yóu*
Ointment	*Yóugāo*
Olfactory	*Xiùjúe qìguan*
Orange	*Chéng*
Oriental	*Dōngfāng de*
Perfume	*Xiāngshǔi*
Powder	*Hùazhūangfěn*
Powdery	*Fěnzhūang de*
Rouge	*Yānzhi*
Salts	*Yán*
Scent	*Xiāngwèi*
Smell	*Qìwèi*
Spicy	*Xiāngliào*
Soap	*Féizào*
Toiletries	*Hùazhūang yòngjù*
Top note	*Gāodiào*

PHARMACEUTICAL, MEDICAL AND DENTAL

Anesthesia	*Mázùi*
Antibiotics	*Kàngshēngsù*
Approve (to)	*Pīzhǔn*
Approval	*Pīzhǔn*
Capsule	*Jiāonáng*
Checkup	*Jiǎnchá*
Clean (to)	*Qīngjié*
Cleaning	*Qīngjié*
Chemistry	*Huàxúe*
Clinical trials	*Línchúang shìyàn*
Disease	*Jíbìng*
Double-blind data	*Shūangdìng shùjù*
Drugs	*Yàowù*
Drug trials (Phase I, Phase II, Phase III)	*Yàowù shìyàn (yī qī, èr qī, sān qī)*
Exam	*Zhěndùan*
Examine (to)	*Zhěndùan*
Filling	*Tiánchōng*
Generic drugs	*Pǔtōng yàowù*
Hospital	*Yīyùan*
Laboratory	*Shíyànshì*
Manufacture (to)	*Jiāgōng zhì zhào*
Magnetic Resonance Imaging (MRI)	*Cígòngzhèn yǐngxiàng*
Over-the-counter	*Gùitái xiāoshòu*
Patent	*Zhūanlì*
Patent (to)	*Zhūanlì*
Patented drug	*Zhūanlì yàowù*
Patient	*Bìngrén*

Pharmaceutical company	*Zhìyào gōngsī*
Pharmacologist	*Yàowùxúejiā*
Pharmacy	*Yàofáng*
Pharmacist	*Yàojìshī*
Pills	*Yàowán*
Placebo	*Kūanxīnwán*
Poison	*Dúyào*
Prescribe (to)	*Kāi yàofāng*
Prescription	*Yàofāng*
Prescription drugs	*Chǔfāng yàowù*
Proprietary drug	*Zhūannmài yàowù*
Rash (skin)	*Fāzhēn (pífū)*
Release (to)	*Chūyùan*
Research	*Yánjiū*
Root canal	*Yá Gēngǔan*
Tablets	*Yàopiàn*
Test (to)	*Cèshì*
Testing	*Cèshì*
Tests	*Cèshì*
Toxicology	*Dúwùxúe*
Treatment	*Zhìliáo*
Veterinary drug	*Shòuyī yàowù*
Vitamins	*Wéishēngsù*
X ray	*X gūang*

PUBLISHING

Acknowledgments	*Xièyì/Míng xiè*
Advance	*Yùfù*
Advanced sales	*Tíqián xiāoshòu*
Appendix	*Fùlù*
Art	*Yìshù*
Asterisk	*Xīnghào*

Author	*Zùozhě*
Author's corrections	*Zùozhě dìngzhèng*
Back ad	*Bèimiàn gǔanggào*
Backlist	*Jiùshū mùlù/Chóng bǎn shū mùlù/ Cúnshū mùlù*
Best-seller	*Chàngxiāoshū*
Binding	*Zhūangdìng*
Blockbuster	*Qiánglì yǐnbào/ Jùxíngzhàdàn/ Húanghúang jù zhù*
Blurb	*Dàsì xūanchúan*
Body	*Zhǔtǐ*
Bold type	*Zhǔtǐ xíngtài*
Book	*Shū*
Book jacket	*Shū wàitào*
Book store	*Shūdiàn*
Border	*Biānyúan*
Box	*Xiāngzi*
Broadsheet newspaper	*Dàfú bàozhǐ*
Bullet points	*Yúandiǎn*
Byline	*Biānxiàn/Shǔ míngde Yīháng*
Caps (capital letters)	*Dàxiě zìmǔ*
Caption	*Biāotí*
Chapter	*Zhāng*
Circulation	*Liútōng*
Color	*Cǎisè*
Color photos	*Cǎisè zhàopiān*
Contents	*Nèiróng*
Contrast	*Dùibǐ*
Copy editor	*Shěngǎo*
Copyright	*Bǎnqúan*
Cover	*Fēngmiàn*
Cropping	*Jiǎncái*

Dagger	*Jiànhào*
Deadline	*Zùihòu qīxiàn*
Dots per inch	*Měi yīngcùn . . . diǎn*
Double-page spread	*Shuāngyè pái/Dà biāotí*
Double dagger	*Shuāngjiànhào*
Edit (to)	*Biānjí*
Editing	*Biānjí*
Editor	*Biānjí*
Electronic publishing	*Diànzǐ chūbǎn*
End papers	*Shūjì juantóu kòngbǎi/ Fēiyè*
Fact check	*Hédùi shìshí*
Flush left/Flush right	*Zuǒ qí/Yòu qí/Zuǒ biān páiqí/Yòu biān pái qí*
Font	*Zìxíng/Quán tào qiānzì*
Footnote	*Jiǎozhù*
Front-list	*Juàntóu shūdān*
Galley	*Huóbǎnpán*
Galley proof	*Chángtiáo jiàoyàng*
Glossary	*Zìhùi*
Glossy	*Gūang mìan zhào piān*
Graphics	*Túxiàng*
Hardcover	*Yìngzhūang/ Jīngzhūang běn*
Illustration	*Tújiě*
Imprint	*Bǎnběn shuō míng*
Index	*Suǒyǐn*
International paper sizes	*Gúojí zhǐzhāng chǐcùn*
Introduction	*Yǐnyán*
International Standard Book Number (ISBN)	*Gúojí Biāozhǔn Shūhào*

International Standard Serial Number (ISSN)	*Gúojí Biāozhǔn qī Kānbiānhào*
Italics	*Xiétǐ*
Jacket	*Hù fēng*
Justify	*Liǎngtóuqí/Tiáo zhěng bǎnmiàn*
Landscape	*Fēngjǐng hùa/Cháng fāng xíng kāi běn/Biǎntǐzì*
Layout	*Bǎnmiàn shèjì/Hùa bǎnmiàn*
Legend	*Túlì shūomíng*
Logo	*Túbiāo*
Loose-leaf	*Sǎnyè/Húoyé*
Lowercase	*Xiǎoxiětǐ*
Magazine	*Zázhì*
Manuscript	*Shǒugǎo*
Margin	*Biān*
Masthead	*Fāxíngrénlán/Bàotóu lán*
Mock-up	*Dà móxíng/Shí tǐ móxíng*
Newspaper	*Bàozhǐ*
Newsstand	*Bàotān*
Page	*Yè*
Page number	*Yèhào*
Page proof	*Yèmìan jiàoyàng*
Pagination	*Biāo yèshù*
Paperback	*Píngzhūang*
Paragraph	*Dùanlùo*
Paragraph mark	*Dùanlùohào*
Percentage	*Bǎifēnbǐ*
Pica	*12 diǎn húozì*

Point	*Diǎn*
Portrait	*Huàxiàng*
Printing	*Yìnshūa*
Prologue	*Qiányán*
Proof	*Jiàoyàng*
Proofread (to)	*Jiàodùi*
Proofreader	*Jiàodùizhě*
Publisher	*Chūbǎnshāng*
Publishing	*Chūbǎn*
Pulp	*Zhǐjiāng*
Reference	*Cānkǎo*
Reference marks	*Cānkǎohào*
Remaindering	*Shèngyú shūjí*
Reporter	*Jìzhě*
Resolution	*Jiěxīdù/Fēnbiàn lü/Qīngxī dù*
Royalties	*Bǎnshùi*
Section mark	*Fēnjiéhào/Zhāngjiéhào*
Sentence	*Jùzi*
Softcover	*Píngzhuāng fēngmiàn*
Subscript/Superscript	*Xiě zài xiàmiàn/ Shàngmiàn de wénzì*
Subscription	*Dìngyùe*
Tabloid	*Xiǎoxíng huàbào/ Tōngsú xiǎobào*
Template	*Móbǎn*
Text	*Zhèngwén*
Title	*Biāotí*
Trade book	*Jiāohùan shūjí*
Trim	*Qíbiān*
Typeface	*Húozì zìyàng*
Watermark	*Shǔiyìn*
Word wrap	*Zìdòng páiháng*
Writer	*Zùozhě/Zùo jiā*

REAL ESTATE

Agent	*Dàilǐ*
Agreement	*Xiéyì*
Air rights	*Kōngjiān qúanlì*
Amortization	*Fēnqī fùkuǎn*
Annual percentage rate	*Nián lìlǜ*
Apartment	*Gōngyù fángjiān*
Appraisal	*Píngjià*
Appraise (to)	*Píngjià*
Assessment	*Gūdìng/Gūjià*
Assign (to)	*Shǒuràng/Ràng yǔ*
Assume	*Jiǎshè*
Assumption	*Shèxiǎng*
Attached	*Fùjiā*
Attachment	*Fùjiāwù*
Auction	*Pāimài*
Balloon mortgage	*Piāofúshì dǐyā*
Bankruptcy	*Pòchǎn*
Bearing wall	*Chéngqiáng*
Bid (to)	*Tóubiāo*
Binder	*Dìngjīn*
Breach of contract	*Wéifǎn hétóng*
Bridge loan	*Gùodù dàikuǎn*
Broker	*Jīngjìrén*
Building	*Xiūjiàn*
Building codes	*Jiànzhù gūizé*
Building permit	*Xiūjiàn xǔkě*
Buy (to)	*Mǎi*
Buy-down	*Mǎidùan*
Capitalization	*Zīběnhùa*
Capital gains	*Zīběn hùolì*
Cash flow	*Xiànjīn liúliàng*
Caveat emptor	*Hùowù chūmén, gài bù tùihùan*

Closing	*Jiésùan*
Closing costs	*Jiésùan chéngběn*
Collateral	*Dǐyāpǐn*
Commitment	*Chéngfù/Tūofù/ Chéngnùo*
Condemnation	*Zénàn*
Condominium (Condo)	*Gōngyùfáng/Gòngyǒu gōngyù*
Contract	*Hétóng*
Convey (to)	*Chúandā*
Conveyance	*Chúandā*
Cooperative (Co-op)	*Hézùo gōngyù*
Credit report	*Xìnyòng bàogào*
Debt-to-income ratio	*Zhàiwù sǔodě bǐlì*
Deed	*Qìjù/Qì yūe*
Default (to)	*Dǎozhàng*
Depreciation	*Zhéjiù*
Diversified	*Dūoyànghùa*
Down payment	*Tóukǔan*
Earnest money	*Dìngjīn*
Easement	*Dìyìqúan*
Eminent domain	*Zhīpèiqúan*
Equity	*Gǔběn*
Escrow	*Yǒu tiáojiàn qìyūe*
Foreclosure	*Sàngshī húidúqúan*
First mortgage	*Dì yī dǐyā*
Flood insurance	*Shǔizāi bǎoxiǎn*
Free and clear	*Méiyǒu yìwù hé qiānlián*
Freehold	*Wánqúan bǎoyǒu*
General contractor	*Zǒng chéngbāoshāng*
Hazard insurance	*Wēixiǎn bǎoxiǎn*
Hotels	*Lǚguǎn*

Indemnity	*Sǔnhài péicháng*
Industrial	*Gōngyè de*
Industrial park	*Gōngyèyúan*
Insurance	*Bǎoxiǎn*
Interest	*Lìxī*
Jumbo loan or mortgage	*Dàbǐ daìkǔan hùo dǐyā*
Land	*Tǔdì*
Landscaping	*Fēngjǐng*
Lease	*Zūlìn/qìyūe*
Lease (to)	*Zūlìn*
Lessee/Lessor	*Zūhù/Chūzūrén*
Let (to)	*Chūzū*
Lien	*Kòuyāqúan*
Manufactured housing	*Yùzhìfáng*
Mortgage	*Dǐyā*
Note	*Piàojù*
Occupancy	*Zhànyǒu*
Office	*Bàngōngshì*
Option	*Xǔanzéqúan*
Outlet center	*Gōngchǎng zhíxiāo zhōngxīn*
Owner	*Wùzhǔ*
Partition	*Gēbǎn*
Points	*Diǎn*
Power of attorney	*Wěirènshū*
Prefabricated construction	*Yùxiān jiànzào*
Prepayment penalty	*Yùfù fákǔan*
Principal	*Běnjīn*
Private mortgage insurance	*Gèrén dǐyā bǎoxiǎn*
Probate	*Yízhǔ rènzhèng*
Promissory note	*Qīpiào*

Property	*Cáichǎn*
Public sale	*Gōngkāi chūshòu*
Real estate	*Fángdìchǎn*
Real estate investment trusts (REITS)	*Fángdìchǎn tóuzī xìntuō*
Realtor	*Bùdòngchǎn jīngjìrén*
Refinance (to)	*Zài dàikuǎn*
Rent	*Zūjīn*
Rent (to)	*Chūzū*
Rental	*Chūzū de*
Renter	*Zūhù*
Rescind (to)	*Fèichú*
Residential	*Zhùzhái de*
Riparian rights	*Hé'àn jūzhùquán*
Second mortgage	*Dì èr dǐyā*
Self-storage	*Zìzhù chǔcáng*
Sell (to)	*Mài gěi*
Settle (to)	*Jiésùan*
Shopping malls	*Gòuwù zhōngxīn*
Strip mall	*Jiēqū shāngdiàn*
Sublet (to)	*Zhuǎnzū*
Tenant	*Chéngzūrén*
Tenure	*Bǎoyǒu qī*
Title	*Qúanzhùang/Sǔo yǒu qúan píngzhèng*
Title insurance	*Sǔoyǒuqúan bǎoxiǎn*
Title search	*Qúanzhùang sōuxún*
Triple-net	*Sānchóng jìngzhí*
Trust	*Xìntuō*
Utilities	*Shǔidiàn fèi*
Vacant	*Kòngwèi*
Warranty deed	*Bǎozhèng qìyūe*
Zoning	*Chéngshì qūhùa*

SHIPPING AND DISTRIBUTION

Agent	*Dàilǐ*
Air freight	*Kōngyùn*
Airport	*Fēijīchǎng*
Anchor	*Máo*
Barge	*Bóchúan*
Bill	*Zhàngdān*
Bill (to)	*Shōuzhàng*
Bill of lading (B/L)	*Tídān*
Boat	*Chúan*
Box	*Xiāngzi*
Broker	*Jīngjìrén*
Bulk carrier (ship)	*Dàzòng hùochúan*
By air	*Kōngyùn*
By land	*Lùyùn*
By sea	*Hǎiyùn*
Cargo	*Hùowù*
Carload	*Zhūangzàiliàng*
Carrier (ship)	*Yùnhùochúan*
Certificate	*Zhèngshū*
Charter	*Qìyūe*
Charter (to)	*Bāozū*
CIF (Costs, Insurance and Freight)	*Dào'ànjià*
Combine (to)	*Liánhé*
Consign (to)	*Wěitūo/Fāsòng*
Consigner	*Wěitūorén/Fāhùo rén*
Container	*Jízhūangxiāng*
Containerization	*Jízhūanghùa*
Container ship	*Jízhūangchúan*
Corrugated box	*Bōzhūang hézi*
Cost	*Chéngběn*
Crate	*Tiáobǎnxiāng*
Crew	*Shǔishǒu*
Customs	*Hǎigūan*

Deliver (to)	*Sònghùo*
Delivery	*Sònghùo*
Delivery note	*Sònghùo tōngzhī*
Delivery time	*Sònghùo shíjiān*
Depot	*Cāngkù*
Destination	*Zhōngdiǎn*
Dispatch	*Pàiqiǎn/Fā sòng*
Dispatch (to)	*Pàiqiǎn*
Dock	*Mǎtóu*
Dock (to)	*Rù mǎtou*
Double hulls	*Shūangchúan*
Duty	*Gūanshùi*
Estimate	*Gujì*
Estimate (to)	*Gūjì*
Ferry	*Dùkǒu*
Fleet	*Chúandùi*
Free on Board (FOB)	*Lí'àn jià*
Forward	*Zhǔanjì/Zhǔanyùn*
Forwarding	*Zhuǎnjì*
Forklift	*Tūigāojī/Chǎnchē*
Fragile	*Yìsùipǐn*
Freight	*Yùnfèi*
Freight carrier	*Yùnhùochúan*
Freight costs	*Yùnfèi*
Freighter	*Hùochúan*
Freight weights	*Hùowù zhòngliàng*
Full-container load	*Jízhūangxiāng mǎnzài*
Goods	*Hùowù*
Guaranteed arrival date	*Bǎozhèng dǐdá rìqī*
Hazardous materials	*Wēixiǎn wùpǐn*
Hire (to)	*Gùyòng*
Hub	*Zhōngzhǔanzhàn*

Insurance	*Bǎoxiǎn*
Insure (to)	*Bǎoxiǎn*
Island	*Dǎo*
Isothermal container	*Děngwēn jízhuāngxiāng*
Landing day	*Dǐdá rì*
Liner	*Dìngqīchúan*
Load	*Zhūanghuò*
Load (to)	*Zhūanghuò*
Load capacity	*Zhūangzàiliàng*
Loader	*Zhūanghùorén*
Loading	*Zhūanghùo*
Loan	*Dàikǔan*
Locks	*Shǔizhá*
Lots	*Dìkùai*
Manager	*Jīnglǐ*
Manifest	*Hùodān*
Merchant ship	*Shāngchúan*
Message center	*Xìnxí zhōngxīn*
Oil tanker	*Yóulún*
Off load (to)	*Zhūanghùo*
On load (to)	*Xièhùo*
Order	*Dìngdān*
Order (to)	*Dìnggòu*
Overdraft	*Tòuzhī*
Package	*Bāogǔo*
Package (to)	*Bāozhūang*
Packaging	*Bāozhūang*
Pack (to)	*Dǎbāo*
Pallet	*Mùdiàn/Hùopán/Yùn hùo tūo bǎn*
Partial carload	*Bùfèn zhūangzài hùoliàng*

Partial containerload	*Bùfèn jízhuāngxiāng húoliàng*
Pickup (to)	*Tíqǔ*
Port	*Gǎngkǒu*
Profit	*Lìrùn*
Railroad	*Tiělù*
Rails	*Tiěgǔi*
Rail yard	*Tiělù tíngchēchǎng*
Refrigerate (to)	*Lěngdòng*
Refrigerated tank	*Lěngdòngxiāng*
Refrigeration	*Lěngdòng*
Reloading	*Zàizhuāng*
Rent (to)	*Zūlìn*
Route	*Lùxiàn*
Route (to)	*Ānpái lùxiàn*
Scrapping	*Sùipiàn*
Sea	*Hǎi*
Sea-lane	*Hǎishàng hángdào*
Service	*Fúwù*
Ship	*Chúan*
Ship (to)	*Chúanyùn*
Shipper	*Hùozhǔ*
Station	*Zhàn*
Storage	*Chǔcáng*
Supertanker	*Chāojí yóulún*
Surface	*Biǎomiàn*
Tank	*Yóuxiāng*
Tanker	*Yóulún*
Taxes	*Shùiwù*
Tie down (to)	*Kǔnbǎng*
Tonnage	*Dūnwèi*
Track (to)	*Gēnzōng/Yùnxíng*
Tracks (railroad)	*Gǔidào (tiělù)*

Traffic	*Jiāotōng*
Traffic coordinator	*Jiāotōng guǎnlǐyúan*
Train	*Huǒchē*
Transloading	*Jiāochā zhūangxiè*
Transport	*Yùnshū*
Transport (to)	*Yùnshū*
Transport company	*Yùnshū gōngsī*
Transporting	*Yùnshū*
Transporter	*Yùnshūzhě*
Truck	*Kǎchē*
Truck (to)	*Kǎchē yùn*
Trucking	*Kǎchē yùn*
Van	*Xiāngxíngchē/ miànbāochē*
Union	*Gōnghùi*
Union representative	*Gōnghùi dàibiǎo*
Unload (to)	*Xièhùo*
Warehouse	*Cāngkù*
Yard	*Yùanzi*

TELECOMMUNICATIONS
(See Computer Systems under Functional Areas of a Company in Chapter 5)

Analog	*Mónǐ*
Bandwidth	*Dàikūan*
Baud	*Bōtè*
Cable	*Diànlǎn*
Capacity	*Róngliàng*
Cellular	*Xìbāo de/Dūo kǒngde*
Cellular phone	*Xíngdòng diànhùa/ Shǒujī/Dà gēdà*
Data	*Shùjù*

Data transmission	*Shùjù chúansòng*
Dedicated line	*Zhūanyòngxiàn*
Digital	*Shùzì de*
Downlink	*Xiàlián*
DSL line	*Shùzì dìnggòu xiànlù*
E-commerce	*Diànzǐ shāngyè*
E-mail	*Diànzǐ yóujiàn*
Fax/Facsimile	*Chúanzhēn*
Fiber-optic line	*Gūangxiān xiànlù*
Hertz	*Hèzī*
High speed	*Gāo sù*
Internet	*Diànnǎowǎng/ Yīntèwǎng*
Intranet	*Nèibùwǎng*
Identification number (ID number)	*Shēnfèn hàomǎ*
Internet Service Providers (ISPs)	*Diànnǎowǎng tígōngshāng*
Keyboard	*Jiànpán*
Keypad	*Jiàndiàn*
Local Area Network (LAN)	*Qūyùwǎnglùo*
Line	*Xiàn*
Link	*Liánjiē*
Liquid-crystal display	*Yèjīng xiǎnshì*
Local calls	*Shìnèi diànhùa*
Long-distance	*Chángtú*
Megahertz	*Yī bǎi wàn hè*
Menu	*Xǔandān*
Mobile phone	*Yídòng diànhùa*
Modem	*Shùjùjī*
Network	*Wǎnglùo*

Palm	*Zhǎngshàngxíng diànnǎo*
Password	*Mìmǎ*
Personal digital assistant (PDA)	*Gèrén shùzì diànnǎo*
Phone line	*Diànhùa xiàn*
Resolution	*Jiěxīdù/Fēnbiànlǜ/ Qīngxīdù*
Satellite	*Wèixīng*
Security	*Ānqúan*
Server	*Sìfùqì*
Telecommunications	*Diànxùn*
Telegram	*Diànbào*
Telephone	*Diànhùa*
Transmit (to)	*Chúansòng*
Transmission	*Chúansòng*
Uplink	*Shànglián*
Video conferencing	*Yǐngxiàng hùiyì*
Voice and Data transmission	*Shēngyinshùjù chúansòng*
Voice mail	*Yǒushēng yóujiàn*
Web	*Wǎngyè*
Web page	*Wǎngyè*
Web site	*Wǎngzhǐ*
Wireless	*Wúxiàn*
World Wide Web (WWW)	*Qúanqiú zīxúnwǎng*

TEXTILE

Acidity	*Sūandù*
Acrylic	*Bǐngxīsūan de*
Alkalinity	*Jiǎnxìng*
Apparel	*Fúzhūang*
Artists	*Yìshùjiā*

Bonded types	*Dānbǎo zhǒnglèi*
Braids	*Biānzhī*
Braided	*Biānzhī de*
Brocade	*Jǐndùan*
Cloth	*Bù*
Cloth	*Bù*
Clothing	*Yīfú*
Color	*Yánsè*
Composite fabrics	*Hùnfǎng*
Conventional methods	*Chúantǒng fāngshì*
Converter	*Zhúanhùanqì*
Cotton	*Mián*
Crimp	*Zhédié*
Cutting	*Jiǎncái*
Cutting room	*Jiǎncáishì*
Damask	*Hūadùan*
Defect	*Qūexiàn*
Design	*Shèjì*
Dry-cleaning	*Gānxi*
Dyeing	*Rǎnsè*
Dye	*Rǎnsè*
Dye (to)	*Rǎnsè*
Elasticity	*Tánxìng*
Elongation	*Lācháng*
Embroidered	*Cìxiù*
Engineers	*Gōngchéngshī*
Fabric	*Miánliào de*
Fastness of finishes and colors	*Wángōng yǔ sècǎi de sùdù*
Felt	*Shǒugǎn*
Fiber	*Xiānwéi*
Fiber masses	*Xiānwéi zhíliàng*
Fineness	*Chúndù*

Finished cloth	*Wángōng de bùpǐ*
Flame resistance	*Kàng huǒ de*
Flax	*Yàmá*
Flexibility	*Shēnsūoxìng*
Floral	*Hūa de*
Garment	*Yīzhūang/fúzhūang*
Geometric	*Jǐhéxúe de*
Hand operation	*Shǒugōng cāozùo*
Insulation	*Júeyúan*
Interlacing	*Jiāochā biānzhī*
Jute	*Húangmá*
Knit	*Zhēnzhī*
Knitted	*Zhēnzhī de*
Knitting	*Zhēnzhī*
Lace	*Biānzhī*
Laundering	*Xǐtàng*
Layer	*Céng*
Length	*Chángdù*
Licensing	*Zhízhào*
Linen	*Yàmá*
Loom	*Zhībù*
Machinery	*Jīxiè*
Manmade fiber	*Rénzào xiānwéi*
Manufacture	*Jiāgōng/Zhì zào*
Manufacturing operations	*Shēngchǎn jīngyíng*
Moisture absorption	*Xīshīdù*
Natural fiber	*Zìrán xiānwéi*
Needle	*Zhēn*
Needle woven	*Zhēnzhī*
Net	*Wǎng*
Newer construction method	*Xīn de jiànzào fāngfǎ*

Nylon	*Nílóng*
Ornament	*Zhuāngshìpǐn*
Patterns	*Huāyàng*
Polyester	*Dílún*
Polyester filament	*Dílúnsī*
Porosity	*Duōkǒngxìng*
Printed	*Yìnhuā de*
Printing	*Yìnhuā*
Processing	*Chǔlǐ*
Production	*Shēngchǎn*
Quality control	*Zhíliàng kòngzhì*
Quality label	*Zhíliàng biāoqiān*
Rayon	*Rénzàosī*
Reaction to heat, sunlight, chemicals	*Duì rè, yángguāng, huàxuépǐn de fǎnyìng*
Resistance to creases	*Kàngzhòu de*
Resistance to pesticides, disease	*Kàng shāchóngyào, kàngbìng de*
Rug	*Máotǎn*
Sew (to)	*Féngrèn*
Sewing	*Féngrèn*
Silk	*Sī*
Silk-screen (to)	*Sīmò/Sīwǎng*
Spandex	*Tánxìng xiānwéi*
Specialization	*Zhuānyèhùa*
Spinning	*Fǎngshā*
Stable-fiber	*Wěndìng xiānwéi*
Strength	*Lìdù*
Structure	*Jiégòu*
Synthetic fabric	*Héchéng miánliào*
Synthetic fiber	*Héchéng xiānwéi*
Tapestry	*Xiùwéi/Guàtǎn*
Technician	*Jìshī*

Textile

INDUSTRY-SPECIFIC TERMS

Testing	*Cèshì*
Texture	*Zhígǎn*
Thread	*Xiàn*
Trademark	*Shāngbiāo*
Traditional	*Chúantǒng*
Treat (to)	*Chǔlǐ*
Uniform thickness	*Tǒngyī hòudù*
Velvet	*Sīróng*
Volume of production	*Shēngchǎn shùliàng*
Water-repellent	*Fángshǔi de*
Weave	*Biānzhī*
Weave (to)	*Biānzhī*
Weave and yarn structure	*Jīngxīan jiégòu*
Weaving	*Biānzhī*
Weight per unit area	*Biānzhī dānwèi miànjī*
Width	*Kūandù*
Wool	*Yángmáo*
Worsted	*Róngxiàn de*
Woven	*Biānzhī de*
Yarn	*Shāxiàn*
Yard (measurement)	*Mǎ*

TOYS

Action figure	*Dòngzùo rénwù*
Activity set	*Húodòng zǔhé*
Age compression	*Niánlíng yāsūo*
Airplanes	*Fēijī*
Animal	*Dòngwù*
Articulation	*Fāyīn*
Art supplies	*Měishù yòngpǐn*
Ball	*Qiú*
Battery	*Diànchí*

Block	*Zǔzhūangkùai/Jīmù*
Board games	*Zhūoshàng yóuxì*
Boat	*Chúan*
Brand-name toy	*Míngpái wánjù*
Building block	*Jiànzhù zǔzhāungkùai*
Building toy	*Jiànzhù wánjù*
Cars	*Chē*
Character	*Rénwù*
Chemistry set	*Hùaxúe zǔhé wánjù*
Children	*Háizi*
Clay	*Niántǔ*
Computer games	*Diànnǎo yóuxì*
Creator	*Chùangzàozhě*
Doll	*Yángwāwa*
Educational software	*Jiàoyù rǔanjiàn*
Frisbee	*Fēipán*
Fun	*Yǒuqù de*
Fun (to have)	*Shūoxiào/Hǎo wán*
Game	*Yóuxì*
Glue	*Jiāoshǔi*
Hobby kit	*Shìhào zǔhé wánjù*
Hobby horse	*Mùmǎ*
Hoop	*Yúanqūan*
Infant toy	*Yòuér wánjù*
Kaleidoscope	*Wànhūatǒng*
Kit	*Yī zǔ gōngjù*
Kite	*Fēngzheng*
Letter	*Shūxìn*
Marbles	*Dànzǐ*
Microscope	*Xiǎnwēijìng*

Mobile	*Yídòng de*
Models	*Xínghào*
Musical toy	*Yīnyuè wánjù*
Novelty	*Xīnqí de*
Parts	*Bùjiàn*
Picture book	*Liánhúanhùa*
Pegboard	*Yǒu kǒng de bǎnzi*
Play	*Wán*
Play (to)	*Wán*
Playing	*Wán*
Playing card	*Dǎpái*
Plastic	*Sùjiāo/sùliào*
Plush toy	*Biānzhī wánjù*
Preschool activity toy	*Xúeqián értóng wánjù*
Puppet	*Mù'ǒu*
Puzzle	*Cāimí*
Railroad	*Tiělù*
Rattle	*Yīnxiǎngqì*
Reissue	*Chóngxīn fāxíng*
Riding toy	*Kě jiàyù de wánjù*
Rocket	*Hǔojiàn*
Rubber	*Xiàngpí*
Science set	*Kēxúexiāng*
Soldiers	*Shìbīng*
Sports equipment	*Yùndòng shèbèi*
Stuffed animal	*Tiánsāi dòngwù*
Stuffed toy	*Tiánsāi wánjù*
Teddy bear	*Wánjùxióng*
Top	*Shàngdūan*
Trading card	*Jiāohùan kǎ*
Trains	*Hǔochē*
Vehicles	*Chē*

Video game	*Yǐngxiàng yóuxì*
Wagon	*Péngchē*
Wood	*Mùtou*
Wood-burning set	*Shāomù zǔhé*
Yo-yo	*Liūliūqiú/Yáo yáo qiú*

WATCHES, SCALES AND PRECISION INSTRUMENTS

Analog	*Mónǐ*
Apparatus	*Qìjù*
Balances	*Tiānpíng*
Batteries	*Diànchí*
Brass	*Huángtóng*
Chain	*Liàntiáo*
Chronographs	*Jìmiǎobiǎo*
Clock	*Zhōng*
Coil	*Xiànquān*
Digital	*Shùzì de*
Display	*Xiǎnshì*
Friction	*Mócā*
Gear	*Chǐlún*
Gold	*Huángjīn*
Instrument	*Yíbiǎo*
Integrated circuit	*Jíchéng diànlù*
Jewels	*Zhūbǎo*
Laboratory	*Shíyànshì*
Laser	*Jīguāng*
Mainspring	*Zhǔfātiáo*
Measurement	*Cèliáng*

Mechanism	*Jīxiè jiégòu*
Miniature	*Suoxĭng*
Miniaturization	*Sūoxiăo*
Motion	*Yùnxíng*
Movement	*Yùnzhùan*
Optical	*Gūangxúe de*
Oscillate (to)	*Zhèndòng*
Oscillation	*Zhènfú*
Pin	*Biézhēn*
Pivot	*Zhōngxīndiăn*
Polished	*Pāogūang de*
Precision	*Jīngmì*
Scales	*Bàngchèng*
Self-winding	*Zìdòng shàng fătiáo*
Shaft	*Jiàngăn*
Silver	*Báiyín*
Spring	*Tánhúang*
Spring-driven	*Tánhúang fādòng de*
Steel	*Bùxiùgāng*
Stopwatch	*Păobiăo*
Time	*Shíjiān*
Time (to)	*Jìshí*
Timepiece	*Shízhōng*
Torque	*Zhùanjù*
Transistor	*Diànjīngtĭ/Jīngtĭ gŭan*
Watch	*Biăo*
Weight	*Fămă*
Wheel	*Lúnzi*
Wristwatch	*Shŏubiăo*

WINE

| Acidity | *Sūandù* |
| Age (to) | *Chéngshú* |

Aging	*Lǎohùa*
Alcohol	*Jiǔjīng*
Aroma	*Fāngxiāng*
Barrel	*Dàtǒng*
Bordeaux	*Bō'érdūo jiǔ*
Bottle	*Jiǔpíng*
Bottle (to)	*Zhūang píng*
Bottled	*Zhūang píng de*
Bubbles	*Pàomò*
Brandy	*Báilándì*
Burgundy	*Pōliǎngdì jiǔ*
Cask	*Mùtǒng*
Cellar	*Jiǔjiào*
Champagne	*Xiāngbīnjiǔ*
"Character" of a wine	*Jiǔ de tèxìng*
Chardonnay	*Xiàdòngnà jiǔ*
Chianti	*Xiāngdì jiǔ*
Clarifying	*Chéngqīng*
Climate	*Qìhòu*
Color	*Sècǎi*
Cool	*Lěngqùe*
Cork	*Rǔanmùsāi*
Cork (to)	*Sāishàng*
Crush (to)	*Yāsùi*
Crusher	*Yāsùijī*
Drink (to)	*Hē*
Dry	*Bù tián de*
Estate	*Dìchǎn*
Ferment (to)	*Fāxiào*
Fermentation	*Fāxiào*
Flavor	*Fēngwèi*
Flavor (to)	*Jiāwèi*

Flavored wine	*Jiā xiāngliào de jiǔ*
Fortified wines	*Qiánglì jiǔ*
Grape(s)	*Pútáo*
Grow (to)	*Zāipéi*
Harvest	*Shōuhuò*
Herbs	*Yàocǎo*
Humidity	*Shīdù*
Label	*Biāoqiān*
Label (to)	*Tiē biāoqiān*
Merlot	*Fǎguó Mòěrlèjiǔ*
Must	*Pútáozhī*
Oak	*Xiàngmù*
Pinot noir	*Hēibǐnuò pútáojiǔ*
Port	*Gǎngkǒu*
Precipitate	*Chéndiàn*
Pulp	*Zhíjiāng*
Red wine	*Hóng pútáojiǔ*
Refine (to)	*Tíliàn*
Refrigerate (to)	*Lěngdòng*
Refrigeration	*Lěngcáng*
Region	*Qūyù*
Riesling	*Ruìsīlíng*
Rosé wine	*Ruórè jiǔ*
Seeds	*Zhǒngzǐ*
Sherry	*Xuělìjiǔ*
Soil	*Tǔrǎng*
Sparkling wines	*Sūdāshuǐ/Qìjiǔ*
Store (to)	*Chǔcáng*
Sugar	*Táng*
Sweet	*Tián de*
Table wines	*Jìncān jiǔ/Zuǒ cānjiǔ*

Tank	*Jiǔgùi*
Taste (to)	*Pǐncháng*
Tasting	*Pǐncháng*
Varietals	*Biànyìjiǔ*
Vermouth	*Kǔ'àijiǔ*
Vine	*Pútáoshù*
Vineyard	*Pútáoyúan*
Vinifera grapes	*Niàng jǐu yòng pútáo*
Vintage	*Chénnián hǎojǐu*
White wine	*Bái pútáojiǔ*
Wine	*Jiǔ*
Winery	*Niàngjiǔchǎng*
Yeast	*Jiàoomǔjùn*

GENERAL GLOSSARY
English–Chinese

A

Accent	*Kǒuyīn*
Accept (to)	*Jiēshòu*
Acceptable	*Kě jiēshòu de*
Accountability	*Zérèn*
Accounting	*Kùaijì*
Accounts payable	*Yīngfùzhàng*
Accounts receivable	*Yīngshōuzhàng*
Activities	*Húodòng*
Ad	*Gǎunggào*
Address	*Dìzhǐ*
Administration	*Xíngzhèng*
Administrative assistant	*Xíngzhèng zhùlǐ*
Admission	*Jìnrù xǔkě*
Agenda	*Yìchéng*
Agree (to)	*Tóngyì*
Agreement	*Xiéyì*
Airport	*Fēijīchǎng*
Airport shuttle	*Jīchǎng yùnsòngchē*
American	*Měigúo*
Amusement	*Yúlè*
Amusement park	*Yúlèyúan*
Answer	*Húidá*
Answer (to)	*Húidá*
Answering machine	*Liúyánjī*
Apology	*Dàoqiàn*
Appointment	*Yūehùi*
Appraise (to)	*Pínggū*
Arc	*Húxíng*
Area	*Miànji*
Argue (to)	*Zhēnglùn*

Arrow	*Jiàntóu*
Art	*Yìshù*
Art gallery	*Huàláng*
Article	*Wénzhāng*
Ask (to)	*Wèn*
Associate	*Hùiyúan*
Asterisk	*Xīnghào*
Attachment	*Fùjiā*
Attention	*Zhùyì*
Audio	*Yīnxiǎng*
Audit	*Shěnjì*
Audit (to)	*Shěnjì*
Authority	*Qúanwēi*
Authorize (to)	*Shòuqúan*
Auto	*Qìchē*

B

Background	*Bèijǐng*
Badge	*Hūizhāng*
Bag	*Kǒudài*
Balcony	*Yángtái*
Ballet	*Bāléi*
Bar	*Jiǔbā*
Bar chart	*Tiáozhùang tú*
Bargain (to)	*Jiǎngjià/ Tǎojiàhúan jìa*
Basketball	*Lánqiú*
Bathroom	*Yùshì*
Bed	*Chúang*
Begin (to)	*Kāishǐ*
Beginning	*Kāishǐ*
Behavior	*Xíngwéi*
Bell-curve	*Zhōngxíng qū xìan*
Benefits	*Fúlì*

Bill	*Zhàngdān*
Bill of sale	*Fāpiào*
Bin	*Lèsèxiāng/Lājīxiāng*
Black	*Hēisè*
Blackboard	*Hēibǎn*
Blank	*Kòngbái*
Blouse	*Shàngyī*
Blue	*Lánsè*
Board	*Mùbǎn*
Bold	*Yǒnggǎn de*
Bond	*Zhàiquàn*
Bonus	*Hónglì*
Book	*Shūjí*
Bookmark	*Shūqiān*
Booth	*Tānwèi*
Boss	*Lǎobǎn*
Bottom	*Dǐ*
Box	*Hézi*
Box seat	*Bāoxiāng*
Breakfast	*Zǎocān*
Brochure	*Xuǎncèzi*
Brown	*Zōngsè*
Buffet	*Zìzhùcān*
Building	*Jiànzhù*
Bus	*Gōnggòng qìchē*
Business	*Shāngyè*
Business cards	*Míngpiàn*
Business center	*Shāngyè zhōngxīn*
Busy	*Máng*
Buy (to)	*Mǎi*

C

Cabinet	*Gùichú*
Cafe	*Kāfēidiàn*

Cake	*Dàngāo*
Calculus	*Wēijīfēn*
Calendar	*Rìlì*
Call (to)	*Dǎ diànhùa*
Calling card	*Diànhùakǎ*
Camera	*Zhàoxiàngjī*
Capability	*Nénglì*
Car	*Jiàochē*
Career	*Zhíyè*
Car phone	*Chē shàng diànhùa*
Cash	*Xiànjīn*
Cash a check (to)	*Dùihùan zhīpiào*
Cat	*Māo*
Cellular phone	*Xíngdòng diànhùa*
Center	*Zhōngxīn*
Central	*Zhōngyāng de*
Central office	*Zhōngyāng bàngōngshì*
Central thesis	*Zhōngxīn lùnwén*
Centralization	*Zhōngyāng jíqúanhùa*
Certified check	*Bǎofù zhīpiào*
Certified mail	*Gùahàoxìn*
Chair	*Yǐzi*
Chairman	*Zhǔxí*
Chairperson	*Zhǔxí*
Chairwoman	*Nǚzhǔxí*
Chalk	*Fěnbǐ*
Change (to)	*Gǎibiàn*
Chart	*Túbiǎo*
Check	*Zhīpiào*
Check (to)	*Jiǎnchá*
Check in (to)	*Bàodào*
Chicken	*Jīròu*
Child(ren)	*Háizi*
Clothing	*Yīfú*
Church	*Jiàotáng*

Cigar	*Xuějiā*
Cigarette	*Xiāngyān*
Circle	*Yúanqūan*
City	*Chéngshì*
Classical music	*Gǔdiǎn yīnyùe*
Classroom	*Jiàoshì*
Clear (to)	*Míngqùe*
Clock	*Zhōng*
Close (to)	*Gūanbì*
Cloudy	*Dūoyún de*
Coach (to)	*Xùnliàn*
Coaching	*Fǔdǎo*
Coat	*Wàiyī*
Cocktail	*Jīwěijiǔ*
Cocktail party	*Jīwěi jiǔhùi*
Coffee	*Kāfēi*
Cold	*Gǎnmào*
Cold call	*Diànhùa tūixiāo*
Color	*Cǎisè*
Color monitor	*Cǎisè xiǎnshìqì*
Column	*Zhuānlán*
Comedy	*Xǐjù*
Communicate (to)	*Tōngxìn*
Communications	*Tōngxùn*
Compensate (to)	*Bàochóu*
Compensation	*Bǔcháng*
Compete (to)	*Jìngzhēng*
Competition	*Jìngzhēng*
Competitive price	*Jìngzhēng jiàgé*
Computer	*Diànnǎo*
Computer cable	*Diànnǎo diànlǎn*
Computer disk	*Diànnǎo cípán*
Computer monitor	*Diànnǎo xiǎnshìqì*
Concert	*Yīnyùehùi*
Concert hall	*Yīnyùetīng*

295

Concierge	*Ménfáng*
Conference	*Hùiyì*
Conference call	*Diànhùa hùiyì*
Conference center	*Hùiyì zhōngxīn*
Conflict	*Zhēngzhí*
Confirm (to)	*Qùerèn*
Confirmation	*Qùerèn*
Consult (to)	*Zīxún*
Consultant	*Gùwèn*
Convince (to)	*Shùifú*
Cool	*Lěngqùe*
Co-owned	*Gòngyǒu*
Connection	*Liánjiē*
Contact (to)	*Liánlùo*
Contract	*Hétóng*
Contractual obligation	*Hétóng yìwù*
Converter	*Zhǔanhùanqì*
Copier	*Fùyìnjī*
Copy	*Fùyìn*
Copyright	*Bǎnqúan*
Corner office	*Jiǎolùo bàngōngshì*
Cost	*Chéngběn*
Country	*Gúojiā*
Course	*Kèchéng*
Cover	*Fēngmiàn*
Cream	*Nǎiyóu*
Crosshatched	*Wǎngmùxiàn yīnyǐng*
Cultural	*Wénhùa de*
Culture	*Wénhùa*
Curve	*Wānqū/Qūxiàn*
Customer	*Gùkè*
Customer service	*Gùkè fúwù*
Customs	*Hǎigūan*
Cyberspace	*Diànzǐ kōngjiān*

D

Dais	*Gāozhūo/Gāotái/ Jiǎngtái*
Dash	*Pòzhéhào*
Data	*Shùjù*
Database	*Shùjùkù*
Date	*Rìqī*
Day	*Rìzi*
Daughter	*Nǚ'ér*
Deadline	*Zuìhòu qīxiàn*
Deal	*Jiāoyì*
Decentralization	*Dìfāng fēnqúan*
Decide (to)	*Júedìng*
Decision	*Júedìng*
Decision making	*Zùo júedìng*
Deferred compensation	*Yánhòu bàochóu*
Delivery	*Jiāofù*
Delivery date	*Jiāofù rì*
Demonstrate (to)	*Yǎnshì*
Demonstration	*Yǎnshì*
Department	*Bùmén*
Desk	*Shūzhūo*
Design	*Shèjì*
Diagram	*Túshì*
Diagram (to)	*Túshì*
Dial	*Bō hào*
Dial (to)	*Bō*
Dialogue	*Dùihùa*
Dinner	*Wǎncān*
Direct (to)	*Zhǐdiǎn*
Direction	*Fāngxiàng*
Direct line	*Zhíxiàn*
Director	*Zhǔrèn*
Directory	*Zhǐnán*

Disco music	*Liúxíng yīnyuè*
Discuss (to)	*Tǎolùn*
Discussion	*Tǎolùn*
Display	*Zhǎnshì*
Display (to)	*Zhǎnshì*
Distribute (to)	*Fēnfā*
Distribution	*Fēnfā*
Doctor	*Yīshēng*
Document	*Wénjiàn*
Dog	*Gǒu*
Dollar	*Měiyuán*
Door	*Mén*
Download (to)	*Xiàzài*
Down payment	*Tóukuǎn*
Downsize (to)	*Cáijiǎn*
Dotted line	*Xūxiàn*
Drama	*Xìjù*
Due	*Dàoqī de*

E

Easel	*Huàjià*
Earlier	*Zǎo yì diǎn*
Early	*Zǎo*
Edge	*Biānyúan*
Eight	*Bā*
Electrical line	*Diànxiàn*
Electricity	*Diànlì*
Ellipse	*Tuǒyúanxíng*
E-mail	*Diànzǐ yóujiàn*
Enclosure	*Fùjiàn*
Encourage (to)	*Gǔlì*
End	*Zhōngdiǎn*
End (to)	*Jiéshù*
Engineer	*Gōngchéngshī*

English	*Yīngyǔ*
Enjoy (to)	*Xǐhūan*
Enterprise	*Qǐyè*
Entrance	*Rùkǒu*
Entrepreneur	*Qǐyèjiā*
Entrepreneurship	*Chùangyè*
Envelope	*Xìnfēng*
Erase (to)	*Cādiào*
Eraser	*Xiàngpícā*
Espresso	*Nóngkāfēi*
Evening	*Wǎnshang*
Excel software	*Excel rǔanjiàn*
Exhibit	*Zhǎnlǎn*
Exhibit (to)	*Zhǎnshì*
Exit	*Chūkǒu*
Exit (to)	*Chūqù*
Expenses	*Kāizhī*
Experience	*Jīngyàn*
Exponential	*Zhǐshù de*
Export (to)	*Chūkǒu*
Extension	*Yánshēn*
Extension cord	*Yánshēn xiàn*

F

Facilitate (to)	*Cùchéng*
Facilitator	*Cùchéngrén*
Fall (season)	*Qiūtiān*
Family	*Jiātíng*
Fax	*Chúanzhēn*
Fax (to)	*Fā chúanzhēn*
Feedback	*Húikùi*
Feedback (to give)	*Húikùi*
Ferry	*Dùkǒu*
File	*Dǎng'àn*

File (to)	*Gūidǎng*
File cabinet	*Dǎng'àngùi*
Film	*Jiāojǔan*
Finance	*Cáiwù*
Finance (to)	*Gěi jīngfèi*
Financial figures	*Cáiwù shùzì*
Financial report	*Cáiwù bàogào*
Find (to)	*Fāxiàn*
Findings	*Fāxiàn*
First	*Dì yī*
Fish	*Yú*
Five	*Wǔ*
Flat-panel display	*Píngbǎn yíngmù*
Flight	*Hángbān*
Flower	*Hūa*
Folder	*Yìngchíjià/Wénjiànjiā*
Follow up (to)	*Gēnzōng*
Food	*Shíwù*
Football	*Gǎnlǎnqiú*
Foreman	*Lǐngbān*
Forward (to)	*Zhǔandì*
Found	*Zhǎohúi*
Four	*Sì*
Front	*Qiánmiàn*

G

Gain (to)	*Hùolì*
Gallery	*Hùaláng*
Gate	*Dàmén*
Geometry	*Jǐhéxúe*
Give (to)	*Gěi*
Glass	*Bōlí*
Goal	*Mùbiāo*
Good	*Hǎo*

Good-bye	*Zàijiàn*
Goods	*Huòwù*
Grandparent	*Zǔfùmǔ*
Grant	*Xǔkě*
Graph (to)	*Túshì*
Graphs	*Túbiǎo*
Green	*Lǜsè*
Grid	*Gézhà*
Guarantee	*Bǎozhèng*
Guarantee (to)	*Bǎozhèng*
Guard	*Shǒuwèi*

H

Handout	*Fēnfā yìnshuāpǐn*
Hang up (to)	*Guàdiào*
Hat	*Màozi*
Heading	*Biāotí*
Health	*Jiànkāng*
Hello	*Wèi*
Help (to)	*Bāngzhù*
Helpful	*Yǒu bāngzhù de*
Histogram	*Zhífāngtú*
History	*Lìshǐ*
Hobby	*Shìhào*
Hold (to)	*Bǎochí*
Hope (to)	*Xīwàng*
Horizontal	*Héngxíng de*
Horizontal bar chart	*Héngxiàng tiáoxíng tú*
Horse	*Mǎ*
Hot	*Rè*
Hotel	*Lǚguǎn*
Hour	*Xiǎoshí*
House	*Fángzǐ*
Human resources	*Rénshì guǎnlǐ*

Husband	*Zhàngfu*
Hypertext	*Chāojí wénjiàn*

I

Ice cream	*Bīngqílín*
Idea	*Zhǔyì*
Illustrate (to)	*Tújiě*
Illustration	*Tújiě*
Import (to)	*Jìnkǒu*
Individual	*Gèrén*
Inform (to)	*Gàozhī*
Information	*Xìnxí*
Information desk	*Wènxùntái*
Inside	*Lǐmiàn*
Insight	*Jiànshì/Dòngchá*
Install (to)	*Ānzhuāng*
Installation	*Ānzhuāng*
Insurance	*Bǎoxiǎn*
Intelligence	*Zhìlì*
Intelligent	*Zhìlì gāo de*
International	*Gúojì*
International law	*Gúojì fǎ*
Internet	*Diànnǎo wǎnglùo/Yīn tè wǎng*
Interview	*Miànshì*
Interview (to)	*Miànshì*
Introduce (to)	*Jièshào*
Introduction	*Jièshào*
Inventory	*Wùpǐn qīngdān*
Invest (to)	*Tóuzī*
Investment	*Tóuzī*
Invoice	*Fāpiào*
Invoice (to)	*Kāi fāpiào*
Issue (to)	*Fā*
Item	*Xiàngmù*

J

Jazz	*Júeshìyùe*
Jazz club	*Júeshì jùlèbù*
Jewelry	*Zhūbǎo*
Job	*Gōngzùo*
Joke	*Wánxiào*
Joke (to)	*Kāi wánxiào*

K

Karate	*Kōngshǒudào*
Key issue	*Gūanjiàn wèntí*
Know (to)	*Zhīdào*
Knowledge	*Zhīshi*

L

Label	*Biāoqiān*
Label (to)	*Tiē biaoqiān*
Language	*Yǔyán*
Laptop computer	*Xīshàngxíng diànnǎo*
Last	*Zùihòu*
Late	*Wǎn*
Later	*Wǎn yì diǎn*
Law	*Fǎlǜ*
Lawsuit	*Sùsòng*
Lawyer	*Lǜshī*
Layout	*Píngmiàntú*
Lead (to)	*Yǐndǎo*
Leader	*Lǐngdǎo*
Leadership	*Lǐngdǎo*
Leading	*Yǐndǎo*
Learn (to)	*Xúexí*
Left	*Zǔo*
Legal	*Fǎlǜ de*

Legal costs	*Fǎlǜ fèiyòng*
Letter	*Xìnjiàn*
Liability	*Zhàiwù*
Library	*Túshūgǔan*
Light	*Dēnggǔang*
Lightbulb	*Dēngpào*
Like (to)	*Xǐhūan*
Limousine	*Háohúa jiàochē*
Line	*Xiàn*
Linear	*Xiànxíng de*
Line graph	*Xiàntiáo túshì*
Link	*Liánjiēdiǎn*
List (to)	*Qīngdān*
Listen (to)	*Tīng*
Literature	*Chūbǎnwù/Wénxúe*
Local	*Dìfāng de*
Local call	*Shìnèi diànhùa*
Location	*Dìdiǎn*
Logarithmic scale	*Dùishù gūimó*
Logo	*Túbiāo*
Log off (to)	*Qiānchū*
Log on (to)	*Qiānrù*
Long-distance	*Chángtú*
Long-distance call	*Chángtú diànhùa*
Look (to)	*Xúnzhǎo*
Lotus 1-2-3 software	*Lotus 1-2-3 rǔanjiàn*
Luggage	*Xínglǐ*
Lunch	*Wǔcān*
Luncheon	*Wǔcān*

M

Magazine	*Zázhì*
Mail	*Yóujiàn*
Mail (to)	*Yóujì*
Mailing list	*Yóujì míngdān*

Mail order	*Yóugòu*
Mainframe computer	*Zhǔjī diànnǎo*
Make (to)	*Zhìzào*
Management	*Guǎnlǐ*
Manage (to)	*Guǎnlǐ*
Manager	*Jīnglǐ*
Map	*Dìtú*
Marker	*Biāoshìqì*
Market	*Shìchǎng*
Market (to)	*Tūixiāo*
Marketing	*Tūixiāo*
Marketing report	*Tūixiāo bàogào*
Market value	*Shìchǎng jiàzhí*
Materials	*Cáiliào*
Mathematics	*Shùxúe*
Maximum	*Zùidà jíxiàn*
Maybe	*Hùoxǔ*
Meat	*Ròu*
Media	*Méitǐ*
Mediate (to)	*Tiáojiě*
Meet (to)	*Hùijiàn*
Meeting	*Hùiyì*
Memo	*Bèiwànglù*
Men's room	*Náncèsǔo*
Mentor	*Liángshī yìyǒu*
Mentoring	*Zùo liángshī yìyǒu*
Menu	*Xǔandān* more commonly *càidān*
Message	*Xìnxí*
Message center	*Xìnxí zhōngxīn*
Mezzanine	*Bāoxiāng*
Microphone	*Màikèfēng*
Middle	*Zhōngjiān*
Milk	*Niúnǎi*
Mineral water	*Kùangqúanshǔi*
Minimum	*Zùixiǎo jíxiàn*

Minute	*Fēnzhōng*
Mission	*Shǐmìng*
Model	*Mótè*
Modem	*Shùjùjī*
Money	*Qián*
Monitor	*Xiǎnshìqì*
Month	*Yùe*
Morning	*Shàngwǔ*
Mosque	*Qīngzhēnsì*
Move (to)	*Yídòng*
Movie	*Diànyǐng*
Multimedia	*Dūoméitǐ*
Museum	*Bówùguǎn*
Music	*Yīnyùe*
Musical	*Yīnyùe de*

N

Name	*Míngzi*
Name (to)	*Míngjiào*
Need (to)	*Xūyào*
Negotiate (to)	*Tánpàn*
Negotiating	*Tánpàn*
Network	*Wǎnglùo*
New	*Xīn de*
News	*Xīnwén*
Newsstand	*Bàotān*
Night	*Wǎnshang*
Nine	*Jǐu*
No	*Bù*
Note	*Biàntiáo*
Note (to)	*Zhùyì*
Notepad	*Bǐjìbù*
Number	*Shùzì*
Nurse	*Hùshì*

O

Object	*Wùtǐ*
Objective	*Mùdì*
Offer (to)	*Tígōng*
Office	*Bàngōngshì*
Officer	*Gūanyúan*
Okay (to)	*Pīzhǔn*
One	*Yī*
On-line	*Xiànshàng*
On-line service	*Xiànshàng fúwù*
On/Off	*Kāi/Gūan*
Open (to)	*Dǎkāi*
Opera	*Gējù*
Operate (to)	*Cāozùo*
Operating system	*Cāozùo xìtǒng*
Operations	*Jīngyíng*
Operator	*Jīngyíngzhě*
Option	*Xǔanzhé*
Orange	*Chéng*
Orchestra	*Gǔanxián yùetúan*
Organization	*Zǔzhī*
Organizational chart	*Zǔzhī jiégòutú*
Organize (to)	*Zǔzhī*
Orientation	*Dìngxiàng*
Origin	*Qǐyúan*
Outside	*Wàimiàn*
Overhead projector	*Hùandēngjī*

P

Package	*Bāogǔo*
Package (to)	*Dǎbāo*
Paper	*Zhǐ*
Page	*Yèshù*

Page (to)	*Biān yèshù*
Pager	*Chúanhūjī*
Parent	*Fùmǔ*
Park (car)	*Tíngchēchǎng*
Part	*Bùjiàn*
Participant	*Cānjiāzhě*
Participate	*Cānjiā*
Partner	*Héhǔorén*
Passport	*Hùzhào*
Password	*Mìmǎ*
Past due	*Gùoqī de*
Patent	*Zhūanlì*
Pause (to)	*Tíngdùn*
Payment	*Fùkǔan*
Peer	*Tóngshì*
Pencil	*Qiānbǐ*
Pension	*Yǎnglǎojīn*
Percentage	*Bǎifēnbǐ*
Personnel	*Rénshì de*
Pet	*Chǒngwù*
Philosophy	*Zhéxúe*
Phone	*Diànhùa*
Phone (to)	*Dǎ diànhùa*
Phone call	*Diànhùa*
Photocopy (to)	*Fùyìnjiàn*
Photograph	*Zhàopiàn*
Picture	*Túhùa*
Pie	*Shǔigǔopài*
Pie chart	*Yúanxíng túbiǎo*
Ping-Pong	*Pīngpāngqiú*
Place (to)	*Fàngzhì*
Plan (to)	*Jìhùa*
Play	*Jùběn*
Play (to)	*Biǎoyǎn*
Please	*Qǐng*

Podium	*Zhǐhūitái*
Point of view	*Guāndiǎn*
Point (to)	*Zhǐchū*
Pointer	*Ànshì*
Police man	*Jǐngchá*
Policy	*Zhèngcè*
Polygon	*Duōbiānxíng*
Pork	*Zhūròu*
Portable	*Kěxiédài de*
Portable phone	*Shǒujī*
Portal	*Chúansòngmén*
Porter	*Fúwùshēng*
Position	*Wèizhì*
Post office	*Yóujú*
Postpone (to)	*Tūichí*
Pound key	*Jǐngzìjiàn*
Pound sign	*Jǐngzìhào*
PowerPoint presentation	*PowerPoint zhǎnshì*
Present (to)	*Zhǎnshì*
Presentation	*Zhǎnshì*
Presenting	*Fēngxiàn*
President	*Zǒngcái*
Price	*Jiàgé*
Print (to)	*Dǎyìn*
Printer	*Dǎyìnjī*
Problem	*Wèntí*
Problem solving	*Jiějúe wèntí*
Procedure	*Chéngxù*
Process	*Chǔlǐ*
Procure (to)	*Cǎigòu*
Produce (to)	*Shēngchǎn*
Product	*Chǎnpǐn*
Production	*Shēngchǎn*
Program	*Jiémù*
Promotion	*Tíshēng*

Property	*Cáichǎn*
Propose (to)	*Tíyì*
Proposal	*Xíeyì*
Provide (to)	*Tígōng*
Purchasing agent	*Gòumǎi dàilǐ*
Purple	*Zǐsè*
Purpose	*Mùdì*

Q

Quality	*Zhíliàng*
Quality control	*Zhíliàng kòngzhì*
Query	*Xùnwèn*
Question	*Wèntī*
Question (to)	*Zhìwèn*
Q & Λ	*Wèndá*
Quiet	*Ānjìng*

R

Rain	*Xiàyǔ*
Rainy day	*Yǔ tiān*
Rare	*Nándé de*
Reboot	*Zài qǐdòng*
Receive (to)	*Jiēshōu*
Receiver	*Jiēshōurén*
Reception	*Jiēdài*
Receptionist	*Chúandáyúan/jiēdài yúan*
Recommend (to)	*Tūijiàn*
Recommendation	*Tūijiàn*
Reconsider (to)	*Zài kǎolǜ*
Record	*Jìlù*
Record (to)	*Lùyīn*

Recording	*Lùyīn*
Rectangle	*Chángfāngxíng*
Red	*Hóngsè*
Redial (to)	*Zài bō*
Referral	*Cānzhào*
Reference	*Cānkǎo*
Reference (to)	*Cānzhào*
Refreshments	*Diǎnxīn*
Refund	*Tuìkuǎn*
Register (to)	*Dēngjì*
Regression	*Huígūi*
Regression line	*Huígūixiàn*
Rehearse	*Páiliàn*
Reject (to)	*Jùjúe*
Rent	*Zūlìng*
Rent (to)	*Chūzū*
Reorganize (to)	*Chóngjiàn*
Reply	*Húifù*
Reply (to)	*Dáfù*
Report	*Bàogào*
Request (to)	*Yāoqiú*
Reservation	*Bǎoliú*
Reserve (to)	*Yùyūe*
Reserved	*Yùliú de*
Restaurant	*Cānguǎn*
Rest room	*Xíshǒujiān*
Result	*Jiégǔo*
Resume (to)	*Zài jìxù*
Return (to)	*Húigūi*
Reveal (to)	*Jiēlù*
Right	*Qúanlì*
Right angle	*Zhíjiǎo*
Risk	*Fēngxiǎn*
Risk (to)	*Mào fēngxiǎn*

Room	*Fángjiān*
Row	*Páilìe*
Rugby	*Lāgēbìqiú/Yīng shì gǎn lǎn qiú*

S

Salary	*Xīnshǔi*
Sale	*Xiāoshòu*
Sales call	*Xiāoshòu diànhùa*
Sales reports	*Xiāoshòu bàogào*
Sales tax	*Yíngyèshùi*
Say (to)	*Shūo*
Scale	*Tiānpíng*
Scatter diagram	*Fēnsàn túshì*
Schedule	*Shíjiānbiǎo*
Science	*Kēxúe*
Science fiction	*Kēhùan*
Screen	*Yínmù/Yíngpíng*
Scuba	*Shǔifèi*
Search engine	*Sōusǔo yǐnqǐng*
Season	*Jìjié*
Second	*Dì èr*
Secretary	*Mìshū*
See (to)	*Kàn*
Sell (to)	*Mài*
Selling	*Mài*
Seminar	*Yāntǎohùi*
Send (to)	*Jì*
Service	*Fúwù*
Set up (to)	*Jiànlì*
Seven	*Qī*
Server	*Shìfúqì*
Service	*Fúwù*
Shaded	*Zhēbì*

Shadow	*Yīnyíng*
Ship (to)	*Yùn*
Shipment	*Zhuāngchuán*
Shipping center	*Zhuāngyùn zhōngxīn*
Shoe	*Xiézi*
Show (to)	*Xiǎnshì*
Sightseeing	*Guānguāng*
Sign (to)	*Qiānshǔ*
Six	*Liù*
Skiing	*Huàxuě*
Skill	*Jìshù*
Skirt	*Qúnzi*
Slice	*Báopiàn*
Slide projector	*Huàndēngjī*
Slide	*Huàndēngpiàn*
Snack	*Xiǎochī*
Snow	*Xuě*
Snowy	*Duōxuě de*
Soccer	*Zúqiú*
Sock	*Duǎnwà*
Software	*Ruǎnjiàn*
Solid	*Jiāngù de*
Solid line	*Shíxiàn*
Solve (a problem) (to)	*Jiějué (wèntí)*
Son	*Érzi*
Sound system	*Yīnxiáng xìtǒng*
Souvenir	*Jìniànpǐn*
Space	*Kōngjiān*
Speak (to)	*Yǎnjiǎng*
Speaker	*Yǎnjiǎngrén*
Special delivery	*Xiànshí zhuānsòng*
Specialty	*Tèchǎn*
Specification(s)	*Guīgé*
Speech	*Yǎnshuō*
Spring	*Chūntiān*

Sport	*Yùndòng*
Square	*Guǎngchǎng*
Stack	*Duījī*
Star	*Xīngxīng*
Start	*Kāishǐ*
Steak	*Niúpái*
Stock	*Gǔpiào*
Stockholder	*Gǔdōng*
Stocking	*Chángwà*
Stock options	*Gǔpiào gòumǎi quán*
Stop	*Tíngzhǐ*
Street	*Jiēdào*
Stress	*Zhòngdiǎn*
Style	*Fēnggé*
Subject	*Zhǔtǐ*
Submit	*Dìjiāo*
Suit	*Tàofáng*
Summer	*Xiàtiān*
Supervisor	*Guǎnlǐrén*
Supply	*Gōngjǐ*
Supply (to)	*Gōngyìng*
Support (to)	*Zhīchí*
Surf (to)	*Chōnglàng*
Surf the Web (to)	*Wǎngshàng liúlǎn*
Switch	*Kāigūan*
Switch (to)	*Zhuǎn dào*
Switchboard	*Jiāohùantái*
Synagogue	*Yóutài jiàotáng*
System	*Xìtǒng*

T

Table	*Zhūozi*
Tailor	*Cáifeng*
Talk (to)	*Tánhùa*

Tape recorder	*Lùyīnjī*
Tax	*Shùiwù*
Tax-exempt	*Miǎnshùi de*
Taxi	*Jìchéngchē/Chūzū qì chè*
Tea	*Chá*
Team	*Tuandùi*
Team building	*Tuandùi jiànshè*
Technical support	*Jìshù zhīchí*
Telephone	*Diànhùajī*
Telephone directory	*Diànhùa zhǐnán*
Telephone number	*Diànhùa hàomǎ*
Telephone operator	*Diànhùa jiēxiànshēng*
Television	*Diànshì*
Temperature	*Wēndù*
Ten	*Shí*
Terminology	*Shùyǔ*
Text	*Zhèngwén*
Theater	*Xìyùan*
Theory	*Lǐlùn*
Thesis	*Lùnwén*
Three	*Sān*
3-D chart	*Lìtǐ túbiǎo*
Ticket	*Piào*
Tie	*Lǐngdài*
Time	*Shíjiān*
Time (to)	*Jìshí*
Title	*Tóuxián*
Tobacco	*Yāncǎo*
Today	*Jīntiān*
Tomorrow	*Míngtiān*
Top	*Dǐngdūan*
Tour	*Lǚyóu*
Tour bus	*Lǚyóuchē*
Town	*Chéngzhèn*

Trade	*Màoyì*
Trade (to)	*Jiāoyì*
Trademark	*Shāngbiāo*
Trade show	*Màoyì zhǎnxiāo*
Trade union	*Shāngyè gōnghuì*
Train (to)	*Xùnliàn*
Training	*Péixùn*
Transact (to)	*Bànlǐ*
Transaction	*Jiāoyì*
Transfer (to)	*Zhuǎnràng*
Transparency	*Tòumíng*
Transportation	*Yùnshū*
Transportation charges	*Yùnshū fèiyòng*
Travel	*Lǚxíng*
Travel (to)	*Qù lǚxíng*
Treasurer	*Chūnàyúan*
Triangle	*Sānjiǎo*
Turn (to)	*Zhuǎnwān*
Two	*Èr*
Type	*Zhǒnglèi*
Type (to)	*Dǎzì*
Typewriter	*Dǎzìjī*

U

Umbrella	*Yǔsǎn*
Unacceptable	*Bù kě jiēshòu*
Underline	*Dǐxiàn*
Understand (to)	*Míngbái*
Understanding	*Lǐjiě*
Underwear	*Nèiyī nèikù*
Union	*Gōnghuì*
United States of America	*Měiguó*
U-shaped	*U zìxíng*
U-turn	*U zìxíng wān*

V

Value	Jiàzhí
Value (to)	Biāojià
Value-added tax	Zēngzhíshùi
Vegetable	Shūcài
Vegetarian	Sùshí zhě
Vertical	Chúizhí de
Via	Jīng yóu
Vice president	Fù zǒngcái
Video	Yǐngxiàng
Video (to)	Lùyǐng/shè xiàng
Video conferencing	Yǐngxiàng hùiyì
Video recorder	Lùyǐngjī/Shè xiàngjī
Virtual reality	Xūní xiànshí
Vision	Yǎngūang
Voice mail	Yǒushēng yóujiàn
Voice recognition	Shēngyīn shìbié

W

Wait (to)	Děngdài
Waiting room	Děnghòushì
Want (to)	Yào
Warm	Nǔanhuo
Warranty	Bǎodān
Watch (to)	Gūankàn
Water	Shǔi
Weather	Tiānqì
Web access	Wǎngyè jìnjiē
Web page	Wǎngyè
Week	Zhōu
Well	Hǎo
Well done	Zùo de hǎo
Wife	Qīzi

Window	*Chūanghù*
Wine	*Jiǔ*
Wine list	*Jiǔdān*
Winter	*Dōngtiān*
Women's Room	*Nǔcèsǔo*
Word software	*Word rǔanjiàn*
WordPerfect software	*WordPerfect rǔanjiàn/ Zìcí wán shàn rǔanjìan*
Work (to)	*Gōngzùo*
Workbook	*Liànxíbù*
Workshop	*Chējiān*
Work station	*Gōngzùozhàn*
World Wide Web	*Wǎngjì wǎnglùo*
Write (to)	*Xiě*

X

X-axis	*Héngzhóu*
XY scatter	*XY sànbù*

Y

Y-axis	*Zòngzhóu*
Yellow	*Húangsè*
Yes	*Shì*
Yield	*Chǎnliàng*
You're welcome	*Bù yòng xiè*

Z

Z-axis	*Z zhóu*
Zoo	*Dòngwùyúan*

GENERAL GLOSSARY:
Chinese–English

A

Ānjìng	*Quiet*
Ànshì	*Pointer*
Ānzhuāng	*Install (to)*
Ānzhuāng	*Installation*

B

Bā	*Eight*
Bǎifēnbǐ	*Percentage*
Bāléi	*Ballet*
Bàngōngshì	*Office*
Bāngzhù	*Help (to)*
Bànlǐ	*Transact (to)*
Bǎnquán	*Copyright*
Bǎochí	*Hold (to)*
Bǎochóu	*Compensate (to)*
Bǎodān	*Warranty*
Bàodào	*Check in (to)*
Bǎofù zhīpiào	*Certified check*
Bàogào	*Report*
Bāoguǒ	*Package*
Bǎoliú	*Reservation*
Bàotān	*Newsstand*
Bǎoxiǎn	*Insurance*
Bāoxiāng	*Box seat*
Bāoxiāng	*Mezzanine*
Bǎozhèng	*Guarantee*
Bǎozhèng	*Guarantee (to)*
Bèijǐng	*Background*

Bèiwànglù	*Memo*
Biān yèshù	*Page (to)*
Biàntiáo	*Note*
Biānyúan	*Edge*
Biāojià	*Value (to)*
Biāoqiān	*Label*
Biāoshìqì	*Marker*
Biāotí	*Heading*
Biǎoyǎn	*Play (to)*
Bǐjìbù	*Notepad*
Bīngqìlín	*Ice cream*
Bō	*Dial (to)*
Bō hào	*Dial*
Bōlí	*Glass*
Bópiàn	*Slice*
Bówùguǎn	*Museum*
Bù	*No*
Bù kě jiēshòu	*Unacceptable*
Bù yòng xiè	*You're welcome*
Bǔcháng	*Compensation*
Bùjiàn	*Part*
Bùmén	*Department*

C

Cáichǎn	*Property*
Cáifeng	*Tailor*
Cǎigòu	*Procure (to)*
Cáijiǎn	*Downsize (to)*
Cáiliào	*Materials*
Cǎisè	*Color*
Cǎisè xiǎnshìqì	*Color monitor*
Cáiwù	*Finance*
Cáiwù bàogào	*Financial report*
Cáiwù shùzì	*Financial figure*

Cāngǔan	*Restaurant*
Cānjiā	*Participate*
Cānjiāzhě	*Participant*
Cānkǎo	*Reference*
Cānzhào	*Reference (to)*
Cāozùo	*Operate (to)*
Cāozùo xìtǒng	*Operating system*
Chá	*Tea*
Cādiào	*Erase (to)*
Chángfāngxíng	*Rectangle*
Chángtú	*Long-distance*
Chángtú diànhùa	*Long-distance call*
Chángwà	*Stocking*
Chǎnliàng	*Yield*
Chǎnpǐn	*Product*
Chāojí wénjiàn	*Hypertext*
Chē shàng diànhùa	*Car phone*
Chējiān	*Workshop*
Chén	*Orange*
Chéngběn	*Cost*
Chéngshì	*City*
Chéngxù	*Procedure*
Chéngzhèn	*Town*
Chóngjiàn	*Reorganize (to)*
Chōnglàng	*Surf (to)*
Chǒngwù	*Pet*
Chúandáyúan	*Receptionist*
Chúang	*Bed*
Chūanghù	*Window*
Chùangyè	*Entrepreneurship*
Chúanhūjī	*Pager*
Chúansòngmén	*Portal*
Chúanzhēn	*Fax*
Chūbǎnwù	*Literature*
Chúizhí de	*Vertical*

Chūkǒu	*Exit*
Chūkǒu	*Export (to)*
Chǔlǐ	*Process*
Chūnàyúan	*Treasurer*
Chūntiān	*Spring*
Chūqù	*Exit (to)*
Chūzū	*Rent (to)*
Cùchéng	*Facilitate (to)*
Cùchéngrén	*Facilitator*

D

Dǎ diànhùa	*Call (to)*
Dǎ diànhùa	*Phone (to)*
Dǎbāo	*Package (to)*
Dáfù	*Reply (to)*
Dǎkāi	*Open (to)*
Dàmén	*Gate*
Dǎng'àn	*File*
Dǎng'àngùi	*File cabinet*
Dàngāo	*Cake*
Dàoqī de	*Due*
Dàoqiàn	*Apology*
Dǎyìn	*Print (to)*
Dǎyìnjī	*Printer*
Dǎzì	*Type (to)*
Dǎzìjī	*Typewriter*
Děngdài	*Wait (to)*
Dǐngdūan	*Top*
Dēnggūang	*Light*
Děnghòushì	*Waiting room*
Dēngjì	*Register (to)*
Dēngpào	*Lightbulb*
Dǐ	*Bottom*
Dì èr	*Second*

Dì yī	*First*
Diànhùa	*Phone*
Diànhùa	*Phone call*
Diànhùa hàomǎ	*Telephone number*
Diànhùa hùiyì	*Conference call*
Diànhùa jiēxiànshēng	*Telephone operator*
Diànhùa tūixiāo	*Cold call*
Diànhùa zhǐnán	*Telephone directory*
Diànhùajī	*Telephone*
Diànhùakǎ	*Calling card*
Diànlì	*Electricity*
Diànnǎo	*Computer*
Diànnǎo cípán	*Computer disk*
Diànnǎo diànlǎn	*Computer cable*
Diànnǎo wǎnglùo	*Internet*
Diànnǎo xiǎnshìqì	*Computer monitor*
Diànshì	*Television*
Diànxiàn	*Electrical line*
Diǎnxīn	*Refreshments*
Diànyǐng	*Movie*
Diànzǐ kōngjiān	*Cyberspace*
Diànzǐ yóujiàn	*E-mail*
Dìdiǎn	*Location*
Dìfāng de	*Local*
Dìfāng fēnqúan	*Decentralization*
Dìjiāo	*Submit*
Dìngxiàng	*Orientation*
Dìtú	*Map*
Dǐxiàn	*Underline*
Dìzhǐ	*Address*
Dōngtiān	*Winter*
Dòngwùyúan	*Zoo*
Dǔanwà	*Sock*
Dùihúa	*Dialogue*
Dùihùan zhīpiào	*Cash a check (to)*

Dūijī	*Stack*
Dùishù gūimó	*Logarithmic scale*
Dùkǒu	*Ferry*
Dūobiānxíng	*Polygon*
Dūoméitǐ	*Multimedia*
Dūoxǔe de	*Snowy*
Dūoyún de	*Cloudy*

E

Èr	*Two*
Érzi	*Son*
Excel rǔanjiàn	*Excel software*

F

Fā	*Issue (to)*
Fā chúanzhēn	*Fax (to)*
Fǎlǜ	*Law*
Fǎlǜ de	*Legal*
Fǎlǜ fèiyòng	*Legal costs*
Fángjiān	*Room*
Fāngxiàng	*Directions*
Fàngzhì	*Place (to)*
Fángzi	*House*
Fāpiào	*Bill of sale*
Fāpiào	*Invoice*
Fāxiàn	*Find (to)*
Fāxiàn	*Finding*
Fēijīchǎng	*Airport*
Fěnbǐ	*Chalk*
Fēnfā	*Distribute (to)*
Fēnfā	*Distribution*
Fēnfā yìnshūapǐn	*Handout*

Fēnggé	Style
Fēngmiàn	Cover
Fèngxiàn	Presenting
Fēngxiǎn	Risk(s)
Fēnsàn túshì	Scatter diagram
Fēnzhōng	Minute
Fù zǒngcái	Vice president
Fǔdǎo	Coaching
Fùjiā	Attachment
Fùjiàn	Enclosure
Fùkuǎn	Payment
Fúlì	Benefits
Fùmǔ	Parent
Fúwù	Service
Fúwù	Service (to)
Fúwùshēng	Porter
Fùyìn	Copy (to)
Fùyìnjī	Copier
Fùyìnjiàn	Photocopy

G

Gǎibiàn	Change (to)
Gǎnlǎnqiú	Football
Gǎnmào	Cold
Gàozhī	Inform (to)
Gāozhuō	Dais
Gǎunggào	Ad
Gěi	Give (to)
Gěi jīngfèi	Finance (to)
Gējù	Opera
Gēnzōng	Follow up (to)
Gèrén	Individual
Gézhà	Grid
Gōngchéngshī	Engineer

Gōngjǐ	*Supply*
Gōnggòng qìchē	*Bus*
Gōnghùi	*Union*
Gōngyìng	*Supply (to)*
Gòngyǒu	*Co-owner*
Gōngzùo	*Job*
Gōngzùo	*Work (to)*
Gōngzùozhàn	*Work station*
Gǒu	*Dog*
Gòumǎi dàilǐ	*Purchasing agent*
Gùadiào/Bǎ . . . guà qǐlái	*Hang up (to)*
Gùahàoxìn	*Certified mail*
Gūandiǎn	*Point of view*
Gūanbì	*Close (to)*
Gǔangchǎng	*Square*
Gūangūang	*Sightseeing*
Gūanjiàn wènteí	*Key issues*
Gūankàn	*Watch (to)*
Gǔanlǐ	*Management*
Gǔanlǐ	*Manage (to)*
Gǔanlǐrén	*Supervisor*
Gǔanxián yùetúan	*Orchestra*
Guānyuán	*Officer*
Gǔdiǎn yīnyùe	*Classical music*
Gǔdōng	*Stockholder*
Gùichú	*Cabinet*
Gùidàng	*File (to)*
Gūigé	*Specification(s)*
Gùkè	*Customer*
Gùkè fúwù	*Customer service*
Gǔlì	*Encourage (to)*
Gúojì	*International*
Gúojì fǎ	*International law*
Gúojiā	*Country*
Gùoqī de	*Past due*

Gǔpiào	*Stock*
Gǔpiào gòumǎi qúan	*Stock option*
Gùwèn	*Consultant*

H

Hǎigūan	*Customs*
Háizi	*Child*
Hángbān	*Flight*
Hǎo	*Good*
Hǎo	*Well*
Háohúa jiàochē	*Limousine*
Héhǔorén	*Partner*
Hēibǎn	*Blackboard*
Hēisè	*Black*
Héngxiàng tiáoxíng tú	*Horizontal bar chart*
Héngxíng de	*Horizontal*
Héngzhóu	*X-axis*
Hétóng	*Contract*
Hétóng yìwù	*Contractual obligation*
Hézi	*Box*
Hónglì	*Bonus*
Hóngsè	*Red*
Hūa	*Flower*
Hùajià	*Easel*
Hùaláng	*Art gallery*
Hùaláng	*Gallery*
Húandēngjī	*Overhead projector*
Húandēngjī	*Slide projector*
Húandēngpiàn	*Slides*
Húangsè	*Yellow*
Húaxǔe	*Skiing*
Húidá	*Answer*
Húidá	*Answer (to)*
Húifù	*Reply*

Húigūi	*Regression*
Húigūi	*Return (to)*
Húigūixiàn	*Regression line*
Hùijiàn	*Meet (to)*
Húikùi	*Feedback*
Húikùi	*Feedback (to give)*
Hùiyì	*Conference*
Hùiyì	*Meeting*
Hùiyì zhōngxīn	*Conference center*
Hùiyúan	*Associate*
Hūizhāng	*Badge*
Húodòng	*Activities*
Hùolì	*Gain (to)*
Hùowù	*Goods*
Hùoxǔ	*Maybe*
Hùshì	*Nurse*
Húxíng	*Arc*
Hùzhào	*Passport*

J

Jì	*Send (to)*
Jiàgé	*Price*
Jiǎnchá	*Check (to)*
Jiǎngjià	*Bargain (to)*
Jiāngù de	*Solid*
Jiànkāng	*Health*
Jiànlì	*Setup (to)*
Jiànshí/Dòng chá	*Insight*
Jiàntóu	*Arrow*
Jiànzhù	*Building*
Jiàochē	*Car*
Jiāofù	*Delivery*
Jiāofù rì	*Delivery date*
Jiāohùantái	*Switchboard*

Jiāojuǎn	*Film*
Jiǎoluò bàngōngshì	*Corner office*
Jiàoshì	*Classroom*
Jiàotáng	*Church*
Jiāoyì	*Deal*
Jiāoyì	*Trade (to)*
Jiāoyì	*Transaction*
Jiātíng	*Family*
Jiàzhí	*Value*
Jīchǎng yùnsòngchē	*Airport shuttle*
Jīchéngchē/Chūzū qìchē	*Taxi*
Jiēdài	*Reception*
Jiēdào	*Street*
Jiēguǒ	*Result*
Jiějué (wèntí)	*Solve (a problem) (to)*
Jiějué wèntí	*Problem solving*
Jiēlù	*Reveal (to)*
Jiémù	*Program*
Jièshào	*Introduce (to)*
Jièshào	*Introduction*
Jiēshòu	*Accept (to)*
Jiēshōu	*Receive (to)*
Jiēshōurén	*Receiver*
Jiéshù	*End (to)*
Jǐhéxué	*Geometry*
Jìhùa	*Plan (to)*
Jìjié	*Season*
Jìlù	*Record*
Jīng yóu	*Via*
Jǐngchá	*Police man*
Jīnglǐ	*Manager*
Jīngyàn	*Experience*
Jīngyíng	*Operation*
Jīngyíngzhě	*Operator*
Jìngzhēng	*Compete (to)*
Jìngzhēng	*Competition*

Jīngzhēng jiàgé	*Competitive price*
Jǐngzìhào	*Pound sign*
Jǐngzìjiàn	*Pound key*
Jìniànpǐn	*Souvenir*
Jìnkǒu	*Import (to)*
Jìnrù	*Admission*
Jīntiān	*Today*
Jīròu	*Chicken*
Jìshí	*Time (to)*
Jìshù	*Skill*
Jìshù zhīchí	*Technical support*
Jiǔ	*Nine*
Jiǔ	*Wine*
Jiǔbā	*Bar*
Jiǔdān	*Wine list*
Jīwěi jiǔhùi	*Cocktail party*
Jīwěijiǔ	*Cocktail*
Jùběn	*Play*
Júedìng	*Decide (to)*
Júedìng	*Decision*
Júeshì jùlèbù	*Jazz club*
Júeshìyuè	*Jazz*
Jùjúe	*Reject (to)*

K

Kāfēi	*Coffee*
Kāfēidiàn	*Cafe*
Kāi fāpiào	*Invoice (to)*
Kāi wánxiào	*Joke (to)*
Kāi/Gūan	*On/Off*
Kāigūan	*Switch*
Kāishǐ	*Begin (to)*
Kāishǐ	*Beginning*
Kāishǐ	*Start*
Kāizhī	*Expenses*

Kàn	*See (to)*
Kě jiēshòu dc	*Acceptable*
Kèchéng	*Course*
Kēhùan	*Science fiction*
Kěxíedài de	*Portable*
Kēxúe	*Science*
Kòngbái	*Blank*
Kōngjiān	*Space*
Kōngshǒudào	*Karate*
Kǒudài	*Bag*
Kǒuyīn	*Accent*
Kùaijì	*Accounting*
Kùangqúanshǔi	*Mineral water*

L

Lāgēbìqiú	*Rugby*
Lánqiú	*Basketball*
Lánsè	*Blue*
Lǎobǎn	*Boss*
Lěngqùe	*Cool*
Lèsèxiāng/Lājīxiāng	*Bin*
Liángshī yìyǒu	*Mentor*
Liánjiē	*Connection*
Liánjiēdiǎn	*Link*
Liánlùo	*Contact (to)*
Liànxíbù	*Workbook*
Lǐjiě	*Understanding*
Lǐlùn	*Theory*
Lǐmiàn	*Inside*
Lǐngbān	*Foreman*
Lǐngdài	*Tie*
Lǐngdǎo	*Leader*
Lǐngdǎorén	*Leadership*
Lìshǐ	*History*
Lìtǐ túbiǎo	*3-D chart*

Liù	*Six*
Liúxíng yīnyuè	*Disco music*
Liúyánjī	*Answering machine*
Lotus 1-2-3 ruǎnjiàn	*Lotus 1-2-3 software*
Lǚguǎn	*Hotel*
Lùnwén	*Thesis*
Lǜsè	*Green*
Lǜshī	*Lawyer*
Lǚxíng	*Travel*
Lùyīn	*Record (to)*
Lùyīn	*Recording*
Lùyǐng	*Video (to)*
Lùyǐngjī	*Video recorder*
Lùyīnjī	*Tape recorder*
Lǚyóu	*Tour*
Lǚyóuchē	*Tour bus*

M

Mǎ	*Horse*
Mǎi	*Buy (to)*
Mài	*Sell (to)*
Mài	*Selling*
Màikèfēng	*Microphone*
Máng	*Busy*
Māo	*Cat*
Mào fēngxiǎn	*Risk (to)*
Màoyì	*Trade*
Màoyì zhǎnxiāo	*Trade show*
Màozi	*Hat*
Měigúo	*American*
Měigúo	*United States of America*
Méitǐ	*Media*
Měiyúan	*Dollar*

Mén	*Door*
Ménfáng	*Concierge*
Miànjī	*Area*
Miànshì	*Interview*
Miànshì	*Interview (to)*
Miǎnshùi de	*Tax-exempt*
Mìmǎ	*Password*
Míngbái	*Understand (to)*
Míngjiào	*Name (to)*
Míngpiàn	*Business card*
Míngqùe	*Clear (to)*
Míngtiān	*Tomorrow*
Míngzi	*Name*
Mìshū	*Secretary*
Mótè	*Model*
Mùbǎn	*Board*
Mùbiāo	*Goal*
Mùdì	*Objective*
Mùdì	*Purpose*

N

Nǎiyóu	*Cream*
Náncèsǔo	*Men's room*
Nándé	*Rare*
Nèiyī nèikù	*Underwear*
Nénglì	*Capability*
Niúnǎi	*Milk*
Niúpái	*Steak*
Nóngkāfēi	*Espresso*
Nǔanhuo	*Warm*
Nǔcèsǔo	*Women's Room*
Nǔ'ér	*Daughter*
Nǚzhǔxí	*Chairwoman*

P

Páiliè	*Row*
Páiliàn	*Rehearse*
Péixùn	*Training*
Piào	*Ticket*
Píngbǎn yíngmù	*Flat-panel display*
Pínggū	*Appraise (to)*
Píngmiàntú	*Layout*
Pīngpāngqiú	*Ping-Pong*
Pīzhǔn	*Okay (to)*
PowerPoint zhǎnshì ruǎnjiàn	*PowerPoint presentation*
Pòzhéhào	*Dash*

Q

Qī	*Seven*
Qián	*Money*
Qiānbǐ	*Pencil*
Qiānchū	*Log off (to)*
Qiánmiàn	*Front*
Qiānrù	*Log on (to)*
Qiānshǔ	*Sign (to)*
Qìchē	*Auto*
Qǐng	*Please*
Qīngdān	*List (to)*
Qīngzhēnsì	*Mosque*
Qiūtiān	*Fall (season)*
Qǐyè	*Enterprise*
Qǐyèjiā	*Entrepreneur*
Qǐyuán	*Origin*
Qīzi	*Wife*
Qù lǚxíng	*Travel (to)*
Quánlì	*Right*

Qúanwēi	*Authority*
Qùerèn	*Confirm (to)*
Qùerèn	*Confirmation*
Qúnzi	*Skirt*

R

Rè	*Hot*
Rénshì de	*Personnel*
Rénshì gǔanlǐ	*Human resources*
Rìlì	*Calendar*
Rìqī	*Date*
Rìzǐ	*Day*
Ròu	*Meat*
Rǔanjiàn	*Software*
Rùkǒu	*Entrance*

S

Sān	*Three*
Sānjiǎo	*Triangle*
Shāngbiāo	*Trademark*
Shàngwǔ	*Morning*
Shāngyè	*Business*
Shāngyè gōnghùi	*Trade union*
Shāngyè zhōngxīn	*Business center*
Shàngyī	*Blouse*
Shèjì	*Design*
Shēngchǎn	*Produce (to)*
Shēngchǎn	*Production*
Shěnjì	*Audit*
Shěnjì	*Audit (to)*
Shēngyīn shìbié	*Voice recognition*
Shí	*Ten*

Shì	*Yes*
Shìchǎng	*Market*
Shìchǎng jiàzhí	*Market value*
Shìhào	*Hobby*
Shíjiān	*Time*
Shíjiānbiǎo	*Schedule*
Shǐmìng	*Mission*
Shìnèi diànhùa	*Local call*
Shíwù	*Food*
Shíxiàn	*Solid line*
Shǒujī	*Portable phone*
Shòuqúan	*Authorize (to)*
Shǒuwèi	*Guard*
Shūcài	*Vegetable*
Shǔi	*Water*
Shǔifèi	*Scuba*
Shùifú	*Convince (to)*
Shǔigǔopài	*Pie*
Shùiwù	*Tax*
Shūjí	*Book*
Shùjù	*Data*
Shùjùjī	*Modem*
Shùjùkù	*Database*
Shūo	*Say (to)*
Shūqiān	*Bookmark*
Shùxúe	*Mathematics*
Shùyǔ	*Terminology*
Shùzì	*Number*
Shūzūo	*Desk*
Sì	*Four*
Sìfùqì	*Server*
Sōusǔo yǐnqíng	*Search engine*
Sùshí zhě	*Vegetarian*
Sùsòng	*Lawsuit*

Tánhùa	Talk (to)
Tánpàn	Negotiate (to)
Tánpàn	Negotiating
Tānwèi	Booth
Tàofáng	Suit
Tǎolùn	Discuss (to)
Tǎolùn	Discussion
Tèchǎn	Specialty
Tiānpíng	Scale
Tiānqì	Weather
Tiáojiě	Mediate (to)
Tiáozhùang tú	Bar chart
Tiē biāoqiān	Label (to)
Tígōng	Offer (to)
Tígōng	Provide (to)
Tīng	Listen (to)
Tíngchēchǎng	Park
Tíngdùn	Pause (to)
Tíngzhǐ	Stop
Tíshēng	Promotion
Tíyì	Propose (to)
Tóngshì	Peer
Tōngxìn	Communicate (to)
Tōngxùn	Communications
Tóngyì	Agree (to)
Tóukuǎn	Down payment
Tòumíng	Transparency
Tóuxián	Title
Tóuzī	Invest (to)
Tóuzī	Investment
Túandùi	Team
Túandùi jiànshè	Team building
Túbiǎo	Chart

Túbiǎo	*Graphs*
Túbiāo	*Logo*
Túhùa	*Picture*
Tūichí	*Postpone (to)*
Tūijiàn	*Recommend (to)*
Tūijiàn	*Recommendation*
Tùikǔan	*Refund*
Tuīxìao bàogào	*Marketing report*
Tūixiāo	*Market (to)*
Tūixiāo	*Marketing*
Tújiě	*Illustrate (to)*
Tújiě	*Illustration*
Tǔoyúanxíng	*Ellipse*
Túshì	*Diagram*
Túshì	*Diagram (to)*
Túshì	*Graph (to)*
Túshūgǔan	*Library*

U

U zìxíng	*U-shaped*
U zìxíng wān	*U-turn*

W

Wàimiàn	*Outside*
Wàiyī	*Coat*
Wǎn	*Late*
Wǎn yì diǎn	*Later*
Wǎncān	*Dinner*
Wǎngjì wǎnglùo	*World Wide Web*
Wǎnglùo	*Network*
Wǎngmùxiàn yīnyǐng	*Crosshatched*
Wǎngshàng liúlǎn	*Surf the Web (to)*

Wǎngyè	*Web page*
Wǎngyè jìnjie	*Web access*
Wānqū/Qū xiàn	*Curve*
Wǎnshang	*Evening*
Wǎnshang/Yèli	*Night*
Wánxiào	*Joke*
Wèi	*Hello*
Wēijīfēn	*Calculus*
Wèizhì	*Position*
Wèn	*Ask (to)*
Wèndá	*Q & A*
Wēndù	*Temperature*
Wénhùa	*Culture*
Wénhùa de	*Cultural*
Wénjiàn	*Document*
Wèntí	*Problem*
Wèntí	*Question*
Wènxùntái	*Information desk*
Wénzhāng	*Article*
Word rǔanjiàn	*Word software*
WordPerfect rǔanjiàn/Zìcí wán shàn rǔanjìan	*WordPerfect software*
Wǔ	*Five*
Wǔcān	*Lunch*
Wǔcān	*Luncheon*
Wùpǐn qīngdān	*Inventory*
Wùtǐ	*Object*

X

Xiàn	*Line*
Xiàngmù	*Item*
Xiàngpícā	*Eraser*
Xiāngyān	*Cigarette*

Xiànjīn	*Cash*
Xiànshàng	*Online*
Xiànshàng fúwù	*Online service*
Xiǎnshì	*Show (to)*
Xiànshí zhuānsòng	*Special delivery*
Xiǎnshìqì	*Monitor*
Xiàntiáo túshì	*Line graph*
Xiànxíng de	*Linear*
Xiǎocèzi	*Brochure*
Xiǎochī	*Snack*
Xiǎoshí	*Hour*
Xiāoshòu	*Sale*
Xiāoshòu bàogào	*Sales report*
Xiāoshòu diànhùa	*Sales call*
Xiàtiān	*Summer*
Xiàyǔ	*Rain*
Xiàzài	*Download (to)*
Xiě	*Write (to)*
Xiéyì	*Agreement*
Xiéyì	*Proposal*
Xiézi	*Shoes*
Xǐhuan	*Enjoy (to)*
Xǐhuan	*Like (to)*
Xǐjù	*Comedy*
Xìjù	*Drama*
Xīn de	*New*
Xìnfēng	*Envelope*
Xíngdòng diànhùa	*Cellular phone*
Xīnghào	*Asterisk*
Xínglǐ	*Luggage*
Xíngwéi	*Behavior*
Xīngxīng	*Star*
Xíngzhèng	*Administration*
Xíngzhèng zhùlǐ	*Administrative assistant*

Xìnjiàn	*Letter*
Xīnshǔi	*Salary*
Xīnwén	*News*
Xìnxí	*Information*
Xìnxí	*Message*
Xìnxí zhōngxīn	*Message center*
Xíshàngxíng diànnǎo	*Laptop computer*
Xǐshǒujiān	*Rest room*
Xìtǒng	*System*
Xīwàng	*Hope (to)*
Xìyùan	*Theater*
Xuǎndān	*Menu*
Xuǎnzhé	*Option*
Xuě	*Snow*
Xuějiā	*Cigar*
Xúexí	*Learn (to)*
Xǔkě	*Grant*
Xūnǐ xiànshí	*Virtual reality*
Xùnliàn	*Coach (to)*
Xùnliàn	*Train (to)*
Xùnwèn	*Query*
Xúnzhǎo	*Look (to)*
Xūxiàn	*Dotted line*
Xūyào	*Need (to)*
XY sànbù	*XY scatter*

Y

Yāncǎo	*Tobacco*
Yǎnglǎojīn	*Pension*
Yángtái	*Balcony*
Yǎngūang	*Vision*
Yánhòu bàochóu	*Deferred compensation*
Yǎnjiǎng	*Speak (to)*
Yǎnjiǎngrén	*Speaker*

Yánshēn	*Extension*
Yánshēn xiàn	*Extension cord*
Yǎnshì	*Demonstrate (to)*
Yǎnshì	*Demonstration*
Yǎnshūo	*Speech*
Yántǎohùi	*Seminar*
Yào	*Want (to)*
Yāoqiú	*Request (to)*
Yèshù	*Page*
Yī	*One*
Yìchéng	*Agenda*
Yídòng	*Move (to)*
Yīfú	*Clothing*
Yǐndǎo	*Lead (to)*
Yǐndǎo	*Leading*
Yìngchíjià/Wénjìanjīa	*Folder*
Yīngfùzhàng	*Accounts payable*
Yínmù/Yíngpíng	*Screen*
Yīngshōuzhàng	*Accounts receivable*
Yǐngxiàng	*Video*
Yǐngxiàng hùiyì	*Video conferencing*
Yíngyèshùi	*Sales tax*
Yīngyǔ	*English*
Yīnxiǎng	*Audio*
Yīnxiǎng xìtǒng	*Sound system*
Yīnyǐng	*Shadow*
Yīnyùe	*Music*
Yīnyùe de	*Musical*
Yīnyùehùi	*Concert*
Yīnyùetīng	*Concert hall*
Yīshēng	*Doctor*
Yìshù	*Art*
Yǐzi	*Chair*
Yǒnggǎn de	*Bold*
Yǒu bāngzhù de	*Helpful*

Yóugòu	*Mail order*
Yóujì	*Mail (to)*
Yóujì míngdān	*Mailing list*
Yóujiàn	*Mail*
Yóujú	*Post office*
Yǒushēng yóujiàn	*Voice mail*
Yóutài jiàotáng	*Synagogue*
Yú	*Fish*
Yūanqūan	*Circle*
Yúanxíng túbiǎo	*Pie chart*
Yùe	*Month*
Yūehùi	*Appointment*
Yúlè	*Amusement*
Yúlèyúan	*Amusement park*
Yùliú de	*Reserved*
Yùn	*Ship (to)*
Yùndòng	*Sport*
Yùnshū	*Transportation*
Yùnshū fèiyòng	*Transportation charges*
Yúsǎn	*Umbrella*
Yùshì	*Bathroom*
Yǔ tiān	*Rainy day*
Yǔyán	*Language*
Yùyūe	*Reserve (to)*

Z

Z zhóu	*Z-axis*
Zài bō	*Redial (to)*
Zài jìxù	*Resume (to)*
Zài kǎolǜ	*Reconsider (to)*
Zài qǐdòng	*Reboot*
Zàijiàn	*Good-bye*
Zǎo	*Early*
Zǎo yì diǎn	*Earlier*

Zǎocān	Breakfast
Zázhì	Magazine
Zēngzhíshùi	Value-added tax
Zérèn	Accountability
Zhàiqùan	Bond
Zhàiwù	Liability
Zhàngdān	Bill
Zhàngfu	Husband
Zhǎnlǎn	Exhibit
Zhǎnshì	Display
Zhǎnshì	Display (to)
Zhǎnshì	Exhibit (to)
Zhǎnshì	Present (to)
Zhǎnshì	Presentation
Zhǎohúi	Found
Zhàopiān	Photograph
Zhàoxiàngjī	Camera
Zhēbì	Shaded
Zhèngcè	Policy
Zhèngwén	Text
Zhēngzhí	Conflict
Zhēnglùn	Argue (to)
Zhéxúe	Philosophy
Zhǐ	Paper
Zhīchí	Support (to)
Zhǐchū	Point (to)
Zhīdào	Know (to)
Zhǐdiǎn	Direct (to)
Zhífāngtú	Histogram
Zhǐhūitái	Podium
Zhíjiǎo	Right angle
Zhìlì	Intelligence
Zhìlì gāo de	Intelligent
Zhíliàng	Quality
Zhíliàng kòngzhì	Quality control

Zhǐnán	*Directory*
Zhīpiào	*Check*
Zhīshi	*Knowledge*
Zhǐshì/cānzhào	*Referral*
Zhǐshù de	*Exponential*
Zhìwèn	*Question (to)*
Zhíxiàn	*Direct line*
Zhíyè	*Career*
Zhìzào	*Make (to)*
Zhōng	*Clock*
Zhōngdiǎn	*End*
Zhòngdiǎn	*Stress*
Zhōngjiān	*Middle*
Zhǒnglèi	*Type*
Zhōngxīn	*Center*
Zhōngxīn lùnwén	*Central thesis*
Zhōngxíng qūxiàn	*Bell-curve*
Zhōngyāng bàngōngshì	*Central office*
Zhōngyāng de	*Central*
Zhōngyāng jíquánhuà	*Centralization*
Zhōu	*Week*
Zhuǎn dào	*Switch (to)*
Zhuǎndì	*Forward (to)*
Zhuāngchúan	*Shipment*
Zhuāngyùn zhōngxīn	*Shipping center*
Zhǔanhùanqì	*Converter*
Zhuānlán	*Column*
Zhuānlì	*Patent*
Zhuǎnràng	*Transfer (to)*
Zhuǎnwān	*Turn (to)*
Zhūbǎo	*Jewelry*
Zhǔjī diànnǎo	*Mainframe computer*
Zhǔrèn	*Director*
Zhūròu	*Pork*
Zhǔtí	*Subject*

Zhǔxí	Chairman
Zhǔxí	Chairperson
Zhùyì	Attention
Zhǔyì	Idea
Zhùyì	Note (to)
Zǐsè	Purple
Zīxún	Consult (to)
Zìzhùcān	Buffet
Zǒngcái	President
Zōngsè	Brown
Zòngzhóu	Y-axis
Zǔfùmǔ	Grandparent
Zùidà jíxiàn	Maximum
Zùihòu	Last
Zùihòu qīxiàn	Deadline
Zùixiǎo jíxiàn	Minimum
Zūlìn	Rent
Zǔo	Left
Zùo de hǎo	Well done
Zùo júedìng	Decision making
Zùo liángshī yìyǒu	Mentoring
Zhūozi	Table
Zúqiú	Soccer
Zǔzhī	Organization
Zǔzhī	Organize (to)
Zǔzhī jiégòutú	Organization chart

INDEX